AF380440

World YEAR BOOK 2022

www.dishapublication.com
Books & ebooks for School & Competitive Exams

www.mylearninggraph.com
Etests for Competitive Exams

Write to us at feedback_disha@aiets.co.in

Preface

We bring you another attractive title *World Year Book 2022*. How is it going to help you? It presents **World Historical Events** in year-wise format. The book will take you through **world's major civilizations and ages.**

The tallest, smallest, biggest, sobriquets, people who have influenced the world and books that have made impact on our minds, and so on, have been covered in the **World Panorama** section.

The book provides continent-wise information like history, geography and culture about **countries of the world.** Grouping of countries, what we call **'families of countries'** is introduced. All international organizations and groups are also highlighted, including **international agreements, treaties and pacts**.

Contemporary issues of **technology development** in different fields such as space, defence, inventions, etc. are taken care of.

Environment issues are on everybody's mind, which are highlighted in detail covering almost every topic.

The book informs on **major resources available** in the world; the major religions followed and languages spoken by the people.

Games and Sports have become an integral part of our modern life and so have **awards and honours**, which the book highlights.

For the last two years, **Covid-19** is on everybody's mind so you will find all the info about it in the book.

In the end, an end product which you would like to buy, read and keep in your shelf. It is going to make you proud owning it. Get your copy now.

CONTENTS

MAJOR CIVILIZATIONS

The Mesopotamian Civilization, Indus Valley Civilization, Egyptian Civilization, The Mayan Civilization, The Chinese Civilization, Greek Civilization, The Persian Civilization, Roman Cvilization, Aztec Civilization, Incan Civilization,

Modern world history, World Wars: I & II, Major Geographical Discoveries, Major Wars in History,

Tallest, Smallest, Biggest around the World, First in the world, Sobriquets, Important Boundary lines, Important People Forever, Important places, Wonders of the world, Most powerful intelligence agencies, News agencies and news papers, Fathers of various fields, National emblems of various countries, Important International days, Trade Organisations of the world

Continent wise : Asia, Africa, Europe, North America, South America, Austraila/ Oceania, Antarctica

Balkans, Central America, Latin America, Middle East, Polynesia, Southeast Asia, Scandinavia, Union of Soviet Socialist Republics (USSR), United Arab Emirates, United Kingdom of Great Britain and Northern Ireland

United Nations: WTO, WMO, WIPO, UNESCO, OECD, IAEA, OPEC, IMO, FAO, NATO, ASEAN, APEC, SAARC, UNEP, UNHCR, UNODC, UNDRR, ICAO, UNDP, IFAD, ITU, UNWTO, ICJ, UNCTAD, WFP, OHCHR, INTERPOL

Major Discoveries In The Field Of Science

World at a Glance

- **195 countries** in the world; 193 countries are member states of the United Nations & 2 countries non-member observer states: the Holy See and the State of Palestine.
- World Population (2021 Projection) 7.9 Billion (As of October 2021, United Nations estimates elaborated by Worldometer)
- Urban population: 56.6% of total population (2021)
- The "Greenwich Mean Time" refers to the time zone at the zero degree of longitude that runs through the London suburb of Greenwich and takes its name from it.
- It is also called the zero meridians. The time difference between Greenwich Mean Time and our Central European Standard Time (CET) is -1 hour.
- Arabic, Chinese (Mandarin), English, French, Russian, and Spanish (Castilian) - are the mother tongue or second language of about 45% of the world's population, and are the official languages in more than half the states in the world
- Approximately 2,300 languages are spoken in Asia, 2,140, in Africa, 1,310 in the Pacific, 1,060 in the Americas, and 290 in Europe (2020)

World Geography

- The earliest widely accepted date for life appearing on earth is 3.48 billion years ago, but this date is conservative and may get pushed back further.
- The world is now thought to be about 4.55 billion years old, just about one-third of the 13.8-billion-year age estimated for the universe
- Total Area: 510.072 million sq km
- Land: 148.94 million sq km
- Water: 361.9 million sq km
- 70.9% of the world's surface is water, 29.1% is land
- 7 continents: Asia, Africa, North America, South America, Antarctica, Europe, and Australia (listed from largest to smallest in size)
- 5 oceans: the Pacific Ocean, Atlantic Ocean, Indian Ocean, Southern Ocean, and Arctic Ocean.
- Highest point: Mount Everest 8,849 m
- Lowest point: Denman Glacier (Antarctica) more than -3,500 m

Top 10 Largest Water Bodies

Pacific Ocean 155,557,000 sq km; Atlantic Ocean 76,762,000 sq km; Indian Ocean 68,556,000 sq km; Southern Ocean 20,327,000 sq km; Arctic Ocean 14,056,000 sq km; Coral Sea 4,184,100 sq km; South China Sea 3,595,900 sq km; Caribbean Sea 2,834,000 sq km; Bering Sea 2,520,000 sq km; Mediterranean Sea 2,469,000 sq km

Top 10 Largest Landmasses

Asia 44,568,500 sq km; Africa 30,065,000 sq km; North America 24,473,000 sq km; South America 17,819,000 sq km; Antarctica 14,200,000 sq km; Europe 9,948,000 sq km; Australia 7,741,220 sq km; Greenland 2,166,086 sq km; New Guinea 785,753 sq km; Borneo 751,929 sq km

Top 10 Largest Islands

Greenland 2,166,086 sq km; New Guinea (Indonesia, Papua New Guinea) 785,753 sq km; Borneo (Brunei, Indonesia, Malaysia) 751,929 sq km; Madagascar 587,713 sq km; Baffin Island (Canada) 507,451 sq km; Sumatra (Indonesia) 472,784 sq km; Honshu (Japan) 227,963 sq km; Victoria Island (Canada) 217,291 sq km; Great Britain (United Kingdom) 209,331 sq km; Ellesmere Island (Canada) 196,236 sq km.

Top 10 Highest Mountains (Measured from Sea Level)

Mount Everest (China-Nepal) 8,849 m; K2 (Pakistan) 8,611 m; Kanchenjunga (India-Nepal) 8,598 m; Lhotse (Nepal) 8,516 m; Makalu (China-Nepal) 8,463 m; Cho Oyu (China-Nepal) 8,201 m; Dhaulagiri (Nepal) 8,167 m; Manaslu (Nepal) 8,163 m; Nanga Parbat (Pakistan) 8,125 m; Anapurna (Nepal) 8,091 m.

Top 10 Longest Mountain Ranges (land-based)

Andes (Venezuela, Colombia, Ecuador, Peru, Bolivia, Chile, Argentina) 7,000 km; Rocky Mountains (Canada, US) 4,830 km; Great Dividing Range (Australia) 3,700 km; Transantarctic Mountains (Antarctica) 3,500 km; Kunlun Mountains (China) 3,000 km; Ural Mountains (Russia, Kazakhstan) 2,640 km; Atlas Mountains (Morocco, Algeria, Tunisia) 2,500 km; Appalachian Mountains (Canada, US) 2,400 km; Himalayas (Pakistan, Afghanistan, India, China, Nepal, Bhutan) 2,300 km; Altai Mountains (Kazakhstan, Russia, Mongolia) 2,000 km; note - lengths are approximate; if oceans are included, the Mid-Ocean Ridge is by far the longest mountain range at 40,389 km.

Top 10 Largest Forested Countries (sq km and percent of land)

Russia 8,149,310 (49.8%); Brazil 4,935,380 (58.9%); Canada 3,470,690 (38.2%); United States 3,103,700 (33.9%); China 2,098,640 (22.3%); Democratic Republic of the Congo 1,522,670 (67.2%); Australia 1,250,590 (16.3%); Indonesia 903,250 (49.9%); Peru 738,054 (57.7%); India 708,600 (23.8%) (2016 est.)

Top 10 Largest (non-polar) Deserts

Sahara (Algeria, Chad, Egypt, Libya, Mali, Mauritania, Niger, Western Sahara, Sudan, Tunisia) 9,200,000 sq km; Arabian (Saudi Arabia, Iraq, Jordan, Kuwait, Oman, Qatar, United Arab Emirates, Yemen) 2,330,000 sq km; Gobi (China, Mongolia) 1,295,000 sq km; Kalahari (Botswana, Namibia, South Africa) 900,000 sq km; Patagonian (Argentina) 673,000 sq km; Syrian (Syria, Iraq, Jordan, Saudi Arabia) 500,000 sq km; Chihuahuan (Mexico) 362,000 sq km; Kara-Kum (Turkmenistan) 350,000 sq km; Great Victoria (Australia) 348,750 sq km; Great Basin (United States) 343,169 sq km; note - if the two polar deserts are included, they would rank first and second: Antarctic Desert 14,200,000 sq km and Arctic Desert 13,900,000 sq km.

10 Driest Places on Earth (Average Annual Precipitation)

McMurdo Dry Valleys, Antarctica 0 mm (0 in); Arica, Chile 0.76 mm (0.03 in); Al Kufrah, Libya 0.86 mm (0.03 in); Aswan, Egypt 0.86 mm (0.03 in); Luxor, Egypt 0.86 mm (0.03 in); Ica, Peru 2.29 mm (0.09 in); Wadi Halfa, Sudan 2.45 mm (0.1 in); Iquique, Chile 5.08 mm (0.2 in); Pelican Point, Namibia 8.13 mm (0.32 in); El Arab (Aoulef), Algeria 12.19 mm (0.48 in)

Top 10 Largest (non-polar) Deserts

Sahara (Algeria, Chad, Egypt, Libya, Mali, Mauritania, Niger, Western Sahara, Sudan, Tunisia) 9,200,000 sq km; Arabian (Saudi Arabia, Iraq, Jordan, Kuwait, Oman, Qatar, United Arab Emirates, Yemen) 2,330,000 sq km; Gobi (China, Mongolia) 1,295,000 sq km; Kalahari (Botswana, Namibia, South Africa) 900,000 sq km; Patagonian (Argentina) 673,000 sq km; Syrian (Syria, Iraq, Jordan, Saudi Arabia) 500,000 sq km; Chihuahuan (Mexico) 362,000 sq km; Kara-Kum (Turkmenistan) 350,000 sq km; Great Victoria (Australia) 348,750 sq km; Great Basin (United States) 343,169 sq km; note - if the two polar deserts are included, they would rank first and second: Antarctic Desert 14,200,000 sq km and Arctic Desert 13,900,000 sq km.

10 Wettest Places on Earth (Average Annual Precipitation)

Mawsynram, India 11,871 mm (467.4 in); Cherrapunji, India 11,777 mm (463.7 in); Tutunendo, Colombia 11,770 mm (463.4 in); Cropp River, New Zealand 11,516 mm (453.4 in); San Antonia de Ureca, Equatorial Guinea 10,450 mm (411.4 in); Debundsha, Cameroon 10,299 mm (405.5 in); Big Bog, US (Hawaii) 10,272 mm (404.4 in); Mt Waialeale, US (Hawaii) 9,763 mm (384.4 in); Kukui, US (Hawaii) 9,293 mm (365.9 in); Emeishan, China 8,169 mm (321.6 in)

10 Coldest Places on Earth (Lowest Average Monthly Temperature)

Verkhoyansk, Russia (Siberia) -47°C (-53°F) January; Oymyakon, Russia (Siberia) -46°C (-52°F) January; Eureka, Canada -38.4°C (-37.1°F) February; Isachsen, Canada -36°C (-32.8°F) February; Alert, Canada -34°C (-28°F) February; Kap Morris Jesup, Greenland -34°C (-29°F) March; Cornwallis Island, Canada -33.5°C (-28.3°F) February; Cambridge Bay, Canada -33.5°C (28.3°F) February; Ilirnej, Russia -33°C (-28°F) January; Resolute, Canada -33°C (-27.4°F) February.

10 Hottest Places on Earth (Highest Average Monthly Temperature)

Death Valley, US (California) 39°C (101°F) July; Iranshahr, Iran 38.3°C (100.9°F) June; Ouallene, Algeria 38°C (100.4°F) July; Kuwait City, Kuwait 37.7°C (100°F) July; Medina, Saudi Arabia 36°C (97°F) July; Buckeye, US (Arizona) 34°C (93°F) July; Jazan, Saudi Arabia 33°C (91°F) June; Al Kufrah, Libya 31°C (87°F) July; Alice Springs, Australia 29°C (84°F) January; Tamanrasset, Algeria 29°C (84°F) June

◅ **Africa (54):** Algeria, Angola, Benin, Botswana, Burkina Faso, Burundi, Cabo Verde, Cameroon, Central African Republic, Chad, Comoros, Democratic Republic of the Congo, Republic of the Congo, Cote d'Ivoire, Djibouti, Egypt, Equatorial Guinea, Eritrea, Eswatini, Ethiopia, Gabon, The Gambia, Ghana, Guinea, Guinea-Bissau, Kenya, Lesotho, Liberia, Libya, Madagascar, Malawi, Mali, Mauritania, Mauritius, Morocco, Mozambique, Namibia, Niger, Nigeria, Rwanda, Sao Tome and Principe, Senegal, Seychelles, Sierra Leone, Somalia, South Africa, South Sudan, Sudan, Tanzania, Togo, Tunisia, Uganda, Zambia, Zimbabwe;

◅ **Europe (49):** Albania, Andorra, Austria, Azerbaijan*, Belarus, Belgium, Bosnia and Herzegovina, Bulgaria, Croatia, Czech Republic, Denmark, Estonia, Finland, France, Georgia*, Germany, Greece, Holy See (Vatican City), Hungary, Iceland, Ireland, Italy, Kazakhstan*, Kosovo, Latvia, Liechtenstein, Lithuania, Luxembourg, Malta, Moldova, Monaco, Montenegro, Netherlands, North Macedonia, Norway, Poland, Portugal, Romania, Russia*, San Marino, Serbia, Slovakia, Slovenia, Spain, Sweden, Switzerland, Turkey*, Ukraine, United Kingdom (* indicates part of the country is also in Asia);

◅ **Asia (48):** Afghanistan, Armenia, Azerbaijan*, Bahrain, Bangladesh, Bhutan, Brunei, Burma, Cambodia, China, Cyprus, Georgia*, India, Indonesia, Iran, Iraq, Israel, Japan, Jordan, Kazakhstan*, North Korea, South Korea, Kuwait, Kyrgyzstan, Laos, Lebanon, Malaysia, Maldives, Mongolia, Nepal, Oman, Pakistan, Philippines, Qatar, Russia*, Saudi Arabia, Singapore, Sri Lanka, Syria, Tajikistan, Thailand, Timor-Leste, Turkey*, Turkmenistan, United Arab Emirates, Uzbekistan, Vietnam, Yemen (* indicates part of the country is also in Europe);

◅ **North America (23):** Antigua and Barbuda, The Bahamas, Barbados, Belize, Canada, Costa Rica, Cuba, Dominica, Dominican Republic, El Salvador, Grenada, Guatemala, Haiti, Honduras, Jamaica, Mexico, Nicaragua, Panama, Saint Kitts and Nevis, Saint Lucia, Saint Vincent and the Grenadines, Trinidad and Tobago, United States;

◅ **Oceania (14):** Australia, Fiji, Kiribati, Marshall Islands, Federated States of Micronesia, Nauru, New Zealand, Palau, Papua New Guinea, Samoa, Solomon Islands, Tonga, Tuvalu, Vanuatu;

◅ **South America (12):** Argentina, Bolivia, Brazil, Chile, Colombia, Ecuador, Guyana, Paraguay, Peru, Suriname, Uruguay, Venezuela

Top 100 Countries in the World by Population (2021)

S.No.	Country	Population (2020)	Density (P/Km²)	Land Area (Km²)	World Share
1	China	1,439,323,776	153	9,388,211	18.47 %
2	India	1,380,004,385	464	2,973,190	17.70 %
3	United States	331,002,651	36	9,147,420	4.25 %
4	Indonesia	273,523,615	151	1,811,570	3.51 %
5	Pakistan	220,892,340	287	770,880	2.83 %

S.No.	Country	Population (2020)	Density (P/Km²)	Land Area (Km²)	World Share
6	Brazil	212,559,417	25	8,358,140	2.73 %
7	Nigeria	206,139,589	226	910,770	2.64 %
8	Bangladesh	164,689,383	1,265	130,170	2.11 %
9	Russia	145,934,462	9	16,376,870	1.87 %
10	Mexico	128,932,753	66	1,943,950	1.65 %
11	Japan	126,476,461	347	364,555	1.62%
12	Ethiopia	114,963,588	115	1,000,000	1.47%
13	Philippines	109,581,078	368	298,170	1.41%
14	Egypt	102,334,404	103	995,450	1.31%
15	Vietnam	97,338,579	314	310,070	1.25%
16	DR Congo	89,561,403	40	2,267,050	1.15%
17	Turkey	84,339,067	110	769,630	1.08%
18	Iran	83,992,949	52	1,628,550	1.08%
19	Germany	83,783,942	240	348,560	1.07%
20	Thailand	69,799,978	137	510,890	0.90%
21	United Kingdom	67,886,011	281	241,930	0.87%
22	France	65,273,511	119	547,557	0.84%
23	Italy	60,461,826	206	294,140	0.78%
24	Tanzania	59,734,218	67	885,800	0.77%
25	South Africa	59,308,690	49	1,213,090	0.76%
26	Myanmar	54,409,800	83	653,290	0.70%
27	Kenya	53,771,296	94	569,140	0.69%
28	South Korea	51,269,185	527	97,230	0.66%
29	Colombia	50,882,891	46	1,109,500	0.65%
30	Spain	46,754,778	94	498,800	0.60%
31	Uganda	45,741,007	229	199,810	0.59%
32	Argentina	45,195,774	17	2,736,690	0.58%
33	Algeria	43,851,044	18	2,381,740	0.56%
34	Sudan	43,849,260	25	1,765,048	0.56%
35	Ukraine	43,733,762	75	579,320	0.56%
36	Iraq	40,222,493	93	434,320	0.52%

S.No.	Country	Population (2020)	Density (P/Km²)	Land Area (Km²)	World Share
37	Afghanistan	38,928,346	60	652,860	0.50%
38	Poland	37,846,611	124	306,230	0.49%
39	Canada	37,742,154	4	9,093,510	0.48%
40	Morocco	36,910,560	83	446,300	0.47%
41	Saudi Arabia	34,813,871	16	2,149,690	0.45%
42	Uzbekistan	33,469,203	79	425,400	0.43%
43	Peru	32,971,854	26	1,280,000	0.42%
44	Angola	32,866,272	26	1,246,700	0.42%
45	Malaysia	32,365,999	99	328,550	0.42%
46	Mozambique	31,255,435	40	786,380	0.40%
47	Ghana	31,072,940	137	227,540	0.40%
48	Yemen	29,825,964	56	527,970	0.38%
49	Nepal	29,136,808	203	143,350	0.37%
50	Venezuela	28,435,940	32	882,050	0.36%
51	Madagascar	27,691,018	48	581,795	0.36%
52	Cameroon	26,545,863	56	472,710	0.34%
53	Côte d'Ivoire	26,378,274	83	318,000	0.34%
54	North Korea	25,778,816	214	120,410	0.33%
55	Australia	25,499,884	3	7,682,300	0.33%
56	Niger	24,206,644	19	1,266,700	0.31%
57	Taiwan	23,816,775	673	35,410	0.31%
58	Sri Lanka	21,413,249	341	62,710	0.27%
59	Burkina Faso	20,903,273	76	273,600	0.27%
60	Mali	20,250,833	17	1,220,190	0.26%
61	Romania	19,237,691	84	230,170	0.25%
62	Malawi	19,129,952	203	94,280	0.25%
63	Chile	19,116,201	26	743,532	0.25%
64	Kazakhstan	18,776,707	7	2,699,700	0.24%
65	Zambia	18,383,955	25	743,390	0.24%
66	Guatemala	17,915,568	167	107,160	0.23%
67	Ecuador	17,643,054	71	248,360	0.23%

S.No.	Country	Population (2020)	Density (P/Km²)	Land Area (Km²)	World Share
68	Syria	17,500,658	95	183,630	0.22%
69	Netherlands	17,134,872	508	33,720	0.22%
70	Senegal	16,743,927	87	192,530	0.21%
71	Cambodia	16,718,965	95	176,520	0.21%
72	Chad	16,425,864	13	1,259,200	0.21%
73	Somalia	15,893,222	25	627,340	0.20%
74	Zimbabwe	14,862,924	38	386,850	0.19%
75	Guinea	13,132,795	53	245,720	0.17%
76	Rwanda	12,952,218	525	24,670	0.17%
77	Benin	12,123,200	108	112,760	0.16%
78	Burundi	11,890,784	463	25,680	0.15%
79	Tunisia	11,818,619	76	155,360	0.15%
80	Bolivia	11,673,021	11	1,083,300	0.15%
81	Belgium	11,589,623	383	30,280	0.15%
82	Haiti	11,402,528	414	27,560	0.15%
83	Cuba	11,326,616	106	106,440	0.15%
84	South Sudan	11,193,725	18	610,952	0.14%
85	Dominican Republic	10,847,910	225	48,320	0.14%
86	Czech Republic (Czechia)	10,708,981	139	77,240	0.14%
87	Greece	10,423,054	81	128,900	0.13%
88	Jordan	10,203,134	115	88,780	0.13%
89	Portugal	10,196,709	111	91,590	0.13%
90	Azerbaijan	10,139,177	123	82,658	0.13%
91	Sweden	10,099,265	25	410,340	0.13%
92	Honduras	9,904,607	89	111,890	0.13%
93	United Arab Emirates	9,890,402	118	83,600	0.13%
94	Hungary	9,660,351	107	90,530	0.12%
95	Tajikistan	9,537,645	68	139,960	0.12%
96	Belarus	9,449,323	47	202,910	0.12%

S.No.	Country	Population (2020)	Density (P/Km²)	Land Area (Km²)	World Share
97	Austria	9,006,398	109	82,409	0.12%
98	Papua New Guinea	8,947,024	20	452,860	0.11%
99	Serbia	8,737,371	100	87,460	0.11%
100	Israel	8,655,535	400	21,640	0.11%

Top 100 Largest Countries by Area

S.No.	Country	Total Area (Km²)	Land Area (Km²)	% of World landmass
1	Russia	17,098,242	16,376,870	11.00%
2	Canada	9,984,670	9,093,510	6.10%
3	China	9,706,961	9,388,211	6.30%
4	United States	9,372,610	9,147,420	6.10%
5	Brazil	8,515,767	8,358,140	5.60%
6	Australia	7,692,024	7,682,300	5.20%
7	India	3,287,590	2,973,190	2.00%
8	Argentina	2,780,400	2,736,690	1.80%
9	Kazakhstan	2,724,900	2,699,700	1.80%
10	Algeria	2,381,741	2,381,740	1.60%
11	DR Congo	2,344,858	2,267,050	1.50%
12	Greenland	2,166,086	410,450	0.30%
13	Saudi Arabia	2,149,690	2,149,690	1.40%
14	Mexico	1,964,375	1,943,950	1.30%
15	Indonesia	1,904,569	1,811,570	1.20%
16	Sudan	1,886,068	1,765,048	1.20%
17	Libya	1,759,540	1,759,540	1.20%
18	Iran	1,648,195	1,628,550	1.10%
19	Mongolia	1,564,110	1,553,560	1.00%
20	Peru	1,285,216	1,280,000	0.90%
21	Chad	1,284,000	1,259,200	0.80%
22	Niger	1,267,000	1,266,700	0.90%
23	Angola	1,246,700	1,246,700	0.80%
24	Mali	1,240,192	1,220,190	0.80%
25	South Africa	1,221,037	1,213,090	0.80%
26	Colombia	1,141,748	1,109,500	0.70%
27	Ethiopia	1,104,300	1,000,000	0.70%

S.No.	Country	Total Area (Km²)	Land Area (Km²)	% of World landmass
28	Bolivia	1,098,581	1,083,300	0.70%
29	Mauritania	1,030,700	1,030,700	0.70%
30	Egypt	1,002,450	995,450	0.70%
31	Tanzania	945,087	885,800	0.60%
32	Nigeria	923,768	910,770	0.60%
33	Venezuela	916,445	882,050	0.60%
34	Pakistan	881,912	770,880	0.50%
35	Namibia	825,615	823,290	0.60%
36	Mozambique	801,590	786,380	0.50%
37	Turkey	783,562	769,630	0.50%
38	Chile	756,102	743,532	0.50%
39	Zambia	752,612	743,390	0.50%
40	Myanmar	676,578	653,290	0.40%
41	Afghanistan	652,230	652,860	0.40%
42	Somalia	637,657	627,340	0.40%
43	Central African Republic	622,984	622,980	0.40%
44	South Sudan	619,745	610,952	0.40%
45	Ukraine	603,500	579,320	0.40%
46	Madagascar	587,041	581,795	0.40%
47	Botswana	582,000	566,730	0.40%
48	Kenya	580,367	569,140	0.40%
49	France	551,695	547,557	0.40%
50	Yemen	527,968	527,970	0.40%
51	Thailand	513,120	510,890	0.30%
52	Spain	505,992	498,800	0.30%
53	Turkmenistan	488,100	469,930	0.30%
54	Cameroon	475,442	472,710	0.30%
55	Papua New Guinea	462,840	452,860	0.30%
56	Sweden	450,295	410,340	0.30%
57	Uzbekistan	447,400	425,400	0.30%
58	Morocco	446,550	446,300	0.30%
59	Iraq	438,317	434,320	0.30%
60	Paraguay	406,752	397,300	0.30%
61	Zimbabwe	390,757	386,850	0.30%

S.No.	Country	Total Area (Km²)	Land Area (Km²)	% of World landmass
62	Japan	377,930	364,555	0.20%
63	Germany	357,114	348,560	0.20%
64	Philippines	342,353	298,170	0.20%
65	Congo	342,000	341,500	0.20%
66	Finland	338,424	303,890	0.20%
67	Vietnam	331,212	310,070	0.20%
68	Malaysia	330,803	328,550	0.20%
69	Norway	323,802	365,268	0.20%
70	Côte d'Ivoire	322,463	318,000	0.20%
71	Poland	312,679	306,230	0.20%
72	Oman	309,500	309,500	0.20%
73	Italy	301,336	294,140	0.20%
74	Ecuador	276,841	248,360	0.20%
75	Burkina Faso	272,967	273,600	0.20%
76	New Zealand	270,467	263,310	0.20%
77	Gabon	267,668	257,670	0.20%
78	Western Sahara	266,000	266,000	0.20%
79	Guinea	245,857	245,720	0.20%
80	United Kingdom	242,900	241,930	0.20%
81	Uganda	241,550	199,810	0.10%
82	Ghana	238,533	227,540	0.20%
83	Romania	238,391	230,170	0.20%
84	Laos	236,800	230,800	0.20%
85	Guyana	214,969	196,850	0.10%
86	Belarus	207,600	202,910	0.10%
87	Kyrgyzstan	199,951	191,800	0.10%
88	Senegal	196,722	192,530	0.10%
89	Syria	185,180	183,630	0.10%
90	Cambodia	181,035	176,520	0.10%
91	Uruguay	181,034	175,020	0.10%
92	Suriname	163,820	156,000	%.10%
93	Tunisia	163,610	155,360	0.10%
94	Bangladesh	147,570	130,170	0.10%
95	Nepal	147,181	143,350	0.10%

S.No.	Country	Total Area (Km²)	Land Area (Km²)	% of World landmass
96	Tajikistan	143,100	139,960	0.10%
97	Greece	131,990	128,900	0.10%
98	Nicaragua	130,373	120,340	0.10%
99	North Korea	120,538	120,410	0.10%
100	Malawi	118,484	94,280	0.10%

Top 10 Mega Cities of the World

Rank	Mega city	Country	Population
1	Shanghai	China	24,870,900
2	Chongqing	China	22,251,500
3	Beijing	China	21,893,100
4	Guangzhou	China	18,676,600
5	Delhi	India	18,498,200
6	Kinshasa	Democratic Republic of the Congo	14,970,000
7	Karachi	Pakistan	14,910,400
8	Shenzhen	China	14,678,000
9	Istanbul	Turkey	14,670,000
10	Lagos	Nigeria	14,234,000

Top 10 Smallest Countries by Area

Rank	Country	Area	Population	Population per km²
1	Holy See (Vatican City)	0.4 km²	1,000	2,272.73
2	Monaco	2.0 km²	39,244	19,427.72
3	Gibraltar *	6.8 km²	33,691	4,954.56
4	Tokelau *	12.2 km²	1,647	135
5	Cocos Islands *	14.2 km²	596	41.97
6	Saint Barthelemy *	21.0 km²	7,116	338.86
7	Nauru	21.1 km²	10,834	513.46
8	Tuvalu	26.0 km²	11,792	453.54
9	Macao *	30.4 km²	649,342	21,359.93
10	Saint Martin *	34.0 km²	40,812	1,200.35

***Not independent and sovereign states**

Top 10 Countries by Nominal GDP at Current US Dollar Exchange Rates

Country	Nominal GDP (in trillions)	PPP Adjusted GDP (in trillions)	Annual Growth (%)	GDP Per Capita (in thousands)
US	$21.43	$21.43	2.20%	$65,298
China	$14.34	$23.52	6.10%	$10,262
Japan	$5.08	$5.46	0.70%	$40,247
Germany	$3.86	$4.68	0.60%	$46,445
India	$2.87	$9.56	4.20%	$2,100
UK	$2.83	$3.25	1.50%	$42,330
France	$2.72	$3.32	1.50%	$40,493.90
Italy	$2.00	$2.67	0.30%	$33,228.20
Brazil	$1.84	$3.23	1.10%	$8,717
Canada	$1.74	$1.93	1.70%	$46,195

Top 10 Airports by Passengers (2019)

Atlanta (ATL) 110,531,300; Beijing (PEK) - 100,011,438; Los Angeles, CA (LAX) 88,068,013; Dubai, UAE (DXB) 86,396,757; Tokyo (HND) 85,505,054; Chicago (ORD) 84,649,115; London (LHR) 80,888,305; Shanghai (PVG) 76,153,455; Paris (CDG) 76,150,009; Dallas/Fort Worth, TX (DFW) 75,066,956;

Water ways – Top 10 Longest Rivers

Nile (Africa) 6,693 km; Amazon (South America) 6,436 km; Mississippi-Missouri (North America) 6,238 km; Yenisey-Angara (Asia) 5,981 km; Ob-Irtysh (Asia) 5,569 km; Yangtze (Asia) 5,525 km; Yellow (Asia) 4,671 km; Amur (Asia) 4,352 km; Lena (Asia) 4,345 km; Congo (Africa) 4,344 km.

Historical Events

4.5 billion B.C.	: Planet Earth formed.
3 billion B.C.	: First signs of primeval life (bacteria and blue-green algae) appear in oceans.
600 million B.C.	: Earliest date to which fossils can be traced.
4.4 million B.C.	: Earliest known hominid fossils (Ardipithecus ramidus) found in Aramis, Ethiopia, 1994.
4.2 million B.C.	: Australopithecus anamnesis found in Lake Turkana, Kenya, 1995.
3.2 million B.C.	: Australopithecus afarenis (nicknamed -Lucy) found in Ethiopia, 1974.
2.5 million B.C.	: Homo habilis (Skillful Man). First brain expansion; is believed to have used stone tools.
1.8 million B.C.	: Homo erectus (Upright Man). Brain size twice that of Australopithecine species.
1.7 million B.C.	: Homo erectus leaves Africa.
100,000 B.C.	: First modern Homo sapiens in South Africa.
70,000 B.C.	: Neanderthal man (use of fire and advanced tools).
35,000 B.C.	: Neanderthal man replaced by later groups of Homo sapiens (i.e., Cro-Magnon man, etc.).
18,000 B.C.	: Cro-Magnons replaced by later cultures.
15,000 B.C.	: Migrations across Bering Straits into the Americas.
10,000 B.C.	: Semi-permanent agricultural settlements in Old World.
10,000-4,000 B.C.	: Development of settlements into cities and development of skills such as the wheel, pottery, and improved methods of cultivation in Mesopotamia and elsewhere.
5500-3000 B.C.	: Predynastic Egyptian cultures develop (5500-3100 B.C.); begin using agriculture (c. 5000 B.C.). Earliest recorded date in Egyptian calendar (4241 B.C.). First year of Jewish calendar (3760 B.C.). First phonetic writing appears (c. 3500 B.C. Copper used by Egyptians and Sumerians. Western Europe is Neolithic, without metals or written records.

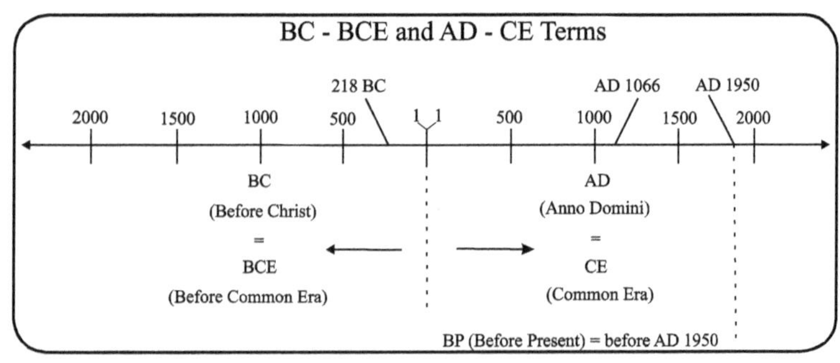

3000- 2000 B.C. : Pharaonic rule begins in Egypt. King Khufu (Cheops), 4th dynasty (2700-2675 B.C.), completes construction of the Great Pyramid at Giza (c. 2680 B.C)

3000-1500 B.C. : The most ancient civilization on the Indian subcontinent, the sophisticated and extensive Indus Valley civilization, flourishes in what is today Pakistan. In Britain, Stonehenge built according to some unknown astronomical rationale. Its three main phases of construction from the time span of 3000-1500 B.C.

2000-1500 B.C. : Hyksos invaders drive Egyptians from Lower Egypt (17th century B.C.). Amosis I frees Egypt from Hyksos (1600 B.C.). Twenty-four-character alphabet in Egypt. Peak of Minoan culture on Isle of Crete-Earliest form of written Greek. Hammurabi, king of Babylon, develops oldest existing code of laws (18th century B.C.).

1500-1000 B.C. : Ikhnaton develops monotheistic religion in Egypt (1375 B.C.). His successor, Tutankhamen, returns to earlier gods. Greeks destroy Troy (1193 B.C.). Chinese civilization develops under Shang Dynasty.

1000-900 B.C. : Hebrew elders begin to write Old Testament books of Bible. Phoenicians colonize Spain with settlement at Cadiz.

900-800 B.C. : Phoenicians establish Carthage (810 B.C.). The Iliad and the Odyssey, perhaps composed by Greek poet Homer.

800-700 B.C. : Prophets Amos, Hosea, Isaiah. First recorded Olympic Games (776 B.C.). Legendary founding of Rome by Romulus (753 B.C.)

700-600 B.C. : Founding of Byzantium by Greeks (660 B.C.). Building of the Acropolis in Athens. Solon, Greek lawgiver (640-560 B.C.). Sappho of Lesbos, Greek poet (610- 580 B.C.). Lao-tse, Chinese philosopher and founder of Taoism (born 604 B.C.).

600-500 B.C. : Babylonian King Nebuchadnezzar builds empire, destroys Jerusalem (586 B.C.). Hanging Gardens of Babylon. Cyrus the Great of Persia creates great empire, conquers Babylon (539 B.C.), and frees the Jews. Athenian democracy develops. Confucius (551-479 B.C.) develops ethical and social philosophy in China.

500-400 B.C. : Greeks defeat Persians.

400-300 B.C. : Pentateuch- First five books of the Old Testament evolve in final form. Alexander the Great (356-323 B.C.), who destroys Thebes (335 B.C.), conquers Tyre and Jerusalem (332 B.C.), occupies Babylon (330 B.C.), invades India, and dies in Babylon. His empire is divided among his generals; one of them, Seleucis I, establishes Middle East Empire with capitals at Antioch (Syria) and Seleucia (in Iraq).

300-251 B.C. : First Punic War (264-241 B.C.) Rome defeats the Carthaginians and begins its domination of the Mediterranean.

250-201 B.C. : Second Punic War (219-201 B.C.)Hannibal, Carthaginian general was defeated by Scipio Africanus at Zama (202 B.C.). Great Wall of China built (c. 215 B.C.).

200-151 B.C. : Romans defeat Seleucid King Antiochus III at Thermopylae (191 B.C.).Beginning of Roman world domination.

150-101 B.C. : Third Punic War (149-146 B.C.) Rome destroys Carthage, killing 450,000 and enslaving the remaining 50,000 inhabitants.

| 100-51 B.C. | : Julius Caesar (100-44 B.C.) attacked Britain (55 B.C.) and conquered Gaul (France) (50 B.C.). Cleopatra on Egyptian throne (51-31 B.C.). Chinese develop use of paper (100 B.C.). Virgil, Roman poet (70-19 B.C.). Horace, Roman poet (65-8 B.C.). |
| 50-1 B.C. | : Caesar crosses Rubicon to fight Pompey (50 B.C.). Herod made Roman governor of Judea (37 B.C.). |

AD (Anno Domini)

1 AD	: Scholars evolved the new calendar didn't have the concept of zero, the new Gregorian calendar is calculated to start at year 1, so we go directly from December 31, 1 BC to January 1, 1 AD for making all the easy calculations of date.
9 AD	: Battle of Teutoberg Forest - 20,000 Roman soldiers under the command of Publius Quinctilius Varus in Germany are killed while in a long convoy line through the Teutoberg Forest.
12 AD	: The supremacy of Latin completed; the last known Etruscan inscription is carved.
30-33 AD	: Christianity set up as the new religion when Jesus is crucified.
70 AD	: The Romans under the direction of Titus destroy Jerusalem killing one and a half million Jews. The gold taken from the Temple finances the Colosseum back in Rome.
85-165	: Claudius Ptolemy devises a structure of Astronomy which will last for 1400 years. He calculates pi as 3+8/60+30/602 which in decimals is "3.1416666...".
97	: Chinese General Pan Chao sends an embassy to the Roman Empire.
235	: The 'Crisis of the Third Century' starts. The Eternal City struggled with civil wars, plagues, barbarian invasion, and climate change.
250	: Beginning of the Classic period for the Maya arises to the spread of scientific knowledge and architecture.
271	: Roman Emperor Aurelian starts building the walls around Rome which would run for 12 miles and were 11 feet thick and 26 feet tall. This is a concrete statement that Rome could no longer hold its enemies back at the border.
313	: When Edict of Milan issued, Christians are tolerated in the Roman Empire.
329	: Saint Basil of Caesarea, Greek bishop of Caesarea Mazaca (modern day Turkey), is born. He will care for the poor and establish what we would consider the first hospital.
400	: The first practical horse collar appears. Earlier versions choked the horse and limited their agricultural use. Horses quickly replaced some oxen since they are more efficient with the new collar.
476	: The Western Roman Empire falls.
496	: King Clovis of the Franks converts to orthodox Christianity.
550	: Persians use windmills to power irrigation pumps.
570	: Prophet Mohammad born. Syria, Jerusalem, Egypt, Persia, & N. Africa fall to Muslim armies after many decades.
632	: Prophet Muhammad dies.

732   : Battle of Tours, Charles Martel stops a Muslim army and the Muslim advance into Western Europe.

793   : Vikings start raiding Ireland.

850   : The Vikings settle Greenland. English farmers grow grapes for wine.

900   : Fall of the Mayan Classic culture. In one of the great mysterious of North America, the Mayan left their amazing cities all over Mesoamerica.

910   : The first nailed iron horseshoe is documented.

999   : Gerbert (940-1003) becomes Pope Sylvester II and writes about "Arabic" numerals.

1024   : The Chinese issue the first paper money.

1099   : The first crusade captures Jerusalem using 15,000 troops and establishes five small Christian states. Roughly, a thousand years earlier when Rome captured Jerusalem of about 60,000 soldiers. The Middle Age's battles were smaller in scope than antiquity.

1140   : Angkor Wat, a huge temple complex - a really huge amazing complex built in Cambodia.

1149   : Oxford University is founded in England.

1175   : The Toltec civilization collapses in Mexico.

1200   : In an amazing navigation feat, Tahitians sail to Hawaii and enslave the local inhabitants who had arrived around 800 years earlier.

1200   : The Mayan culture revives after its collapse in 900ad and survives until the 1450s when it falls shortly before the Europeans arrive.

1206   : Genghis Khan leads the Mongol armies. 30 to 60 million people are killed in their campaigns building the largest known land empire. It stretched from the Pacific Ocean to the Black Sea.

1223   : Genghis Kahn invades Russia.

1250   : European sailors now begin to use the magnetic compass.

1258   : Mongol troops utterly destroy Baghdad, the capital of the Islamic Abbasid Caliphate. The Mongols destroyed so many books by throwing them into Tigris that its water was colored black from the ink.

1275   : Marco Polo starts on his alleged trip to China. He returns in 1295 to Venice.

1285   : Spectacles for the farsighted are invented in Italy.

1300   : Eyeglasses are common in Rome for scholars.

1300   : Gunpowder used for warfare in England after being introduced to Europe in 1242.

1315   : Great Famine of 1315-1317 Torrential rains and cool weather, perhaps the result from a volcano, devastate crops in Europe. Millions die from starvation.

1337   : Timur-i Lang (Tamerlane) a Muslim conqueror of Mongol descent was born. He conquers a huge territory in the Middle East and Asia.

1346	: The Bubonic plague starts in China and moves westward aided by the ease of travel in the Mongol empire.
1348	: The Black Plague (aka Bubonic) in Europe kills about 75 million.
1431	: Joan of Arc burned at the stake. She is credited with leading the French in victory over the English. The English had been dominating France since Agincourt. Joan of Arc was helped by artillery that could now damage castle walls of the English.
1441	: First documented black African slaves imported into Europe.
1455	: German inventor Johann Gutenberg revolutionizes knowledge transfer. He improves or invents three items: the printing press, movable metal type, and an oil-based ink. His first work is the 42-line Bible.
1498, May 20	: Captain Vasco da Gama becomes the first European to travel to India by way of the sea. He arrives near the city of Calicut and receives a hostile welcome from the traders.
1514	: Nicolas Copernicus (1473-1543) returns to Poland convinced that the earth revolves around the sun. He dedicates his work to his friend Pope Paul III.
1536	: John Calvin wrote The Institutes of the Christian Religion.
1550	: Greek, Latin, and Hebrew scholar Robertus Stephanus publishes a Greek New Testament, the Textus Receptus, became the basis for many translations into common languages for centuries to come. This is the first Bible to have our familiar chapter and verse notations.
1556	: Earthquake in China kills 830,000.
1559, January 15	: Elizabeth Tudor, after surviving many attempts on her life, crowned queen of England ushering in the English Renaissance where England becomes a major world power.
1564, April 23	: William Shakespeare, titan of English literature, is born in Stratford-on-Avon in England.
1686	: Isaac Newton writes Mathematical Principles of Natural Philosophy which shows the laws of the heavens are the same as the laws of earth.
1776	: The American colonies declared themselves independent of Great Britain.
1795	: The Metric system of measurement is introduced into France.
1804	: Napoleon is crowned Emperor of France.
1815, June 18	: Napoleon defeated at Waterloo
1816	: Mary Shelley is forced inside and writes Frankenstein.
1824	: Mexico's new constitution abolishes slavery.
1833	: Charles Babbage designs the Difference Machine - a forerunner of the modern computer. Traditionally it was thought to fail because metallurgy was not yet advanced enough.
1836	: Slavery, which had been outlawed in Mexico, is reintroduced into Texas with the birth of the Republic of Texas.
1848, February 26	: Karl Marx and Fredrick Engels publish a little pamphlet, The Communist Manifesto.

1856	:	Louis Pasteur shows that disease is spread from tiny, little organisms, instead of bad vapors. Germ theory is born.
1859	:	Charles Darwin publishes Origin of Species.
1860	:	James Clerk Maxwell completes his four equations of electromagnetism.
1860	:	Herman Hollerith invents an electronic tabulator for the US Census. He starts a company that eventually becomes IBM.
1863, January 1	:	President Lincoln signs the Emancipation Proclamation freeing the slaves in rebelling states. This makes British intervention on behalf of the Confederacy less likely due to the strong anti-slavery sentiments there.
1866	:	North America and Europe are connected by a 2,500 mile long telegraph table.
1872, March 1	:	Yellowstone, the world's first national park is created in the western US.
1873	:	The Colt Firearms company debuts the revolutionary Colt Single Action Army Revolver, or Peacemaker, which employs metal cartridges.
1876-1878	:	Between 30 and 60 million people die in the Great Famine as the rains fail in India, China, and many other countries.
1882, September 30	:	World's first hydroelectric dam is built in Appleton Wisconsin.
1895	:	Wilhelm Roentgen accidentally discovers X-Rays. Within a year, X-Rays are being used in the medical field to set bones and peer into the body. For his research, Wilhelm was awarded the first Nobel Prize in physics in 1901.
1905	:	Albert Einstein publishes his theory of relativity and also states energy equals matter ($E = mc^2$).
1911	:	Rutherford proposes the 'Solar System' model of the atom.
1912, April 15	:	The Titanic sank down after collided with an iceberg and 1,500 people died.
1915, September 6	:	The first military tank rolls off the assembly line in England to break the stalemate of trench warfare in WWI. Although the first tank, Little Willie, is woefully underpowered, it is a sign of things to Come.
1916	:	Einstein publishes his 'General Relativity' paper.
1917, April 6	:	The United States enters World War I against Germany. The tide of the war is already against the Germans. 10 million people will die from the war.
1918, November 11	:	On the 11th hour of the 11th day of the 11th month, World War I is officially over. During this war, 6 hours 2,738 soldiers died. 320 of those were American.
1918	:	The influenza virus kills over 50 million people. About a quarter of the US population catches it, and 2 to 3% die from it.
1939, September 1	:	Germany invades Poland starting World War II.
1939, September 3	:	German submarine U-30 sinks the civilian ship Athena starting the "longest, largest, and most complex" naval battle in history, the "Battle for the Atlantic".

1942, February 23	:	A Japanese submarine shells an oil refinery near Santa Barbara California.
1942, May 7	:	Carrier groups of Japanese and Americans fight the Battle of the Coral Sea. This is the first time that the ships fighting never had sight of each other; airplanes did the damage.
1945, March 9-10	:	The most deadly single day air raid in WWII occurs when Tokyo is fire-bombed resulting in over 100,000 causalities.
1945, July 16	:	The earth witnesses the first nuclear explosion as the Manhattan Project comes to fruition in the Trinity test of a plutonium bomb.
1945, August 9	:	8 kg of plutonium-239 on Nagasaki, Japan. (The B-29 program cost 3 billion dollars, while the atomic bomb cost less, 2 billion).
1945, August 14	:	Japan surrenders in WWII eight days after the second atom bomb is dropped.
1947, August 15	:	British Empire back off from Indian subcontinent.
1947, November 29	:	The United Nations (UN) General Assembly passes Resolution 181 calling for the partition of Palestine into Arab and Jewish states.
1948, May 14	:	Since the British mandate over Palestine is about to expire, David Ben-Gurion and the Jewish People's Council announce the new State of Israel.
1949	:	Half of all the gold mined in history, 22,000 tons, is in the United States due in part to the US selling weapons and supplies during WWII.
1949, July 27	:	The Comet, the world's first jet powered airliner, takes flight revolutionizing the airline industry.
1950, June 25	:	North Korean soldiers invade South Korea starting the Korean War.
1952, November 1	:	The world's first thermonuclear bomb is detonated on Eniwetok Atoll bringing the fire of the sun to our planet.
1953, May 29	:	Edmund Hillary of New Zealand and Tenzing Norgay, a Nepalese Sherpa, reach the summit of Everest. News of this once-in-a-species event reached England on the day of Queen Elizabeth II's coronation.
1954, January 21	:	Nautilus, the first nuclear powered submarine launched.
1957	:	Sputnik I becomes the first man-made satellite.
1958	:	The deaths of 45 million people during the famine phase existed in the China.
1961, August 12	:	Communist East Germany starts erecting barbed wire fences and later concrete walls in what will become an indication of the cold war, the Berlin Wall.
1961, April 11	:	Yuri A. Gargarin becomes the first human in space and to orbit the earth
1968, March 16	:	504 Vietnamese were killed in the My Lai Massacre in Vietnam.
1969, July 20	:	Neil Armstrong becomes the first man to walk on the moon.
1969	:	The Chemical Bank of Rockville Center New York presents the world with the first ATM machine.
1975, April 30	:	After 11 years, 58,000 American dead, and 2 million Vietnamese killed, the Vietnam War finally ends.
1984	:	Largest bio-terrorist attack in the United States modern history

		occurs in The Dales, Oregon. 751 people become ill with the salmonella bacteria spread by followers of Bhagwan Shree Rajneesh in places like salad bars.
1989, November 9	:	East and West Germans tear down the Berlin wall and pave the way for the uniting of Germany a year later. The Cold War ends and the Soviet Union will be dissolved.
1991, January 16	:	President George Herbert Walker Bush with allies launches the First Iraqi War with Operation Desert Storm to push the Iraqi army out of the tiny kingdom of Kuwait.
1994, April 27	:	Nelson Mandela wins South Africa's first multiracial election.
2001, September 11	:	Nineteen al-Qaeda militants hijack four commercial airplanes. Two of the planes fly into the twin towers of the World Trade Center in New York City, the third plane crashes into the Pentagon.
2001, October 7	:	Under the direction of President George Bush, US forces invade Afghanistan to deny Al-Qaeda a base of operations begun the war in American history.
2005, August 29	:	Hurricane Katrina slams into the Gulf Coast and becomes the worst natural disaster in the US to date. The government will be heavily criticized for its slow response to aid citizens.
2011, December 15	:	Osama Bin Laden founder of Al-Qaeda killed in Pakistan by the US Senate army.
2012	:	Barrack Obama re-elected as the US President.
2013	:	The West African Ebola virus epidemic becomes the most widespread outbreak of Ebola virus disease in history
2015	:	Nepal is devastated by a massive 7.8 earthquake - nearly 9,000 dead, 22,000 injured, 3.5 million people homeless; Greece dives into severe debt, pressuring EU. Zika virus epidemic spreads rapidly across South America.
2017	:	India's ISRO set the world record for the largest number of satellites ever launched successfully on a single rocket - 104 satellites
2018	:	US-China trade war began
2019	:	ISIS chief Abu Bakr al-Baghdadi killed by the US military. Sri Lanka Easter bombings: 259 people killed, over 500 injured after 3 churches and 3 luxury hotels are objectified in a series of coordinated terrorist suicide bombing.
2020	:	The World Health Organization announced Jan. 9 that a deadly corona virus had emerged in Wuhan, China. After a while, the virus has spread across the globe to more than 20 million people, resulting in at least 3 million deaths worldwide.
2021	:	Joe Biden became new elected US President. COVID-19 came back with various types of new variants in many countries. The total area of 2,270,232 ha burnt in the wildfires escalated in the areas of US, Canada, and some parts of Europe as well. Taliban sieges Kabul, capital of Afghanistan.

The Mesopotamian Civilization

Period: 3500 BC–500 BC

Native Location: Northeast by the Zagros Mountains, southeast by the Arabian plateau

Present Location: Iraq, Syria, and Turkey

Meaning: Land between rivers (ancient Greek)

Major Highlights: First civilization in the world

Occupation/ Trade: Agriculture.

Currency: Mesopotamian shekel

The name Mesopotamia originated from Greek word mesos, meaning middle and potamos, meaning "land between the rivers". Mesopotamia is considered the beginning of civilization. The rivers are the Tigris and Euphrates. Mesopotamia is also implied by a changing succession of ruling bodies from different areas and cities that seized control over a period of thousands of years.

The civilization is well known for its prosperity, city life and its rich literature, mathematics and astronomy. Mesopotamian religion was polytheistic, with followers worshipping various prime gods and thousands of minor gods. The three main gods were Ea (Sumerian: Enki), the god of wisdom and magic, Anu (Sumerian: An), the sky god, and Enlil (Ellil), the god of earth, storms and agriculture and the controller of fates. Hammurabi's (who ruled 1792–1750 B.C.) most famous contribution is his list of laws, titled as the "Code of Hammurabi", formulated around 1772 B.C. Mesopotamia at first glance does not look like an ideal place for a civilization to flourish. It is hot and very dry. However, snow, melting in the mountains at the source of these two rivers, created an annual flooding.

- The flooding deposited silt, which is fertile, rich, soil, on the banks of the rivers every year. This is why Mesopotamia is part of the Fertile Crescent, an area of land in the Middle East that is rich in fertile soil and crescent-shaped.
- Associated with Mesopotamia are ancient cultures like the Sumerians, Assyrians, Akkadians, and Babylonians.
- Lower Mesopotamia is located the modern country of Iraq, while Upper Mesopotamia is in Syria and Turkey.

◁   The Sumerians were the first people to migrate to Mesopotamia, they created a great civilization. The wheel, ploy, and writing (a system which we call cuneiform) are examples of their achievements. The farmers in Sumer created levees to hold back the floods from their fields and cut canals to channel river water to the fields.

◁   Some evidences of metalwork in art come from southern Mesopotamia, a silver statuette of a kneeling bull from 3000 B.C.

Popular Terms

Code of Hammurabi - It was set in place by Babylonian King Hammurabi. It is one of the oldest detailed recordings of a code of law in world history.

Cuneiform - One of the earliest forms of writing originated by the Sumer. It uses wedge shaped marks to make picture symbols on clay tablets. Cylinder seal - An engraved stone cylinder used to create a seal or signature on clay tablets.

Fertile Crescent - A large area in the Middle East that is shaped like a crescent on a map. It stretches from the Persian Gulf, along the Tigris and Euphrates rivers, over to the Mediterranean Sea, and downwards the Nile River Valley of Egypt.

Indus Valley Civilization

Period: 3300 BC–1900 BC

Native Location: Around the basin of the Indus river

Present Location: Northeast Afghanistan to Pakistan and northwest India

Major Highlights: One of the most widespread civilizations, covering 1.25 million km

Occupation/ Trade: Agriculture.

Currency: Barter Exchange System

The Indus River Valley Civilization, 3300-1300 BCE, also called as the Harappa Civilization, stretched from modern-day northeast Afghanistan to Pakistan and northwest India. Indus Valley excavation sites have shown a number of different evidences of the culture's art, including sculptures, seals, pottery, gold jewellery, and detailed structures figurines in terracotta, bronze, and steatite. It's another name because of its location in the valley of the Indus River; it is also commonly called Indus-Sarasvati Civilization and the Harappan Civilization.

◁   The lifespan of the Indus Valley Civilization is often separated into three phases: Early Harappa Phase (3300-2600 BCE), Mature Harappa Phase (2600-1900 BCE) and Late Harappa Phase (1900-1300 BCE).

◁   It is considered a Bronze Age society, and inhabitants of the ancient Indus River Valley developed new techniques in metallurgy—the science of working with copper, bronze, lead, and tin. They also performed intricate handicraft, especially using products made of the semi-precious gemstone Carnelian, as well as seal carving— the cutting of patterns into the bottom face of a seal used for stamping.

- ◁ The Indus cities are known for their urban planning, baked brick houses, elaborate drainage systems, water supply systems, and clusters of large, non-residential buildings.
- ◁ The Indus Valley Civilization is also known as the Harappa Civilization, after Harappa, the first of its sites to be excavated in the 1920s, in what was then the Punjab province of British India and is now in Pakistan.
- ◁ Mohenjo-Daro is considered to have been built in the 26th century BCE and became not only the largest city of the Indus Valley Civilization but one of the world's earliest, major urban centres.
- ◁ Located west of the Indus River in the Larkana District, Mohenjo-Daro was one of the most sophisticated cities of the period, with sophisticated engineering and urban planning.
- ◁ Mohenjo-Daro was left around 1900 BCE when the Indus Civilization went into sudden decline.

Popular Terms

Steatite: Also known as Soapstone, steatite is a talc-schist, which is a type of metamorphic rock. It is very soft and has been a medium for carving for thousands of years.

Chalcolithic period: A period also known as the Copper Age, which lasted from 4300-3200 BCE.

Citadels: A central area in a city that is heavily fortified.

Harappa and Mohenjo-Daro: Two of the major cities of the Indus Valley Civilization during the Bronze Age.

Egyptian Civilization

Period: 3150 BC–30 BC

Native Location: Banks of the Nile

Present Location: Egypt

Major Highlights: Construction of pyramids

Occupation/ Trade: Farming, Craft ship, Soldiers, Scribes, Priests and Priestesses. Farmers

Currency: Egyptians used gold currency was called shat.

Egyptian civilization grew along the Nile River in huge portion because the river's annual flooding ascertains the reliable, rich soil for growing crops. The Egyptians kept written records using a writing system known as hieroglyphics. The history of Egypt is divided into three "kingdom" periods—Old, Middle, and New—with shorter intermediate periods segregating the kingdoms. Old Kingdom ruled from 2686-2181 BCE. Old Kingdom rulers built the first pyramids, which were both tombs and monuments for the kings who had them built. The time period in which Middle Kingdom ruled 2000-1700 BCE. The Middle Kingdom saw Egypt unified again as kings found ways to take back power from regional governors. The time period in which New Kingdom ruled from 1550-1077 BCE. This period was Egypt's most prosperous time and marked the peak of its power.

◄ The term pharaoh, which called to the king's palace, became an appellation for the king himself during this period, later emphasizing the idea of divine kingship. Egyptian civilization has flourished continuously since prehistoric times.

◄ The civilization has always been strongly connected with other parts of the world, bringing in and exporting goods, religions, food, people and ideas.

◄ The country was also occupied by other powers — the Persians, Nubians, Greeks and Romans all conquered the country at different points in time.

◄ Ancient Egypt was rich in culture including government, religion, arts, and writing. The government and religion were tied together as the leader of the government, the Pharaoh, was also leader of the religion. Writing was also important in keeping the government running.

◄ The pharaohs of Egypt were often buried in giant pyramids or in secret tombs. They believed that they needed treasure to be buried with them to help them in the afterlife.

◄ As a result, archaeologists have a lot of well preserved artefacts and tombs to examine in order to find out how the ancient Egyptians lived.

Popular Terms

Mummy - A dead body that has been specially preserved by embalming so that it won't rot.

Nefertiti - A queen of Egypt who was popular for her beauty.

Osiris – The god of afterlife in the Egyptian mythology.

Pharaoh - The supreme ruler of all of Ancient Egypt. He or she was considered as a god.

Pyramid - A huge tomb built for the pharaohs of Egypt. It was made from stone and had four sides that came to a point at the top in a pyramid shape.

Rosetta stone - A special stone that had the same inscription written both in Greek and in Egyptian hieroglyphics. It was very useful in translating and understanding hieroglyphics.

Sphinx - A mythological beast with the body of a lion and the head of a pharaoh or god. The Egyptians constructed sphinx statues to protect tombs.

The Mayan Civilization

Period: 2600 BC–900 AD

Native Location: Around present-day Yucatan

Present Location: Yucatan, Quintana Roo, Campeche, Tabasco, and Chiapas in Mexico and south through Guatemala, Belize, El Salvador, and Honduras

Major Highlights: Complex understanding of astronomy

Occupation/ Trade: Priest, Epigrapher, Mayanist.

Currency: Barter Exchange System

The term "Maya" describes to both a modern-day group of people who live across the globe and their ancestors who built an ancient civilization that stretched across much of Central America. The Maya civilization was one of the most dominant Indigenous societies of Mesoamerica (a term used to describe Mexico and Central America before the 16th century Spanish conquest).The Classic Period, which began around A.D. 250, was the golden age of the Maya Empire. The Maya civilization reached its peak during the first millennium A.D., and Maya ruins can still be seen across Central America.

- The earliest Maya inhabitants date to around 1800 B.C., or the starting of what is called the Pre classic or Formative Period.
- The Classic Maya built many of their temples and palaces in a stepped pyramid shape, decorating them with elaborate reliefs and inscriptions.
- The Maya had a perplex number of gods, with at least 166 named deities. Because each of the gods had many aspects and facts.
- The Maya were proficient at agriculture, pottery, hieroglyph writing, calendar-making and mathematics, and left behind an astonishing amount of impressive architecture and symbolic artwork.
- The Late pre-classic city of Mirador, in the northern Peten, was one of the greatest cities ever built in the pre-Columbian Americas.

Popular Terms

Kukulcan - The serpent god of the Maya.

Lintel - An architectural element often found over doorways in Maya architecture.

Obsidian - A hard rock that was employed to make sharp edges and tools.

Popol Vuh - A book or codex that described Maya religion and mythology.

Pre-classic Period - The period of Maya history began from starting of the Maya civilization around 2000 BC to the start of the Classic Period in 250 AD.

Post-classic Period - The period of Maya history began from the end of the Classic Period in 900 AD to the end of the Maya civilization in 1500 AD.

The Chinese Civilization

Period: 1600 BC–1046 BC
Native Location: Yellow River and Yangtze region
Present Location: Country of China
Major Highlights: Invention of paper and silk
Occupation/ Trade: Agriculture.
Currency: Yuanbao is a small metal ingot.

The name 'China' comes from the Sanskrit word 'Cina (derived from the name of the Chinese Qin Dynasty, pronounced 'Chin') which was translated as 'Cin' by the Persians. The prehistoric Xia Dynasty existed in the time period of 2070-1600 BCE. In the year 1046 BCE, King Wu, of the province of Zhou, battled against King Zhou of Shang and his forces at the Battle of Muye, establishing the Zhou Dynasty (c. 1046- 256 BCE). It is found that tea was first cultivated in Yunnan during the Shang Dynasty era. 1046-771 BCE signifies the Western Zhou Period whereas 771-226 BCE signifies the Eastern Zhou Period. The Shang ruled in the Yellow River valley, which is commonly organized to be the framework of Chinese civilization. Shi Huangdi set up the Qin Dynasty (221-206 BCE) which is also called as the Imperial Era in China. Shi Huangdi's original wall (The Great Wall of China) built under his rule.

- Confucius was a philosopher and teacher who lived from 551 to 479 B.C.E.
- Scholars have discovered that some characters such as the word for father, □ fù, look somewhat similar to the characters that the Shang wrote. Their inscriptions have been found on tens of thousands of oracle bones and on their surviving bronze metal creations.
- The Shang produced large, heavy, and geometrically intricate bronze objects in characteristic styles that the Zhou clan who were initially subjects of the Shang Dynasty continued after they took over the empire.
- Jade objects had religious significance, and this is an unusual tradition of ancient culture that many modern Chinese retain. They consider it to be quite an auspicious material, and many still wear it as an amulet as you can observe in China today.
- Green tea brewing is another ancient Chinese tradition carried on in modern times.
- The earliest example of silk fabric dates from 3,630 BC in Henan. Silk cloth manufacture was well advanced during the Shang Dynasty era.

Popular Terms

Confucianism - A religion or philosophy based on the teaching of Confucius.

Dragon - A sacred mythical creature that has the long body of a serpent, sharp teeth, four legs with sharp talons, and can fly.

Great Wall of China - A 5500 mile long wall built along the northern border of China. It was built to keep out the Mongol invaders.

Pagoda - A religious temple that is built as a tower with many tiers and roofs.

Porcelain - A type of ceramic invented by the Chinese. It is thin, strong, and beautiful. It is often called "china" in the west.

Silk - A luxurious material made from the cocoons of silkworms. Silk was highly prized in ancient China and was only worn by wealthy nobles.

Silk Road - A trade route that ran from northern China to Europe.

Taoism - One of the three major religions or philosophies of Ancient China, Taoism follows the teachings of Lao-Tzu.

Three Perfections - The Three Perfections were the three most important art forms of Ancient China: painting, poetry, and calligraphy.

Three Ways - Refers to the three major philosophies of Ancient China: Confucianism, Taoism, and Buddhism.

Yin and Yang - A part of the philosophy of Taoism, the yin and yang are opposites that balance each other throughout nature such as "light and dark", "hot and cold", and "male and female".

Greek Civilization

Period: 2700 BC–479 BC

Native Location: Italy, Sicily, North Africa, and as far west as France

Current Location: Greece

Major Highlights: Concepts of democracy and the Senate, the Olympics

Occupation/ Trade: Agriculture, Soldier, Teacher, Government worker, and craft ship.

Currency: Drachma is a silver coin of ancient Greece.

The term Ancient or Archaic, Greece refers to the years 700-480 B.C., not the Classical Age (480-323 B.C.) known for its art, architecture and philosophy. Ancient Greek civilization was the period following Mycenaean civilization, which ended about 1200 BCE, to the death of Alexander the Great, in 323 BCE. It was a period of political, philosophical, artistic, and scientific achievements that made a legacy with unparalleled influence on Western civilization. Surrounding the city was the farmland of the city-state. Many of the citizens lived within the city walls and walked out to their fields each day to work. Farms were very small – mere plots of land of a few acres. As the Greek cities grew in size and wealth, their societies became more complex. New classes appeared, of prosperous craftsmen, sailors and traders, to stand alongside the older classes of aristocrats, peasants and slaves. Women lived very sheltered lives, first under the authority of their father or another male relative, and then under that of their husband. Pythagoreans were another group of early Greek thinkers (6th-5th century BC). They formed a strange combination of philosophical school and religious brotherhood. They believed that all things could be explained by numbers. As a result, they did much mathematical speculation. However, they believed in such religious ideas as the transmigration of the soul. They lived simple, ascetic lives. Greek philosophy reached its high point in the careers of three thinkers who lived and worked in Athens, Socrates, Plato and Aristotle.

- The classical period offered a series of political reforms that created the system of Ancient Greek democracy known as demokratia, or "rule by the people".
- The epic poet Homer, from Ionia, produced his "Iliad" and "Odyssey" during the archaic period.
- Primarily, the two sects exist in the Greek civilization viz., Dorian and Ionian. Classical periods had the firm belief in 'Dorianism' as a linguistic and religious concept. Between 750 B.C. and 600 B.C., Greek colonies emerged from the Mediterranean to Asia Minor, from North Africa to the coast of the Black Sea.
- Larger houses were constructed around a courtyard, with rooms leading off. These houses were of two storeys, and were equipped with bathrooms and toilets. The walls of the reception rooms and family quarters were painted with large, colourful scenes.
- The Greeks worshipped a pantheon of gods and goddesses, headed by the chief of the gods, Zeus. Other gods included Hera, Zeus's wife; Athena, goddess of wisdom and learning; Apollo, god of music and culture; Aphrodite, goddess of love; Dionysus, god of wine; Hades, god of the underworld; and Diana, goddess of the hunt.

Popular Terms

Acropolis - An acropolis is a mound shaped citadel within a larger city. The popular acropolis is the Acropolis of Athens.

Agora - The agora was the central meeting place in Ancient Greek cities. Democracy was originated at the agora in Athens.

Alexander the Great - A ruler of Ancient Greece who conquered much of the civilized world from Greece to India including Egypt.

Democracy - A form of government where citizens have right to express the views and opinions in choosing their rulers and leaders and abiding by the laws.

Homer - A Greek epic poet who wrote the Iliad and the Odyssey.

Macedonia - A region of northern Ancient Greece, Macedonia was home to the Greek kings Philip II and Alexander the Great.

Olympics - An athletic event held by the Ancient Greeks every four years.

The Persian Civilization

Period: 550 BC–331 BC

Native Location: Egypt in the west to Turkey in the north, and through Mesopotamia to the Indus River in the east

Present Location: Modern-day Iran

Major Highlights: Constructed Royal roads.

Occupation/ Trade: Agriculture, Clothes making and Cattle Raising.

Currency: The Persian Daric (a gold coin).

The Persian Civilization is a series of dynasties centred in modern-day Iran that passed over the several centuries—from the sixth century B.C. to the twentieth century A.D. Cyrus was a ruler of one tribe who has beaten many nearby tribes including Media, Lydia and Babylon, confluence them under one rule. The first Persian Empire, founded by Cyrus the Great around 550 B.C., became one of the largest empires in history, stretching from Europe's Balkan Peninsula in the West to India's Indus Valley in the East. The Persian Empire came to the fore under the leadership of Cyrus II, who conquered the neighbouring Median Empire ruled by his grandfather.

- The Persians were the first people to establish regular routes of communication between three continents—Africa, Asia and Europe. They built many new roads and developed the world's first postal service.
- The first Persian Empire under Cyrus the Great soon became the world's first superpower.
- It united under one government three important sites of early human civilization in the ancient world: Mesopotamia, Egypt's Nile Valley and India's Indus Valley.
- The artefacts included a small golden chariot, coins and bracelets decorated in a griffon motif. (The griffon is a mythical creature with the wings and head of an eagle and the body of a lion, and a symbol of the Persian capital of Persepolis.)
- Named after the Persian prophet Zoroaster (also known as Zarathustra), Zoroastrianism is one of the world's oldest monotheistic religions. It's still practiced today as a minority religion in parts of Iran and India.

Popular Terms

Persian Wars- These were a series of conflicts between the Achamenid empire of Persia and Greek city states that began in 499 BC and ended until 449 BC.

Royal Roads- These roads were an ancient highway reorganized and rebuild by the Persian King Darius the great (Darius I) of the Archemanid Empire in the 5th Century BC. He built the road to serve the trade purpose.

Roman Cvilization

Period: 550 BC–465 AD

Native Location: Village of the Latini

Present Location: Rome

Major Highlights: Most powerful ancient civilization

Occupation/ Trade: Agriculture, doctors, engineers, architects, teachers, shopkeepers, craftsmen, soldiers, sailors, fisherman, writers, poets, musicians, statesmen, bankers, traders, merchants, accountants, government officials including tax collectors, smiths, jewellers, construction workers, temple workers, entertainers, artists, and slaves.

Currency: Sestertius, Aureus, Solidus

As per the legend, Rome was founded in 753 BC by twin sons Romulus and Remus who were raised by a she-wolf. During its twelve-century history, the Roman civilization shifted from a monarchy to an oligarchic republic to a immense empire. There is another Roman foundation legend, which has its sources lies in ancient Greece, tells of how the mythical Trojan Aeneas founded Lavinium and started a dynasty that would lead to the birth of Romulus and Remus several centuries later. In the Iliad, an epic Greek poem composed by Homer in the eighth century B.C., Aeneas was the only major Trojan hero to survive the Greek destruction of Troy. A passage told of how he and his descendants would rule the Trojans, but since there was no record of any such dynasty in Troy, Greek scholars proposed that Aeneas and his followers relocated. In the first century B.C., the Roman poet Virgil developed the Aeneas myth in his epic poem the Aeneid, which said about Aeneas' journey to Rome. Augustus, the first Roman emperor and emperor during Virgil's time, and Julius Caesar, his great-uncle and predecessor as Roman ruler, were mentioned as to be descended from Aeneas.

- The Roman Empire began in 27 BCE when Augustus became the sole ruler of Rome.
- Augustus and his successors tried to maintain the imagery and language of the Roman Republic to justify and preserve their personal power.
- Starting from Augustus, emperors built far more monumental structures, which changed the city of Rome in a dynamic way.

Popular Terms

Julius Caesar-The Roman ruler that declared himself emperor

Carthage- a city in northern Africa that Romans conquered

Republic- a form of government where the people choose their leaders
Pax Romana- Latin for Roman peace
Caesar Augustus- emperor during the time known as "Pax Romana"
Senate- the oldest and most powerful branch of the Roman Empire - made up of Patricians
Plebeian- the largest group in Roman society made up of farmers, traders and craftsman
Concrete- a building material first made by Romans
Mosaic- an art form using small bits of glass, brick, or stone set with mortar to form a picture

Aztec Civilization

Period: 1345 AD–1521 AD
Native Location: South-central region of pre-Columbian Mexico
Present Location: Mexico
Major Highlights: Nahuatl became the major language
Occupation/ Trade: Agriculture and Hunting.
Currency: Copper Tajadero (Spanish for chopping knife)

The Aztec civilization was with its capital city at Tenochtitlán (Mexico City) the most well-documented Mesoamerican civilization with sources including archaeology, native books (codices) and lengthy and detailed accounts from their Spanish conquerors - both by military men and Christian clergy. Aztec name derived from Culhua-Mexica, Nahuatl-speaking people who in the 15th and early 16th centuries ruled a large empire now known as the central and southern Mexico. The two principal gods worshipped were Huitzilopochtli (the war and sun god) and Tlaloc (the rain god) and both had a temple on top of the Templo Mayor pyramid at the heart of Tenochtitlan. Aztec religion comprises of mixed and absorbing elements from various other Mesoamerican cultures. Aztec culture is usually grouped with the cultural complex known as the nahuas, because of the common language they shared. They believed they came from a place called Aztlan, thus the name Aztecs.

- The Aztec was fundamentally a culture based on war and agriculture. Their two most important deities were Huitzilopochtli, the god of war, and Tlaloc, the god of rain. The duality of war and agriculture was crucial for the Aztec economy.
- The Aztecs expanded their empire through military conquest and sustained it through tributes imposed on the conquered regions.
- According to scholars, there are six large regions in the world that are the base of civilization. Those regions are Egypt, Mesopotamia, China, the Indus Valley, Mesoamerica, and the Andes, where people developed civilizations independently, boasting large cities and strong states.
- The Aztec religion was mainly polytheist. They had different gods, male and female. The sun god was Tonatiuh. There were many deities, and they were revered in monthly festivities with rich offerings.
- There is the black legend that only the Aztecs used human sacrifices in their religious rituals, when there is evidence that they existed in many other ancient cultures that were mostly agricultural societies.

Popular Terms

Adobe - A building substance made from mixing sand, clay, and water together and after that dry in the sun. Some of the Aztec homes were built from adobe.

Amanteca - Aztec craftspeople who worked with feathers. They fabricated clothing and headdresses for the nobility.

Nahuatl - The language spoken by the Aztecs. It is still spoken by some people in central Mexico today.

Tribute - A tax contributed by the city-states to the Aztec Emperor in the capital city of Tenochtitlan.

Incan Civilization

Period: 1438 AD–1532 AD

Native Location: Present-day Peru

Present Location: Ecuador, Peru, and Chile

Major Highlights: Largest Empire in South America in the pre-Columbian era

Occupation/ Trade: Government Official, Sorcerers, Weavers, Potters, Craft ship, Herders.

Currency: Barter Exchange System

The Inca civilization spread in ancient Peru between 1400 and 1533 CE, and their empire passed across western South America from Quito in the north to Santiago in the south. It is the largest empire ever seen in the Americas and the largest in the world at that time. The Incas kept record of their kings (Sapa Inca) enlisting such names as Pachacuti Inca Yupanqui (reign c. 1438-63 CE), Thupa Inca Yupanqui (reign c. 1471-93 CE), and Wayna Qhapaq (the last pre-Hispanic ruler, reign c. 1493-1525 CE). Inca society was highly organized and mannered. The Inca religion combined features of animism, fetishism, and the worship of nature gods. One of the most common Inca buildings was the ubiquitous one-room storage warehouse the qollqa. Built in stone and well-ventilated, they were either round and stored maize or square for potatoes and tubers. The kallanka was a very large hall used for community gatherings. More modest buildings include the kancha - a group of small single-room and rectangular buildings (wasi and masma) with thatched roofs built around a courtyard enclosed by a high wall.

- The kancha was a typical architectural feature of Inca towns, and the idea was exported to conquered regions.
- Macchu Picchu settled between the Andes Mountains of modern-day Peru and the Amazon basin and is one of the Inca's most popular existing archaeological sites.
- The Inca crafted magnificent objects from gold and silver, but perhaps their most striking examples of art were in the form of textiles.
- The Inca grew cotton, sheared wool and used looms to create their elaborate textiles. The finest grade of cloth was called cumpi, and was reserved for the emperor and nobility.

Popular Terms

Manco Capac – is the first Sapa Inca, Manco Capac introduced the Kingdom of Cuzco.

Peru - The modern nation where Cuzco and the capital of the Inca Empire was situated.

Middle Ages

The Middle Ages was the period in European history from the fall of Roman civilization in the 5th century CE to the period of the Renaissance (variously interpreted as beginning in the 13th, 14th, or 15th century, depending on the region of Europe and other factors). In the history of Europe, the middle ages or medieval period lasted approximately from the 5th to the late 15th centuries, similarly to the Post-classical period of global history. It began with the fall of the Western Roman Empire and transitioned into the Renaissance and the Age of Discovery.

Features

- During the Middle Ages, classical civilization was changed by exposure with three cultures: Germanic invaders, Christianity, and Islam.
- The period is also described as an "age of chivalry." The code of chivalry emphasised gentility, generosity, concern for the powerless, and a potential for experiencing selfless and passion.
- Medieval literature is dominated by two concerns: the demands of religious faith and the appropriate use of physical force.
- Chaucer spent the first part of his career as a court poet who catered to the narrow tastes of an aristocratic readership, but in The Canterbury Tales he writes about men and women from every social class.
- The most vivid legacy of the Middle Ages is the cast of characters it has contributed to world literature: Roland, Charlemagne, Sir Gawain, Beowulf, the pilgrims in The Canterbury Tales, and the lost souls of the Inferno.
- The medieval attitude toward women was deeply misogynistic; men were associated with reason, intellect, culture, and self-control; women with emotion, nature, and disorder.

1. Medieval European Civilization: During the middle ages, between 900 and 1300, Europe faced one of the longest periods of growth constantly in human history. Hungary, Portugal, Germany, France, England, and Spain were some of the countries which gained independence from the Western Roman Empire during the middle ages.

In the Middle Ages, society was organized in a system of feudalism, where people fell into one of three categories: commoners, clergy, or at the top, nobility. Three major groups that invaded Europe during the Middle Ages were the Vikings, the Magyars, and the Muslims.

Features

- The period of European history which we call "Medieval" is included of the thousand years in the 5th century to the period of the Renaissance in the 15th century.
- From the 5th Century onwards, the invasions led to the breakdown of Roman power in the western provinces. These territories also faced a sharp decline in material civilization.
- The Church was a powerful international organization, challenging and constraining the authority of emperors and kings. Senior churchmen were ministers and high officials to secular rulers, and the servants of the Church – priests, monks, nuns and other "clerks" – were tried in their own courts and by their own system of law.

- One of the special aspects of medieval society was the presence of monks and nuns in the monastery.
- In the late 11th century, a new kind of educational institution made i.e., the university. The first of these was at Bologna, in northern Italy, but other medieval universities soon appeared in Paris, Oxford, Cambridge and other places.
- For the aristocracy, massive stone castles housed powerful nobles, along with their families, retainers and domestic servants.
- A cathedral spire soared above a skyline of most medieval cities, able to be seen for miles around.
- Villagers' clothes were simple, consisting of woolen tunics for men and woolen dresses for women. Shoes were made from the leather of slaughtered animals. Poor townsfolk dressed in much the same way, but wealthier townsmen would have brightly dyed cloaks and gowns to wear, with linen (or, for the wealthiest, silk) undergarments next to their skin.Monks wore habits – plain, woolen garments, often with a hood.
- In medieval Europe, law was a hotchpotch of local custom, feudal practice, Roman law and Church law.

2. African Civilization: The classical African civilizations or African empires are terms that generally refer to the various pre-colonial African kingdoms. The civilizations usually include Egypt, Carthage, Axum, Numidia, and Nubia. The Aksumite Empire is also known as the Kingdom of Aksum (or Axum), this ancient society is the oldest of the African kingdoms on this list and is spread across what is today Ethiopia and Eritrea in an area where proof of farming dates back 10,000 years. Africa's first great civilization emerged in ancient Egypt in c. 3400 BC. The big three of the Ghana Empire, Mali Empire, and Songhai Empire as well as the lucrative trade connections they made with West and North Africa.

Features

- Civilizations Africa has appeared the rise and fall of many great civilizations and empires throughout its history.
- Significant civilizations evolved throughout the continent such as Carthage, the Mali Empire, and the Kingdom of Ghana. You can learn more about these civilizations in the links below.
- The culture of Ancient Africa varied as the geography of the large continent which comprises Sahara Desert of North Africa, the Savannah of West Africa, and the rainforest of Central Africa.
- The geography affected where people could inhabited, essential trade resources such as gold and salt, and trade routes that helped different civilizations to interact and develop.

3. Mongol Empire: During Europe's High Middle Ages the Mongol Empire, the largest adjoining land empire in history, began to rise. The Mongol Empire began in the Central Asian steppes and remained throughout the 13th and 14th centuries. At its greatest expansion, it included all of modern-day Mongolia, China, parts of Burma, Romania, Pakistan, Siberia, Ukraine, Belarus, Cilicia, Anatolia, Georgia, Armenia, Persia, Iraq, Central Asia, and much or all of Russia. The empire unified the nomadic Mongol and Turkic tribes of historical Mongolia under the leadership of Genghis Khan, who was proclaimed ruler of all Mongols in 1206. The empire grew rapidly under his rule and then under his descendants, who sent invasions in every direction. The vast transcontinental empire connected the east with the west with an enforced Pax Mongolica, or Mongol Peace, allowing trade, technologies, commodities, and ideologies to be disseminated and exchanged across Eurasia. The Pax Mongolica implies to the control of the regions under Mongol control during the height of the empire in the 13th and 14th centuries.

Features

◁ The Mongol Empire was known for its sheer military power, a rapid communication system based on relay stations, paper currency, diplomatic immunity and safe travel under Pax Mongolica.

◁ When Marco Polo travelled in the Mongol Empire in 1274, he was surprised to find paper currency, which was not available in medieval Europe at the time. Genghis Khan established paper money; this currency was fully backed by silk and precious metals.

◁ The Mongol Empire law was mainly focused on national issues and resolved disputes between the representatives of various cultural traditions.

◁ The idea that Genghis Khan had the Mandate of Heaven to rule an earthly empire without borders became an official ideology.

4. Arab Civilization: The Arabs were originally the people of the Arabian Desert. They conquered the Middle East from the Sassanian and Byzantine empires and established a succession of Arab-Islamic Middle Eastern empires from Spain to Central Asia and from the Caucasus to India. The Nabataeans, are an Arab people, who formed their Kingdom near Petra in the 3rd century BCE. Arab tribes, most notably the Ghassanids and Lakhmids, began to in the Southern Syrian Desert from the mid 3rd century CE onward, during the mid to later stages of the Roman and Sasanian empires.

Features

◁ Arabian culture is a part of Semitic civilization; because of this and because of the influences of sister Semitic cultures to which it has been subjected at certain epochs, it is often tough to determine what is specifically Arabian.

◁ The Arabian Peninsula was encircled by two more advanced civilizations, the Byzantine and Sassanian Empires.

◁ Arab Civilization is a mixture of certain classical Arab values as the Islamic culture and institutions, the inherited knowledge of the great civilizations of the Old World, and the unity provided by the Arabic language.

◁ The Arabs preserved and built upon existing knowledge in the domains of government, literature, philosophy, history, art and architecture, music, physical and mathematical sciences, biology, medicine, engineering, navigation, and commercial law.

Features

◁ Because Islam originated and has developed in an Arab culture; other cultures which have adopted Islam have tended to be influenced by Arab customs.

◁ The word "Islam" means "submission to the will of God."

◁ Muslims are monotheistic and worship one, all-knowing God, who in Arabic is known as Allah.

◁ Mosques are places where Muslims worship. Some of the significant Islamic holy places include the Kaaba shrine in Mecca, the Al-Aqsa mosque in Jerusalem, and the Prophet Muhammad's mosque in Medina.

◁ The Quran (or Koran) is the major holy text of Islam. The Hadith is another important book.

- ◁ Sunnis accept that the first four caliphs were the true successors to Muhammad. Shiite Muslims believe that only the caliph Ali and his descendants are the real successors to Muhammad.
- ◁ The Islamic calendar, also called the Hijra calendar, is a lunar calendar used in Islamic religious worship. The calendar began in the year 622 A.D., celebrating the journey of Muhammad from Mecca to Medina.
- ◁ The crescent moon and star has been adopted in some predominantly Muslim countries as a symbol of Islam, though the crescent moon and star image is believed to pre-date Islam and was originally a symbol of the Ottoman Empire.
- ◁ Islam's legal system is known as Sharia Law.

The European era between 14th to 17th centuries AD was designated as the Age of Renaissance generally known for **"Revival of Learning"**. The Florence city of Italian region **Tuscany** was well known as the birth place of Renaissance.

Reformation

Reformation was a social movement initiated by **Martin Luther** during **16th** century in Europe against **Roman Catholic Church**. He started criticizing the selling of self indulgence of higher authorities in the church by highlighting the fact that the Pope had no authority over the purgatory and there was no evidence of catholic doctrine of the merits of the saints in the gospel.

Major Revolutions

Glorious Revolution (1688)

It was otherwise known as the **Bloodless Revolution** primarily focused on securing freedom of worship from Catholics and unifying Whigs and Tories of Anglican church against the Roman Catholic ruler James II.

Industrial Revolution

It was the process of change in earning livelihood by adopting industrial processes rather than agriculture. It started during mid 18th century in Britain with the invention of several technological aids such as **spinning jenny** by **James Hargreaves** in 1764, water-powered spinning frame by Richard Arkwright in 1769, spinning mule by Samuel Crompton in 1779, **power loom** by **Edmund Cartwright** in 1785, **steam engine** by **James Watt** in 1769 etc.

American Revolution

It was the mutiny of people living in thirteen colonies of England in North America in late 18th century. Various factors such as French and Indian War, Stamp Act, Townshend Acts, Boston Massacre, Boston Tea Party (1773/Intolerable Acts, can be considered as the triggering fact of this revolution in 1775-83.

- ◁ On 4th July 1776, the **Declaration of Independece** was issued by Thomas Jafferson.
- ◁ The war ended with the Treaty of Paris in 1783.

French Revolution

It was one of the greatest revolutions of eighteenth century which put an end to French monarchy. It lasted from 1789 to 1799, and partially carried forwarded by Napoleon during the later expansion of the French Empire.

- ◁ **Liberty, Equality and Fraternity** were the watch of the revolution.
- ◁ **Montesquieu, Voltaire** and **Rousseau** were the French writers and thinkers of the period.

Russian Revolution

Based on the ideology of Marxism, Russian revolution took place in 1917 and eventually ended up in creating the Russian Soviet Union. The prime causes of these revolutions were the autocratic rule of Czars, inefficient and vigorous use of power, low living standard of people in the society, to support church forcefully.

Great Litterateur of Renaissance

Italian	Dante – Book Divine Comedy Petarch – Founder of Humanism. Boccacio- Book Dacemeron.
French	Rabelais – Pantagruel
Spanish	Cewantes – Don Quixote
German	Thomas Kempis – The Imitation of Christ

World Wars: I & II

Event	World War I	World War II
Countries Involved	Germany, Austria,Hungary, Bulgaria, Turkey vs. France, Russia, Britain, US, Italy.	Britain, France, USSR, US, Other nations vs. Germany, Italy, Japan
Duration of War	July 28, 1914 – November 11, 1918	September 1, 1939 – September 2, 1945
Causes	**Immediate** Murder of Austrian King **Archduke Ferdinand** at **Serajevo** by a Serbian which resulted in strong hostility between Austria-Hungary and Serbia **Associated** Militarism Nationalism or Competitive Patriotism Economic Imperialism Anglo-German Rivalry and the charter of William II Lack of International Organization	**Immediate** Germany's ultimatum and Poland's rejection for surrender of Port Dazing. Refusal of Poland to establish rail link between Germany and West Prussia through Polish corridor. **Associated** The **Treaty of Versailles** (1919) Nationalist movement of Germany & Italy. Ideological conflict between Dictatorship and Democracy Inefficiency of League of Nation Colonial and commercial rivalry Aggressiveness of Berlin-Rome – Tokyo axis

Consequences	End of the German, Russian, Ottoman and Austro-Hungarian empires Formation of new countries in Europe and the Middle East. Transfer of German colonies and regions of the former Ottoman Empire to other powers Establishment of the **League of Nations**	Collapse of Nazi Germany Fall of Japanese and Italian Empires Creation of the **United Nations** Emergence of the United States and the Soviet Union as **superpowers** Beginning of the **Cold War**

Major Geographical Discoveries

Discovery	Year	Discoverer Name
Cape of Good Hope	1487	Bartholomew, Portugal
America	1492	Christropher Columbus, Spain
Newfoundland	1497	John Cabot, England
Sea-route of India	1498	Vasco da Gama, Portuguese
New Zealand	1642	Tasman, Holland

Major Wars in History

Trojan War

Participants: City of Troy vs City of Sparta

Duration of War: 10 years

Causes of War: The war resulted due to the kidnapping of Queen Helen from her husband, the king of Sparta by the Trojan Prince.

Outcome of war: The war ended with victory of Greek and destruction of Troy.

Persian War

Participants: Greek vs. Persia

Duration of War: 499 BC – 449 BC

Causes of War: The king of Persia, Darius I attacked Athens when the series of Greek uprisings were suppressed.

Outcome of war: The Greek had its victory against Persia.

Peloponnesian War

Participants: Athens vs. Sparta

Duration of War: 431 BC – 404 BC

Causes of War: The war occurred due to the political fragmentation and mutual two city states of Greece, Athens and Sparta.

Outcome of War: Eventually Sparta registered its victory by defeating Athens in Decelean war (known to be the third phase of Peloponnesian War), with the help of Persian Empire.

Punic Wars

First

Participants: Rome vs. Carthage

Duration of War: 264 BC -241 BC

Causes of War: The war broke out as the Carthaginians established a base of island that seemed to be a potential threat to Rome.

Outcome of War: The Romans won the war.

Second

Participants: Greek vs. Trojan

Duration of War: 218 BC- 201 BC

Causes of War: The war occurred when Carthage started expanding its power in Spain and striving for the coastal city of Saguntum (the present day Sagunto) which was allied with Rome.

Outcome of War: Finally Rome won over Carthage in the Battle of Zama forcing the Carthaginians to give up Spanish territories and its navy.

Third

Participants: Greek vs. Persian

Duration of War: 149 BC- 146 BC

Causes of War: The fear of Carthaginian resurgence led to the war in the city streets of Carthage

Outcome of War: Ultimately Romans destroyed the city of Carthage

Hundred Years' War

Participants: France vs. England

Duration of War: 1337 BC -1453 BC

Causes of War: The war broke out after King Edward III of England invaded the country of France and continued to seize its land and became its ruler.

Outcome of War: At the end France managed to defy the England's reign with the help of Scotland.

Russo-Japan War

Participants: Russia vs. Japan

Duration of War: 1904 – 05 AD

Causes of War: The war took place for having imperial authority over Manchuria and Korea.

Outcome of War: Japanese won the war.

Vietnam War

Participants: Democratic Republic of Vietnam allied with Soviet Union vs. China.

Duration of War: 1955 – 75 AD

Causes of War: The war was fought for checking communism spread all over South-Asia.

Outcome of War: The war ended with the victory of North Vietnam by empowering the Communist government in South Vietnam, Laos and Cambodia with annexure of South Vietnam. The American-led forces had to back out from Indochina.

Iraq–Iran War

Participants: Islamic Republic of Iran and the Republic of Iraq

Duration of War: 1980 – 88 AD

Causes of War: The war started with the invasion of republic of Iran resulting from a border dispute of two Republics.

Outcome of War: Iraq failed to take over the east bank of the Shatt al-Arab and strengthen Arab separatism in the region of Khuzestan. The Iranian invasion failed and the idea of deposing Saddam Hussein was shattered.

World Panorama

Type	Place
Tallest Animal	Giraffe
Tallest Building	Burj Khalifa (828 m)
Tallest Monument	Gateway Arch (USA)
Smallest Bird	Humming Bird
Smallest Continent	Australia
Smallest Planet	Mercury
Biggest Country by Area	Russia
Biggest Planet	Jupiter
Biggest Ocean	Pacific Ocean
Hottest Place	Death Valley, California, USA.
Deepest Lake	Baikal (Siberia)
Deepest Ocean	Pacific Ocean

Type	Place
Largest Continent	Asia
Largest Delta	Ganges Delta (consists of Bangladesh and the state of West Bengal, India)
Largest Desert	Sahara Desert (covers a surface area of 3.5 million square miles)
Largest Island	Greenland
Largest Dam	Three Gorges Dam (spans the Yangtze River in China)
Largest Library	United State Library of Congress, Washington D.C.
Largest Sea Bird	Albatross
Largest city in population	Tokyo, Japan
Largest Peninsula	Arabian Peninsula
Largest Solar Plant	Yanchi Solar Park, China

Type	Place
Longest River	Nile
Longest Railways	Trans-Siberian Railway
Longest Road Tunnel	Laedal Tunnel, Norway (24.51 km long)
Longest Railway Platform	Gorakhpur (Uttar Pradesh, India)

Type	Place
Longest Ship Canal	St. Laurence Seaway (USA and Canada)
Longest River Dam	Hirakud Dam, Odisha, India
Longest Mountain Range	Andes (South America, Length = 5500m)
Longest Wall	Wall of China

Type	Place
Highest Mountain Peak	Mt. Everest
Highest Mountain Range	Greater Himalayas
Highest Plateau	Pamir Tibet (Roof of World)
Highest Railway Station	Tanggula railway station
Highest Lake	Lake Titicaca
Highest Fall	Angel Falls (Venezuela, located on a tributary of the Rio Caroni)
Metal with highest Melting and Boiling Point	Tungsten
Highest Capital City	La Paz (Bolivia)

The first person to reach Mount Everest	Sherpa Tenzing, Edmund Hillary
The first person to reach the North Pole	Robert Peary
The first person to reach the South Pole	Amundsen
The first country to print book	China
The first religion of the world	Hinduism
The first country to issue paper currency	China
The first European to reach China	Marco Polo
The first country to host the modern Olympics	Greece
The first country to launch Artificial satellite in the space	Russia
The first country to send a man to the moon	U.S.A.
The first person to sail around the world	Magellan
The first person to fly an aeroplane	Wright Brothers
The first European to attack India	Alexander, The Great
The first country to host NAM summit	Belgrade (Yugoslavia)
The first Governor-General of Pakistan	Mohd. Ali Jinnah
The first country to prepare a constitution	U.S.A.
The first country to win the football World cup	Uruguay
The first Governor-General of the United Nations	Trygve Lie (Norway)

The first Prime Minister of Britain	Robert Walpole
The first President of the U.S.A	George Washington
The first woman Prime Minister of a country	Mrs. S. Bandamaike (Sri Lanka)
The first woman to climb Mount Everest	Mrs. Junko Tabei (Japan)
The first woman cosmonaut of the world	Velentina Tereshkova (Russia)
The first woman President of the U.N. General Assembly	Vijaya Lakshmi Pandit
The first man to fly into space	Yuri Gagarin (Russia)
The first batsman to score three test century in three successive tests on debut	Mohd. Azharuddin
The first man to have climbed Mount Everest Twice	Nawang Gombu
The first Muslim Prime Minister of a country	Benazir Bhutto (Pakistan)
The first woman Prime Minister of England	Margaret Thatcher
The first spacecraft to reach on Mars	Viking—I
The first shuttle to go in space	Columbia
The first person to land on the moon	Neil Armstrong followed by Edwin E. Aldrin
The first city on which the atom bomb was dropped	Hiroshima (Japan)
The first U.S. President to resign Presidency	Richard Nixon

SOBRIQUETS

Sobriquets	Primary Names
America's Motor	Detroit
Blue Mountains	Nilgiri Hills (India)
Britain of the South	New Zealand
Bengal's Sorrow	Damodar River (India)
China's Sorrow	River Hwang Ho
City of Dreaming Spires	Oxford (England)
City of Eternal Springs	Quito (South America)
City of Flowers	Cape Town (South Africa)
City of Golden Gate	San Francisco (USA)
City of Golden Temple	Amritsar (India)
City of Magnificient Buildings	Washington (USA)
City of Palaces	Kolkata (India)
City of Quiet	Thoroughfares Venice
City of Seven Hills	Rome (Italy)
City of Skyscrapers	New York (USA)
Cockpit of Europe	Belgium

Dark Continent	Africa
Emerald Isle	Ireland
Empire City	New York
Eternal City of Hopes	Rome, Italy
Forbidden City	Lhasa (Tibet)
Garden City	Chicago
Garden in the desert	Ethiopia
Garden of England	Kent (England)
Gate of tears	Strait of bab-el-Mandeb
Gateway of India	Mumbai
Golden City	Johannesburg
Gibraltar of Indian	Ocean Aden
Gift of Nile	Egypt
Granite City	Aberdeen
Hanging Valleys	Valley of Switzerland
Hermit Kingdom	Korea
Herring Pond	Atlantic Ocean
Holy Land	Palestine
Human Equator of the Earth	Himalayas
Island Continent	Australia
Island of Cloves	Zamzibar
Island of Pearls	Bahrain (Persian Gulf)
Islands of Sunshine	West Indies
Kashmir of Europe	Switzerland
Key to Mediterranean	Gibraltar
Land of Five Seas	South West Asia
Land of Five Rivers	Punjab, India
Land of Lakes	Scotland
Land of Golden Pagoda	Myanmar
Land of Kangaroo	Australia
Land of Golden Fleece	Australia
Land of Lilies	Canada
Land of Maple	Canada
Land of Midnight Sun	Norway
Land of Morning Calm	Korea
Land of Rising Sun	Japan
Land of Setting Sun	United Kingdom

Land of Thousand Elephants	Laos
Land of Thousand Lakes	Finland
Land of Thunderbolt	Bhutan
Land of White Elephant	Thailand
Loneliest Island	Tristan De Gumha (Mid. Atlantic)
Manchester of Japan	Osaka (Japan)
Pillars of Hercules	Straits of Gibraltar
Pink City	Jaipur, India
Play Ground of Europe	Switzerland
Quaker City	Philadelphia
Queen of the Adriatic	Venice
Roof of the World	The Pamirs (Tibet)
River in the Sea	Gulf Stream
Sickman of Europe	Turkey
Sugar Bowl of the world	Cuba
Venice of the East	Bangkok
Venice of the North	Stockholm
White City	Belgrade
Windy City	Chicago
Workshop of Europe	Belgium
World's Loneliest Island	Tristan Da Cunha
Yellow River	River Hwang Ho (China)

IMPORTANT BOUNDARY LINES

Boundary line	Location
Durand Line	Boundary between India and Afghanistan. It was drawn up in 1896 by the then Foreign Secretary of (British) India Sir Henry Mortimer Durand. This line is approximately 2,640 kilometers long.
Hindenburg Line	Divides Germany and Poland. Germans retreated to this line in 1917 during World War I.
Inter-Entity Boundary Line(IEBL)	Divides Bosnia and Herzegovina into two entities, the Republika Srpska and the Federation of Bosnia and Herzegovina.
Line of Control	Between India and Pakistan
Maginot line	Between France and Germany; built by France on its eastern border during World War to prevent German invasion
Marginal Line	320 km long line of fortification on the Russia-Finland border drawn up by General Mannerheim

Mason-Dixon Line	Line of demarcation between four states in the United State
McMohan Line	Demarcates the frontier between India and China. The line was drawn up by Sir Henry McMahon. China did not recognize the McMahon line and crossed it in 1962.
Order-Neisse Line	The border between Poland and Germany, running along the Order and Neisse rivers, adopted at the Poland Conference (Aug 1945) after World War II.
Parallel north	The boundary line between Iraq and Iran.
Radcliffe Line	It was named after its architect, Sir Cyril Radcliffe, who as chairman of the Border Commissions demarcating the boundary between India and Pakistan and was announced on 17 August 1947.
Siegfried Line	The line of fortification drawn up by Germany on its border with France.
16th Parallel	The boundary line between Angola and Namibia
17th Parallel north	The line which defines the boundary between North Vietnam and south Vietnam established by the Geneva Accords of 1954 before the two were united in the year 1976 following the surrender of the South Vietnamese government.
20th Parallel north	The boundary line between Libya and Sudan.
22nd Parallel north	The boundary line between Egypt and Sudan.
25th Parallel north	The boundary line between Mauritania and Mali.
26th Parallel north	The boundary line between Western Sahara and Mauritania.
38th Parallel north	The parallel of latitude which separates North Korea and South Korea
49th Parallel north	The boundary between USA and Canada.

IMPORTANT PEOPLE FOREVER

Augustus Caesar (63 BC-AD 14) – was the first Roman emperor, reigning from 27 BC until his death in AD 14. His status as the founder of the Roman Principate (the first phase of the Roman Empire) has consolidated a legacy as one of the most effective leaders in human history.

Shih Huang Ti (259 – 210 BC) – was the founder of the Qin dynasty, and first emperor of a unified China.

Euclid (c. 325 – 265 BC) – was a Greek mathematician, often referred to as the "founder of geometry" or the "father of geometry".

Aristotle (384 BC – 322 BC) – was a Greek philosopher and polymath during the Classical period in Ancient Greece. Taught by Plato, he was the founder of the Lyceum, the Peripatetic school of philosophy, and the Aristotelian tradition.

Confucius (551 – 479 BC) – Chinese philosopher and politician of the Spring and Autumn period who was traditionally considered the paragon of Chinese sages.

St. Paul (5 – AD 67) – Paul the Apostle (c. 5 – c. 64/67 AD), commonly known as Saint Paul and also known by his Hebrew name Saul of Tarsus was a Christian apostle (although not one of the Twelve Apostles) who spread the teachings of Jesus in the first-century world.

Christopher Columbus (1451 – 1506) – was an Italian explorer and navigator who completed four voyages across the Atlantic Ocean, opening the way for the widespread European exploration and colonization of the Americas.

Galileo Galilei (1564 – 1642) was an astronomer, physicist and engineer, sometimes described as a polymath, from Pisa, in modern-day Italy.

Nicolaus Copernicus (1473-1543) Renaissance mathematician and astronomer who believed Sun was the centre of the Universe – rather than earth

Constantine the Great (272 AD – 337) Roman Emperor was born in Naissus, Dacia Mediterranea (now Niš, Serbia), was the son of Flavius Constantius (a Roman army officer born in Dacia Ripensis who had been one of the four emperors of the Tetrarchy).

Martin Luther (1483-1546) Sought to reform the Roman Catholic Church – starting the Protestant Reformation.

George Washington (1732 – 1799) – Leader of US forces during American Revolution and 1st President of US.

Karl Marx (1818 — 1883) – German Communist philosopher; Marx's political and philosophical thought had enormous influence on subsequent intellectual, economic and political history.

Genghis Khan (1162 – 1227) – was the founder and first Great Khan (Emperor) of the Mongol Empire, which became the largest contiguous empire in history after his death. He came to power by uniting many of the nomadic tribes of Northeast Asia.

Adam Smith (1723-1790) Scottish social philosopher and pioneer of classical economics; also known as ''The Father of Economics'' or ''The Father of Capitalism,'' Smith wrote two classic works, The Theory of Moral Sentiments (1759) and An Inquiry into the Nature and Causes of the Wealth of Nations (1776).

Alexander the Great (356 — 323 BC) – King of Macedonia and military leader; a member of the Argead dynasty, he was born in Pella—a city in Ancient Greece—in 356 BC. He succeeded his father King Philip II to the throne at the age of 20, and spent most of his ruling years conducting a lengthy military campaign throughout Western Asia and Northeastern Africa.

Napoleon Bonaparte (1769 — 1821) – French military and political leader; usually referred to as simply Napoleon in English, was a French military and political leader who rose to prominence during the French Revolution and led several successful campaigns during the Revolutionary Wars.

Adolf Hitler (1889 – 1945) – Dictator of Nazi Germany; was an Austrian-born German politician who was the dictator of Germany from 1933 to 1945. He rose to power as the leader of the Nazi Party, becoming the chancellor in 1933 and then assuming the title of Führer und Reichskanzler in 1934.

Plato (424 – 348 BC) – was an Athenian philosopher during the Classical period in Ancient Greece, founder of the Platonist school of thought and the Academy, the first institution of higher learning in the Western world.

Oliver Cromwell (1599-1658) – was an English general and statesman who, first as a subordinate and later as Commander-in-Chief, led armies of the Parliament of England against King Charles I during the English Civil War, subsequently ruling the British Isles as Lord Protector from 1653 until his death in 1658.

John Locke (1632-1704) English political philosopher. Locke promoted a theory of liberal democracy and a social contract.

Ludwig van Beethoven (1770 – 1827) German composer of the classical and romantic period.

Simon Bolivar (1783 – 1830) – was a Venezuelan military and political leader who led what are currently the countries of Venezuela, Bolivia, Colombia, Ecuador, Peru, and Panama to independence from the Spanish Empire.

Rene Descartes (1596 – 1650) Dubbed as the father of modern philosophy, Descartes was influential in a new rationalist movement, which sought to question basic presumptions with reason.

Michelangelo (1475 – 1564) known simply as Michelangelo, was an Italian sculptor, painter, architect and poet of the High Renaissance born in the Republic of Florence, who exerted an unparalleled influence on the development of Western art.

Pope Urban II (1042 – 29 July 1099) Influential Pope who ordered the first Crusade to the Holy Land and set up the Papal Court

Asoka (c. 260 – 232 BC) Powerful Indian King who established large empire by conquest before converting to Buddhism and pursuing a peaceful approach.

St. Augustine (354 – 430) Influential Christian saint and writer, who shaped much of Western Christian thought.

John Calvin (1509 – 27 May 1564) Christian theologian who developed a strict brand of Protestant Christianity which stressed the doctrine of predestination.

Francisco Pizarro (1471 – 1541) Spanish Conquistador who claimed Inca lands for Spain.

Hernando Cortes (1485 – 1547) Spanish Conquistador who conquered the Aztec lands of modern-day Mexico.

Thomas Jefferson (1743 – 1826) 3rd President of US; Principle author of the US Declaration of Independence.

Queen Isabella I (1451 – 1504) Queen of Castille, who helped create a powerful and unified state of Spain whose influence spread to the Americas.

Joseph Stalin (1878 – 1953) Absolute ruler of the Soviet Union from 1924 to his death; led the Soviet Union in WWII.

Julius Caesar (100 BC – 44 BC) Roman ruler who oversaw the demise of the Roman Republic to be replaced with a Roman Emperor; militarily strengthened the power of Rome.

William the Conqueror (1028 – 1087) First Norman King of England

Sigmund Freud (1856 – 1939) An Austrian neurologist who founded psychoanalysis, which involved the investigation of the subconscious, dreams and human mind.

Edward Jenner (1749 – 1823) developed the world's first vaccine (the smallpox vaccine). Known as the father of immunology

Johann Sebastian Bach (1685 – 1750) composer and organist; created some of the world's most beautiful music.

Lao Tzu (6th Century BC –) Author of Tao Te Ching and founder of Taoism

Voltaire (1694 – 1778) A key figure of European Enlightenment; his satirical writings played a role in the French Revolution.

Jean-Jacques Rousseau (1712-1778) – French philosopher, author of Social Contract

Nicoli Machiavelli (1469 – 1527) Italian diplomat and Renaissance writer considered the father of political science.

Thomas Malthus (1766 – 1834) English scholar who raised concern over growing population.

John F. Kennedy (1917 – 1963) 38th President of the US; served at the height of the Cold War and helped defuse Cuban Missile Crisis.

Mani (216 –) Iranian founder of Manichaeism, a gnostic religion which for a time was a rival to Christianity.

Lenin (1870 – 1924) Leader of the Russian Revolution and new Communist regime from 1917 to 1924.

Sui Wen Ti (541 – 604) Founder of China's Sui Dynasty and reunifying China in 589.

Vasco da Gama (1460s –1524) Portuguese explorer, first European to reach India and establish a route for imperialism.

Cyrus the Great (600 – 530 BC) Founder of the Achaemenid Empire, the first Persian Empire, relatively enlightened ruler.

Peter the Great (1721 – 1725) Russian Emperor who expanded the Tsarist Empire to make Russia European power.

Mao Zedong (1893 – 1976) Leader of the Communist Revolution and dictator of China from 1949-1974.

Francis Bacon (1561 – 1626) Creator of the scientific method and key figure in Scientific Revolution of the Enlightenment.

Mencius (385–303BC) Chinese philosopher one of the principal interpreters of Confucianism.

Zoroaster (c. 1200 BC) Iranian prophet who founded the religion of Zoroastrianism.

Queen Elizabeth I (1533 – 1603) Queen of England from 1558 to her death in 1603; cemented England as a Protestant country; defeated Spanish Armada.

Menes (c. 3000 BC) Egyptian pharaoh who united Upper and Lower Egypt to found the First Dynasty.

Charlemagne (742 – 814) United Europe to form the Carolingian Empire; first western Emperor since the fall of Rome.

Homer (c. 750 BC) was the reputed author of the Iliad and the Odyssey, the two epic poems that are the foundational works of ancient Greek literature. He is regarded as one of the greatest and most influential writers of all time.

Justinian I (482 –   565) also known as Justinian the Great, was the Byzantine emperor from 527 to 565. His reign is marked by the ambitious but only partly realized renovatio imperii, or "restoration of the Empire".

Mahavira (6th century BC) was the 24th Tirthankara of Jainism. He was the spiritual successor of the 23rd Tirthankara Parshvanatha. Mahavira was born in the early part of the 6th century BCE into a royal Jain family in Bihar, India. Historically, Mahavira, who preached Jainism in ancient India, was an older contemporary of Gautama Buddha.

Nelson Mandela (1918–2013) Campaigned for justice and freedom in his native South Africa. Mandela spent 20 years in jail for his opposition to apartheid. After his release, he became the first President of Democratic South Africa and helped heal the wounds of apartheid by his magnanimous attitude to his former political enemies.

Mikhail Gorbachev (1931–) Had the courage, tenacity and strength of character to give up the absolute power of Soviet Communism. Gorbachev moved the Soviet Union towards democracy and respect for human rights. In doing so he enabled the Berlin Wall to come down and Eastern Europe gained freedom from Communist control.

Martin Luther King (1929–1968) Inspiring leader of the non-violent civil rights movement. Inspired millions of people, black and white, to aspire for a more equal and just society.

William Wilberforce (1759–1833) Fought tirelessly for ending the slave trade, at a time when many accepted it as an 'economic necessity'. He awakened the conscience of many of his fellow countrymen and helped to make slavery appear unacceptable.

Albert Einstein (1879–1955) His theories of relativity were a very significant scientific breakthrough; being a genius scientist, Einstein was also a champion of human rights and campaigned for a more peaceful world.

Thomas Jefferson (1743–1826) One of the United States of America's founding fathers. Jefferson helped draft the Declaration of Independence and he held a deep-seated belief in human rights. Jefferson passed one of the first bills on religious tolerance in his state of Virginia. He sought to improve education and was a noted polymath with a wide range of interests.

Mother Teresa (1910–1997) A modern day saint who sought to identify with and offer compassion to the unloved and destitute. She lived a life of voluntary poverty and service to the poor.

Abraham Lincoln (1809–1865) Abraham Lincoln overcame many setbacks to become the most influential American President. In his famous Gettysburg speech, he inspired the nation with his noble words and helped to bring about the abolishment of slavery.

Leonardo da Vinci (1452–1519) One of the greatest minds in human history; in many areas, he was a couple of centuries ahead of scientific discovery. He helped make great advances in anatomy, astronomy, physics, science and in other fields as well. Amidst all this, he found time to paint the most iconic picture in history – The Mona Lisa.

Helen Keller (1880–1968) Despite disability of both deafness and blindness, she learned to read and write, becoming a champion of social issues and helping to improve the welfare of deaf people.

Joan of Arc (1412–1431) As a young, illiterate peasant girl, Joan of Arc inspired the Dauphin of France to defeat the English. Although burned at the stake for 'heresy', her prophecy of French unity came true after her death.

Benjamin Franklin (1706–1790) Great polymath and promoter of American ideals at home and in the US; a practical man of great dynamism and good character.

Mahatma Gandhi (1869–1948) Gandhi was the principle figurehead of the Indian independence movement; taught a philosophy of non-violence and peaceful protest.

Florence Nightingale (1820–1910) Nightingale volunteered to nurse soldiers during the Crimean War. Her statistical analysis of the pitiful conditions she found, and her management of them, helped to revolutionise the service of nursing and the treatment of patients.

Harriet Tubman (1822–1913) Tubman escaped from slavery but returned on many dangerous missions to Maryland where she helped lead slaves to freedom. She also served as agent and leader during the Civil War.

Winston Churchill (1874–1965) In the worst moments of 1940, the Nazi war machine looked invincible as it swept through Europe. Churchill inspired the free nations to keep alive the fight against the tyranny of Hitler's Germany.

Anne Frank (1929–1945) Anne Frank was nobody special, just an ordinary teenage girl. But she became a symbol of how ordinary people can get caught up in Man's inhumanity. Despite the most testing of conditions, Anne retained an optimistic spirit and faith.

Socrates (469 BC–399 BC) Socrates showed the power and integrity of independent thought. He taught by encouraging people to honestly question their preconceptions. His method of self-enquiry laid the foundations of Western Philosophic thought.

George Orwell (1903–1950) George Orwell was a democratic socialist who fought in the Spanish civil war on the side of the Republicans. He gave up his privileged education to spend time with the unemployed of the Great Depression. His greatest contribution was warning about the dangers of totalitarian regimes, whatever the ideology may be behind them.

Buddha (c 563–483BC) The Buddha was a young prince who gave up the comforts of palace life to seek the meaning of life by meditating in the wilderness. After gaining realisation, the Buddha spent the remainder of his life travelling around India teaching a middle path of meditation and inner peace.

Sri Chinmoy (1931–2007) An Indian spiritual teacher who combined the best of Eastern and Western cultures. He founded the Sri Chinmoy Oneness-Home Peace Run, a worldwide run to promote peace and greater understanding.

William Shakespeare (1564–1616) Shakespeare remains the king of English literature. His plays and poetry captured the richness and diversity of human existence in the most powerful and poetic way.

St Therese de Lisieux (1873–1897) A Carmelite nun, who died aged 24, unknown to the world. Yet after her death, her simple writings had a profound effect, becoming one of the best selling spiritual writings. Her approach was a simple approach of doing the smallest acts with love.

Edward Jenner (1749–1823) Led pioneering work on the development of an inoculation against deadly smallpox. Opened up the way to more immunisation treatments, arguably saving the lives of millions of people around the world.

Akbar (1542–1605) The great Moghul Emperor who went a long way to uniting India under his rule. Although a great warrior, Akbar was also known for his love of culture, music and philosophy. He introduced enlightened laws on religious tolerance in his kingdom and encouraged representatives of different religions to come to his court.

Sir Isaac Newton (1642–1727) One of the greatest scientists of all time; Isaac Newton led the foundation of modern physics with his development of theories of gravity and mechanics.

Leo Tolstoy (1828–1910) Influential Russian author, whose great epics include War and Peace. His philosophy of non-violence and a return to rural simplicity inspired other politicians such as Gandhi.

Emily Dickinson (1830–1886) One of the most popular female poets who wrote unique, uplifting poems which captured the imagination of many people.

J R R Tolkien (1892–1973) Writer and creator of the Lord of the Rings trilogy; Tolkien was a modest professor at Oxford University but found time to create a whole mythical world.

William Blake (1757–1827) Mystical poet and artist; William Blake wrote poems of great depth and power, celebrating both the joys of spirit and nature and also fiercely criticising the injustice of the times.

Mozart (1756–1791) Music genius who composed a range of breathtaking music from piano concertos to his immortal Requiem.

Swami Vivekananda (1863–1902) a direct disciple of Sri Ramakrishna, Vivekananda helped spread Sri Ramakrishna's message and mission to the West.

St Teresa of Avila (1515–1582) Christian mystic and writer; she also played a key role in the Spanish church at a time when women were largely marginalised.

B.R. Ambedkar (1891–1956) Indian social reformer; Ambedkar was born in the Mahar 'untouchable' caste but became a pioneering political activist and social reformer. He was the principal figure in the drafting of the Indian Constitution, which outlawed 'untouchability' and promoted equality.

Marie Curie (1867–1934) Marie Curie is the only person to win a Nobel Prize for both Chemistry and Physics. Her discoveries with radiation helped advance medical science. Her achievements were even more remarkable at a time when few women had the opportunity to gain an education.

Woodrow Wilson (1856–1924) Woodrow Wilson had a vision for a League of Nations a forum where nations could come together to solve disputes. The League of Nations struggled to make an impact before the Second World War, but his vision was important in the development of the United Nations.

Susan B. Anthony (1820–1906) Susan Anthony was an active member of the American Anti-Slavery Society, despite meeting hostility she continued to press for an amendment to the US constitution to outlaw slavery. She was also a prominent women's rights activist who helped push forward the women's suffrage campaign in the Nineteenth Century.

Tom Paine (1737–1809) English-American writer and political activist. He wrote influential pamphlets arguing for independence for the US and the end of slavery. He was a key figure of the enlightenment and age of reason, supporting the revolutionary principles of US and France.

Charles Darwin (1809–1882) Darwin published his Origin of Species detailing a belief in evolution at a time when such a decision was very controversial.

Rabindranath Tagore (1861–1941) Poet, writer, humanitarian, Tagore was the first Indian to be awarded Nobel Prize for Literature.

Maximilian Kolbe (1894–1941) was a Franciscan priest who encouraged devotion to Mary and was committed to praying for those hostile to the Church. In 1941, he was arrested for sheltering Jews and sent to Auschwitz. He volunteered to take the place of a man condemned to death.

Eric Liddell (1902–1945) Eric Liddell won Olympic gold in the 400m in the 1924 Paris Olympics. He is also famed for turning down the opportunity to compete in the 100m because the heats were on a Sunday. Eric was an accomplished sportsman also representing Scotland at rugby union.

Dietrich Bonhoeffer (1906–1945) was a Lutheran Pastor who was an influential critic of Hitler and Nazism, executed in 1945. His theology and writings remain influential today.

Desmond Tutu (1931–) Nobel Peace Prize winner; campaigner against apartheid and instrumental in promoting human rights and justice. Tutu helped to heal the wounds of apartheid in South Africa.

Eleanor Roosevelt (1884–1962) Helped draft United Nations declaration of human rights; strived to improve civil rights in the US; Inspired many people because of her positivity, compassion and self-giving.

Pope Francis (1936–) The first Jesuit pope and the first pope from the Americas, he has sought to reform the Vatican and the Catholic church. Pope Francis has stressed the importance of humility, modesty and concern for the poor. He is seen as a reforming Pope, trying to bring back the tradition of emphasis on the Gospels.

Rosa Parks (1913–2005) Rosa Parks became a well respected figurehead of the American civil rights movement. Rosa showed what ordinary people can do when they stick fast to their beliefs in testing conditions.

Pope John Paul II (1920–2005) Lived through two totalitarian regimes, eventually becoming a priest and then the first Polish pope. He was a charismatic spiritual leader who retained great faith in moral and spiritual values.

Emil Zatopek (1922–2000) Greatest long-distance runner, winning three gold medals at the 1954 Olympics. He was a principled supporter of Czech democracy, being sent to work in mines for his opposition to the Communist government.

Dalai Lama (1938–) The fourteenth Dalai Lama has been awarded the Nobel Prize for his non-violent resistance to Chinese rule. The Dalai Lama teaches a path of tolerance and compassion.

Muhammad Ali (1942–2016) Champion boxer and great character; Ali refused to fight in the Vietnam war and became a champion of civil rights and African interests. When asked how he would like to be remembered, Ali said: "As a man who tried to unite all humankind through faith and love."

Oprah Winfrey (1954–) Influential talk show host. Oprah Winfrey has become a role model for African American women.

Jesse Owens (1913–1980) Jesse Owens' four gold medals at Hitler's 1936 Olympics in Berlin was one of the great moments of sport, which helped to puncture the Nazi ideology of Aryan supremacy. Jesse Owens was a modest hero who remained a great ambassador for Sport.

Malala Yousafzai (1997–) Pakistani schoolgirl who defied threats of the Taliban to campaign for the right to education for girls. She survived being shot in the head by the Taliban and has become a global advocate for women's rights, especially the right to education.

IMPORTANT PLACES

1. The Forbidden City

It is a palace complex in Dongcheng District, Beijing, China, at the center of the Imperial City of Beijing. It is surrounded by numerous opulent imperial gardens and temples including the Zhongshan Park, the sacrificial Imperial Ancestral Temple.

2. St. Peter's Basilica

The Papal Basilica of Saint Peter in the Vatican or simply Saint Peter's Basilica is a church built in the Renaissance style located in Vatican City, the papal enclave that is within the city of Rome.

3. Palace of Versailles

The Palace of Versailles is a former royal residence located in Versailles, west of Paris, France. The palace is owned by the French Republic and has since 1995 been managed, under the direction of the French Ministry of Culture, by the Public Establishment of the Palace, Museum and National Estate of Versailles.

4. Lincoln Memorial

The Lincoln Memorial is a US national memorial built to honour the 16th president of the United States, Abraham Lincoln.

5. Colosseum

The Colosseum is an oval amphitheatre in the centre of the city of Rome, Italy. It is the largest ancient amphitheatre ever built, and is still the largest standing amphitheatre in the world today, despite its age.

6. Parthenon

The Parthenon is a former temple on the Athenian Acropolis, Greece, dedicated to the goddess Athena, whom the people of Athens considered their patroness. Construction started in 447 BC when the Athenian Empire was at the peak of its power.

7. Taj Mahal

The Taj Mahal is an ivory-white marble mausoleum on the right bank of the river Yamuna in the Indian city of Agra. It was commissioned in 1632 by the Mughal emperor Shah Jahan to house the tomb of his favourite wife, Mumtaz Mahal; it also houses the tomb of Shah Jahan himself.

8. Eiffel Tower

The Eiffel Tower is a wrought-iron lattice tower on the Champ de Mars in Paris, France. It is named after the engineer Gustave Eiffel, whose company designed and built the tower.

9. Cologne Cathedral

Cologne Cathedral is a Catholic cathedral in Cologne, North Rhine-Westphalia. It is the seat of the Archbishop of Cologne and of the administration of the Archdiocese of Cologne. It is a renowned monument of German Catholicism and Gothic architecture.

10. Peterhof Palace

The Peterhof Palace is a series of palaces and gardens located in Petergof, Saint Petersburg, Russia, commissioned by Peter the Great as a direct response to the Palace of Versailles by Louis XIV of France.

11. Palace on the Isle

The Palace on the Isle also known as Baths Palace is a classicist palace in Warsaw's Royal Baths Park, the city's largest park, occupying over 76 hectares of the city center.

12. World War II Memorial

The World War II Memorial is a memorial of national significance dedicated to Americans who served in the armed forces and as civilians during World War II.

13. Sagrada Família

The Sagrada Família is a large unfinished Roman Catholic minor basilica in the Eixample district of Barcelona, Catalonia, Spain. Designed by the Spanish architect Antoni Gaudí (1852–1926), his work on the building is part of a UNESCO World Heritage Site. On 7 November 2010, Pope Benedict XVI consecrated the church and proclaimed it a minor basilica.

14. Mysore Palace

The Mysore Palace, officially known as Mysuru Palace, is a historical palace and the royal residence (house) at Mysore in Karnataka, India. It is the official residence of the Wadiyar dynasty and the seat of the Kingdom of Mysore. Mysore is commonly described as the 'City of Palaces', and there are seven palaces including this one.

15. Tower of London

The Tower of London, officially Her Majesty's Royal Palace and Fortress of the Tower of London, is a historic castle on the north bank of the River Thames in central London. It lies within the London Borough of Tower Hamlets, which is separated from the eastern edge of the square mile of the City of London by the open space known as Tower Hill.

16. Statue of Unity

The Statue of Unity is a colossal statue of Indian statesman and independence activist Vallabhbhai Patel (1875–1950), who was the first deputy prime minister and home minister of independent India and an adherent of Mahatma Gandhi during the nonviolent Indian independence movement.

17. Moscow Kremlin

The Moscow Kremlin is a fortified complex in the center of Moscow founded by Russian ruling dynasty of Rurikids. It is the best known of the kremlins (Russian citadels), and includes five palaces, four cathedrals, and the enclosing Kremlin Wall with Kremlin towers.

18. Tulum

Tulum is the site of a pre-Columbian Mayan walled city which served as a major port for Coba, in the Mexican state of Quintana Roo. The ruins are situated on 39 ft tall cliffs along the east coast of the Yucatán Peninsula on the Caribbean Sea in the state of Quintana Roo, Mexico.

19. Edinburgh Castle

Edinburgh Castle is a historic castle in Edinburgh, Scotland. It stands on Castle Rock, which has been occupied by humans since at least the Iron Age, although the nature of the early settlement is unclear.

20. Mosque–Cathedral of Córdoba

The Mosque–Cathedral of Córdoba, officially known by its ecclesiastical name, the Cathedral of Our Lady of the Assumption is the cathedral of the Roman Catholic Diocese of Córdoba dedicated to the Assumption of Mary and located in the Spanish region of Andalusia.

21. Statue of Liberty National Monument

The Statue of Liberty National Monument is a United States National Monument comprising Liberty Island and Ellis Island in the U.S. states of New Jersey and New York. It includes the Statue of Liberty (Liberty Enlightening the World) by sculptor Frédéric Auguste Bartholdi and the Statue of Liberty Museum, both situated on Liberty Island, as well as the former immigration station at Ellis Island which includes the Ellis Island Immigrant Hospital.

22. Royal Palace of Madrid

The Royal Palace of Madrid is the official residence of the Spanish royal family at the city of Madrid, although now used only for state ceremonies. The palace has 1,450,000 sq ft of floor space and contains 3,418 rooms. It is the largest functioning royal palace and the largest by floor area in Europe.

23. Machu Picchu

Machu Picchu is a 15th-century Inca citadel located in the Eastern Cordillera of southern Peru on a 7,970 ft mountain ridge. It is located in the Machupicchu District within Urubamba Province above the Sacred Valley, which is 80 kilometers northwest of Cuzco.

24. Great Wall of China

The Great Wall of China is a series of fortifications that were built across the historical northern borders of ancient Chinese states and Imperial China as protection against various nomadic groups from the Eurasian Steppe. Several walls were built from as early as the 7th century BC, with selective stretches later joined together by Qin Shi Huang (220–206 BC), the first emperor of China.

25. Egyptian pyramids

The Egyptian pyramids are ancient masonry structures located in Egypt. Sources cite at least 118 identified Egyptian pyramids. Most were built as tombs for the country's pharaohs and their consorts during the Old and Middle Kingdom periods.

26. Great Barrier Reef

The Great Barrier Reef is the world's largest coral reef system composed of over 2,900 individual reefs and 900 islands stretching for over 2,300 kilometres over an area of approximately 344,400 square kilometres. The reef is located in the Coral Sea, off the coast of Queensland, Australia.

27. Vatican Museums

The Vatican Museums are the public museums of the Vatican City. They display works from the immense collection amassed by the Catholic Church and the papacy throughout the centuries, including several of the most renowned Roman sculptures and most important masterpieces of Renaissance art in the world.

28. Las Vegas Strip

The Las Vegas Strip is a stretch of Las Vegas Boulevard South in Clark County, Nevada, that is known for its concentration of resort hotels and casinos. The Strip, as it is known, is about 4.2 mi (6.8 km) long, and is immediately south of the Las Vegas city limits in the unincorporated towns of Paradise and Winchester, but is often referred to simply as "Las Vegas".

29. Times Square, New York City

Times Square is a major commercial intersection, tourist destination, entertainment center, and neighbourhood in the Midtown Manhattan section of New York City. Brightly lit by numerous billboards and advertisements, it stretches from West 42nd to West 47th Streets.

30. Central Park, New York City

Central Park is an urban park in New York City located between the Upper West and Upper East Sides of Manhattan. It is the fifth-largest park in the city by area, covering 843 acres (341 ha).

31. Golden Gate Bridge

The Golden Gate Bridge is a suspension bridge spanning the Golden Gate, the 1.6 km strait connecting San Francisco Bay and the Pacific Ocean. The structure links the U.S. city of San Francisco, California—the northern tip of the San Francisco Peninsula—to Marin County, carrying both U.S. Route 101 and California State Route 1 across the strait.

WONDERS OF THE WORLD		
Wonder	Date of construction	Location
Great Wall of China	Since 7th century BCE	China
Petra	c. 100 BCE	Jordan
Christ the Redeemer	Opened October 12, 1931	Brazil
Machu Picchu	c. AD 1450	Peru
Chichen Itza	c. AD 600	Mexico

Wonder	Date of construction	Location
Colosseum	Completed AD 80	Italy
Taj Mahal	Completed c. AD 1648	India
Great Pyramid of Giza (Honorary Candidate)	Completed c. 2560 BCE	Egypt

TOP 10 INTELLIGENCE AGENCIES

SNo.	Name	Headquarters	Founded
1.	CIA (Central Intelligence Agency) USA	Langley Virginia	September 18, 1947
2.	RAW (Research and Analysis Wing), India	New Delhi	September 21, 1968
3.	Mossad, Israel	Tel Aviv-Yafo, Israel	December 13, 1949
4.	ISI (Inter-Services Intelligence), Pakistan	Islamabad	January 1, 1948
5.	MI6 (Secret Intelligence Service), UK	London	July 4, 1909
6.	GRU (Main Intelligence Agency), Russia	Moscow	Founded May 7, 1992
7.	MSS (Ministry of State Security), China	Beijing	July 1, 1983
8.	NIA (National Investigation Agency), India	New Delhi	2009
9.	NSA (National Security Agency), USA	Maryland, US	November 4, 1952
10.	FSS (Federal Security Service), Russia	Moscow	April 12, 1995

TOP NEWS AGENCIES OF THE WORLD

S.No.	Agencies	Countries
1.	Associated Press (AP)	USA
2.	Reuters	UK
3.	Telegraph Agency of the Sovereign States (TASS)	Russia
4.	Malaysian National News Agency (MNNA)	Malaysia
5.	Agenzia Nazionale Stampa Associate (ANSA)	Italy
6.	Associated Israel Press (AIP)	Israel
7.	Agence France Press (A.F.P)	France
8.	Press Trust of India (PTI)	India
9.	Samachar Bharti	India
10.	Univarta	India

11.	Xin Hua	China
12.	Kyodo	Japan
13.	Antara	Indonesia
14.	Islamic Republic news Agency (IRNA)	Iran
15.	Deutsche Presse Agentur (D.P.A.)	Germany
16.	WAFA	Palestine
17.	Australian Associated Press (A.A.P)	Australia
18.	Novosti	Russia
19.	Pakistan Press International (P.P.I) and Associated Press of Pakistan (APP)	Pakistan
20.	Middle East News Agency (MENA)	Egypt
21.	United Press International (UP)	USA

TOP 10 NEWSPAPERS OF THE WORLD

SNO.	Name of Newspaper	Country	Year
1.	USA Today	USA	1982
2.	The Guardian	UK	1821
3.	The New York Times	USA	1851
4.	The Wall Street Journal	USA	1889
5.	The Washington Post	USA	1877
6.	Daily Mail	UK	1896
7.	Yomiuri Shimbun	Japan	1874
8.	Dainik Bhaskar	India	1948
9.	Reference News	China	1931
10.	The Asahi Shimbun	Japan	1879

FATHERS OF VARIOUS FIELDS

Father of Modern Physics	Albert Einstein
Father of the Green Revolution	Norman Ernest Borlaug
Father of the Green Revolution in India	M.S.Swaminathan
Father of Microbiology	Antonie Philips Van Leeuwenhoek
Father of Modern Astronomy	Nicolaus Copernicus
Father of Nuclear Physics	Ernest Rutherford
Father of Nuclear Science	Marie Curie and Pierre Curie
Father of Computer Science	George Boole and Alan Turing
Father of Classification	Carl linneaus

Father of the Green Revolution in India	M. S. Swaminathan
Father of the Indian Constitution	Dr. B. R. Ambedkar
Father of American Football	Walter Chauncey Camp
Father of Evolution	Charles Darwin
Father of modern Olympic	Pierre De Coubertin
Father of Numbers	Pythagoras
Father of Genetics	Gregor Mendel
Father of Internet	Vint Cerf
Father of Botany	Theophrastus
Father of Scientific Management	Frederick Winslow Taylor
Father of Electricity	Benjamin Franklin
Father of Electronics	Michael Faraday
Father of Television	Philo Farnsworth
Father of Nuclear Chemistry	Otto Hahn
Father of Periodic Table	Dmitri Mendeleev
Father of Humanism	Francesco Petrarca
Father of Telephone	Alexander Graham Bell
Father of Mobile Phone	Martin Cooper
Father of Geometry	Euclid
Father of Microscopy	Antonie Philips Van Leeuwenhoek
Father of Laptop	Bill Moggridge
Father of Psychology	Wilhelm Wundt
Father of Surgery	Sushruta
Father of New France	Samuel de Champlain
Father of the American Constitution	James Madison
Father of Plastic Surgery	Sushruta
Father of Ayurveda	Dhanwantari
Father of Western Medicine	Hippocrates
Father of Modern Medicine	Hippocrates
Father of Computer	Charles Babbage
Father of Astronomy	Copernicus
Father of Economics	Adam Smith
Father of Biology	Aristotle
Father of Modern Chemistry	Antoine Lavoisier

Father of History	Herodotus
Father of Classical mechanics	Isaac Newton
Father of Comedy	Aristophanes
Father of English poetry	GeoffreyChaucer
Father of Homeopathy	Heinemann
Father of India's Communication Revolution	Sam Pitroda
Father of Pentium Chip	Vinod Dham
Father of Modern Political science	Niccolo Machiavelli
Father of Quantum mechanics	Max Planck
Father of Relativity	Albert Einstein
Father of Robotics	Joseph F. Engelberger
Father of Thermodynamics	Sadi Carnot
Father of Zoology	Aristotle
Father of Blood groups	Landsteiner
Father of Blood Circulation	William Harvey
Father of Bacteriology	Louis Paster
Father of Artificial Intelligence	John Mccarthy
Father of White Revolution	Varghese khurien
Father of Bio Technology	Karl ereky
Father of Botony	Theophrastus
Father of Vaccination	Edward Jenner
Father of Embiriology	Aristotle
Father of Geography	Erithosthenus
Father of Geometry	Euclid
Father of DNA Fingerprinting	Alec John Jeffreys

NATIONAL EMBLEMS OF VARIOUS COUNTRIES

Name of the Country	Emblem
Australia	Kangaroo
Bangladesh	Water Lily
Barbados	Head of Trident
Belgium	Lion
Canada	White Lily

Chile	Candor and Huemul
Denmark	Beach
Dominica	Sisserou Parrot
France	Lily
Germany	Corn Flower
Hong Kong	Bauhinia (Orchid Tree)
India	Lion Capital
Iran	Rose
Ireland	Shamrock
Israel	Candelabrum
Italy	White Lily
Ivory Coast	Elephant
Japan	Chrysanthemum
Luxembourg	Lion with Crown
Lebanon	Cedar Tree
Mongolia	The Soyombo
Norway	Lion
New Zealand	Kiwi, Southern Cross
Pakistan	Crescent
Papua New Guinea	Bird of Paradise
Spain	Eagle
Sri Lanka	Sword & Lion
Syria	Eagle
Sierra Leone	Lion
Russia	Sickle & Hammer
Turkey	Star and crescent
United Kingdom	Rose
USA	Golden Rod

IMPORTANT INTERNATIONAL DAYS

DATE	EVENT
14 January	World Logic Day
24 January	International Day of Education
27 January	International Day of Commemoration in Memory of the Victims of the Holocaust

11 February	International Day of Women and Girls in Science
13 February	World Radio Day
21 February	International Mother Language Day
4 March	World Engineering Day for Sustainable Development
8 March	International Women's Day
21 March	International Day for the Elimination of Racial Discrimination; International Day of Nowruz
22 March	World Water Day
6 April	International Day of Sport for Development and Peace
15 April	World Art Day
23 April	World Book and Copyright Day
3 May	World Press Freedom Day
5 May	African World Heritage Day
16 May	International Day of Living Together in Peace
21 May	World Day for Cultural Diversity for Dialogue and Development
22 May	International Day for Biological Diversity
5 June	World Environment Day
8 June	World Oceans Day
17 June	World Day to Combat Desertification and Drought
18 July	Nelson Mandela International Day
26 July	International Day for the Conservation of the Mangrove Ecosystem
9 August	International Day of the World's Indigenous People
12 August	International Youth Day
23 August	International Day for the Remembrance of the Slave Trade and its Abolition
8 September	International Literacy Day
15 September	International Day of Democracy
20 September	International Day of University Sport
21 September	International Day of Peace
28 September	International Day for the Universal Access to Information
5 October	World Teachers' Day
11 October	International Day of the Girl Child
13 October	International Day for Disaster Reduction
17 October	International Day for the Eradication of Poverty
24 October	United Nations Day
27 October	World Day for Audiovisual Heritage
2 November	International Day to End Impunity for Crimes against Journalists
5 November	World Day of Romani Language; World Tsunami Awareness Day
10 November	World Science Day for Peace and Development

14 November	International Day against Illicit Trafficking in Cultural Property
16 November	International Day for Tolerance
18 November	International Day of Islamic Art
25 November	International Day for the Elimination of Violence against Women
26 November	World Olive Tree Day
29 November	International Day of Solidarity with the Palestinian People
1 December	World AIDS Day
3 December	International Day of Persons with Disabilities
10 December	Human Rights Day
18 December	International Migrants Day
18 December	World Arabic Language Day

TRADE ORGANISATIONS OF THE WORLD

The World Trade Organization (WTO): In brief, the World Trade Organization (WTO) is the only international organization dealing with the global rules of trade. Its main function is to ensure that trade flows as smoothly, predictably and freely as possible.

The General Agreement on Tariffs and Trade (GATT): The General Agreement on Tariffs and Trade (GATT) is a multilateral agreement regulating international trade. The General Agreement on Tariffs and Trade (GATT) is a multilateral agreement regulating international trade, the purpose of which is the "substantial reduction of tariffs and other trade barriers and the elimination of preferences, on a reciprocal and mutually advantageous basis".

The European Union: The European Union (EU) is an economic and political union made up of 27 member states that are located primarily in Europe.

The North American Free Trade Agreement (NAFTA): NAFTA is an agreement signed by Canada, Mexico, and the United States, creating a trilateral trade bloc in North America.

The Asia-Pacific Economic Cooperation: APEC is a forum for 21 Pacific Rim countries that seeks to promote free trade and economic cooperation throughout the Asia-Pacific region.

The World Bank: The World Bank is an international financial institution that provides loans to developing countries for various programs. The World Bank's official goal is the reduction of poverty. According to the World Bank's Articles of Agreement, all of its decisions must be guided by a commitment to promote foreign investment, international trade, and facilitate capital investment.

The International Monetary Fund (IMF): The IMF seeks to promote international economic cooperation, international trade, employment, and exchange rate stability. The IMF is an international organization that was created on July 22, 1944 at the Bretton Woods Conference. The IMF's stated goal is to stabilize exchange rates and assist the reconstruction of the world's international payment system after World War II.

Major Countries of the World

- Largest of all continents.
- Stretches from 10°S and 8°N latitude and 25°E to 170°W longitude.
- World's highest point- **Mt. Everest**.
- World's lowest point- **Dead Sea**.

Climate

- In summer the Sun shines directly over the Tropic of Cancer, making the interiors of Asia very hot.
- Because of the warm rising air, low pressure develops over vast area.
- Moist winds from the sea all around are sucked into these low pressure centres. These are the **'Summer Monsoon'** winds which bring rain to most parts of South and South East Asia.
- In Winter the Sun shines over the Tropic of Capricorn.

INDIA	
Capital:	New Delhi
Geographical location (Coordinates):	The Country extends between 8° 4' and 37° 6' latitudes north of the Equator, and 68° 7' and 97° 25' longitudes east of it.
Area:	32,87,263 sq. km
Currency:	Rupees (INR)
System of Governance:	Sovereign Socialist Secular Democratic Republic with a Parliamentary system of Government.
Independence:	15 August 1947

Agriculture

India is one of the self-sufficient countries in agricultural production. Agriculture is the primary source of livelihood for more than half of India's population and a major contributor of country's GDP India is among the top producers of several crops like wheat, rice, pulses, sugarcane and cotton. It is the highest producer of milk and second highest producer of fruits and vegetables. India also exports rice, spices, cotton, meat & related products, sugar, etc.

Art & Culture

India is a country where various ancient civilizations flourished. It is full of diverse culture and heritage. It is home to various religious groups (Hindus, Muslims, Jains, Sikhs, Buddhists, Christians, Bahais, Zoroastrians etc.). There are various dance (Bharatnatyam, Kathak, Kathakali, Odissi, Mohiniyattam etc.) forms and music forms in addition to variety of painting styles (Madhubani, Pattachitra, Pahari, Tanjore, Mysore, Jaipur, Miniature) etc. Inside this country there are various languages and dialect with one million or more speakers, including the 22 scheduled langauages. Hindi, Tamil, Telugu, Marathi, Bangla, Malayalam, English, Odia, Assamese are some of the languages. India is called the land of festivals as the country celebrates a plethora of festivals and celebrations throughout the year like Holi, Diwali, Dussehra, Pongal, Eid ul-Fitr, Bakr-Id, Christmas, Baisakhi, Onam, Chhath Puja, Ganesh Chaturthi, Ram Navmi, Shiv-ratri, Guru-Parv, Janmashtami, Bihu, Independence day, Republic day etc.

AFGHANISTAN

Capital:	Kabul	**Capital:**	Kabul
Geographical location (Coordinates):	The Country extends between 33.9391° N, 67.7100° E	**System of Governance:**	Presidential Islamic Republic
Area:	652,864 sq. km	**Independence:**	19 August 1919
Currency:	Afghani (AFN)		

Agriculture

Afghanistan is world's leading producer of opium. A major part of country's economy is derived from the cultivation and sale of opium Additionally it also produces apricots & other dry fruits, pomegranates, sweet melons, grapes etc.

Art & Culture

Afghanistan's population is divided into several ethno-linguistic groups like Pashtun, Tajik, Hazara, Uzbek, Baluch, Turkmen, Nuristani, Pamiri, Arab, Gujar, Brahui, Qizilbash, Aimaq, and Pashai. Pashto and Dari are Afghanistan's official languages. The country as a whole follows the tribal system with different regions of the country practice their own cultures. Majority of population practice Islam with a very small percentage of Christians, Sikhs and Hindus. Music comprises many varieties of classical music and folk music and singing styles like mursia, manqasat, nowheh and rowzeh.

ARMENIA

Capital:	Yerevan	**Capital:**	Yerevan
Geographical location (Coordinates):	The Country extends between 40.0691°N, 45.0382°E	**System of Governance:**	Unitary Parliamentary Republic
Area:	29,800 sq. km	**Independence:**	21 September 1991
Currency:	Dram (AMD)		

Agriculture

Agriculture provides 40% employment out of of total employment and accounts for more than 31% of country's GDP. Pomegranate and apricot are the main agricultural products.

Art & Culture

Several cultures flourished in Armenia such as, Hayasa-Azzi, Mitanni, Trialeti-Vanadzor. Ethnic Armenians make up majority of the population, while Yazidis, Russians, Assyrians, Ukrainians, Caucasus Greeks, etc. are minorities. Christianity is the major religion. A mixture of indigenous folk music like duduk music along with Kef and Christian music is popular.

AZERBAIJAN	
Capital:	Baku
Geographical location (Coordinates):	The Country extends between 40.1431° N, 47.5769° E
Area:	86,600 sq. km
Currency:	Manat
System of Governance:	Unitary Semi-presidential Republic
Independence:	18 October 1991

Agriculture

Azerbaijan produces various cash crops like cotton, tobacco and these accounts for a majority of agri-products. Country also grows various vegetables and fruits such as citrus, grapes etc. Dairy and meat products are also an important part of country's economy.

Art & Culture

The country is rich in various art-forms like jewelery-making, metal-engraving, wood-craving, carpet and rug making, miniature paintings. Opera and ballet is popular in the country.

BAHRAIN	
Capital:	Manama
Geographical location (Coordinates):	The Country extends between 26.07° N, 50.56° E
Area:	778.3 sq. km
Currency:	Bahraini Dinar (BHD)
System of Governance:	Unitary Parliamentary Islamic Constitutional Monarchy
Independence:	15 August 1971

Agriculture

Agriculture played a limited role in country's economy. The major crop is alfalfa which is mainly used as animal fodder. Other products are figs, dates, pomegranates, melons etc.

Art & Culture

Islam is the major religion and divided into Ethnically diverse groups like, Baharna, Ajam, Arabs, Huwala etc. Prevalent art forms are calligraphic art, Expressionism, surrealism while Khaliji, Sawt are music styles.

<table>
<tr><td colspan="2" align="center">BANGLADESH</td></tr>
<tr><td>Capital:</td><td>Dhaka</td></tr>
<tr><td>Geographical location (Coordinates):</td><td>The Country extends between 23.68° N, 90.35° E</td></tr>
<tr><td>Area:</td><td>147,570 sq. km</td></tr>
<tr><td>Currency:</td><td>Taka(BDT)</td></tr>
<tr><td>System of Governance:</td><td>Unitary Parliamentary Constitutional Republic</td></tr>
<tr><td>Independence:</td><td>16 December 1971</td></tr>
</table>

Agriculture

The country is major producer of Rice and jute. Wheat, tea are also grown in large scale. Other products are sugarcane, tobacco, cotton, and various fruits and vegetables.

Art & Culture

Bangladesh has a rich tradition of Art including Terracotta, pottery, Bengal paintings, Monipuri and Sant dances. Drama and Jatra are famous theatre forms. Pahela Baishakh, Eid-ul-Fitr, Durga Puja are some of the major festivals.

<table>
<tr><td colspan="2" align="center">BHUTAN</td></tr>
<tr><td>Capital:</td><td>Thimphu</td></tr>
<tr><td>Geographical location (Coordinates):</td><td>The Country extends between 27.51° N, 90.43° E</td></tr>
<tr><td>Area:</td><td>38,394 sq. km</td></tr>
<tr><td>Currency:</td><td>Ngultrum (BTN)</td></tr>
<tr><td>System of Governance:</td><td>Unitary Parliamentary Constitutional Monarchy</td></tr>
<tr><td>Independence:</td><td>8 August 1949</td></tr>
</table>

Agriculture

Major agricultural produce includes rice (including Bhutanese red rice) apples, citrus, chilies, barley etc. Organic farming and Dairy products are also growing in Bhutan.

Art & Culture

Bhutan is Buddhism is the major religion in Bhutan and as a result the culture is very much influenced by it. It is reflected in Thangkas, wall paintings and sculptures. Masked dances or chham are major dance form. Music ranges from folk to religion to modern, such as rigsar. Tshechu is the biggest festival.

BRUNEI	
Capital:	Bandar Seri Begawan
Geographical location (Coordinates):	The Country extends between 4.53° N, 114.73° E
Area:	5,765 sq. km
Currency:	Brunei Dollar (BND)
System of Governance:	Unitary Islamic absolute monarchy
Independence:	1 January 1984

Agriculture

Agriculture production in Brunei is limited. Country's main products include vegetables, rice, tropical fruits, meat and dairy products.

Art & Culture

Multiculture societies consisting of Malay, Chinese, Indians, Dayaks, Dusuns etc. influenced Brunei culture. Benari/Joget Baju Putih, Aduk-aduk, Jipin are major dance styles. Adai Adai is most popular music form.

CAMBODIA	
Capital:	Phnom Penh
Geographical location (Coordinates):	The Country extends between 12.57° N, 104.99° E
Area:	181,035 sq. km
Currency:	Riel (KHR)
System of Governance:	Unitary one-party parliamentary elective Constitutional Monarchy
Independence:	9 November 1953

Agriculture

The primary agricultural products are rice, maize,cassava and soybean. Rubber, sugarcane, cotton, and tobacco are major cash crops.

Art & Culture

Cambodian culture is highly influenced by Hinduism and Buddhism. Apsara Dance, Khmer and Cambodian folk dances, Shadow Theatres are some of the distinct features of Cambodian culture.

CYPRUS	
Capital:	Nicosia
Geographical location (Coordinates):	The Country extends between 35.12° N, 33.42° E
Area:	9,251 sq. km

Currency:	Euro (EUR)
System of Governance:	Unitary Presidential Constitutional Republic
Independence:	1 October 1960

Agriculture:

Better irrigation facilities are required for cultivation of crops due to hot and dry summers with limited water supply. The major agriculture produce are grapes, kiwi, avocados, citrus fruits and potatoes. Other important products are barley, wheat, grapefruit, oranges, legumes, tomatoes, carrots, carobs, olives, and various other fruits and vegetables.

Animal products like dairy products, meat, eggs and fisheries also play an important role in the economy.

Art & Culture

Majority of the population are of Greek origin, people of Turkish origin are second most in numbers the rest of the populations includes Armenians, British and Lebanese Maronites. Majority follow the Greek Orthodox. Traditional artwoks like Cypriot lacework, silversmithing, sculpture and dance like tsifteteli and traditional music accompanied by Laouto etc. show the distinct Greek and Turkish influences.

CHINA	
Capital:	Beijing
Geographical location (Coordinates):	The Country extends between 35.86° N, 104.19° E
Area:	9,596,961 sq. km
Currency:	Yuan (Renminbi) (CNY)
System of Governance:	Unitary one-party Socialist Republic
Independence:	21 September 1949

Agriculture

Being the country with the highest population, Agriculture remains one of the major contributors of China's economy. China is one among the top producers of Rice, Wheat, Potatoes, Apples, Cotton, and Tea etc.

Art & Culture

With a long old civilization Chinese art encompasses various forms of art, dance (Dragon dance, Lion dance), mbroidery, calligraphy (Cursive, Oracle bone), music (Yayue, Rock), sculpture, architecture, handicrafts (Knot), Pottery (ceramics, Blue-white porcelain) forms, Puppetry (Glove), Bonsai, Painting (Ink & wash, Shan Shui) etc.

TURKEY	
Capital:	Ankara
Geographical location (Coordinates):	The Country extends between 38.96° N, 35.24° E
Area:	783,356 sq. km

Currency:	Turkish Lira (TRY)
System of Governance:	Unitary Presidential Constitutional Republic
Proclamation of Republic	29 October 1923

Agriculture

Major agricultural products include apricots, hazelnuts wheat, sugar beets, cotton, various fruits, vegetables, and animal products like milk and poultry.

Art & Culture

Turkey has a very ancient folk dance tradition which include various forms like Zeybek, Horon, Halay, Hora; Varieties of folk music include Turku, Kosma, Bozlak, Agit, Havasi, Maya, Tekerleme etc. Tureky's Stone work, metal work, painting, architecture and other handcrafts are distinctive.

GEORGIA	
Capital:	Tbilisi
Geographical location (Coordinates):	The Country extends between 42.31° N, 43.36° E
Area:	69,700 sq. km
Currency:	Lari (GEL)
System of Governance:	Unitary Presidential Constitutional Republic
Independence:	26 May 1918 (Pre-Soviet Era) 9 April 1991 (Post-Soviet Era)

Agriculture

Agriculture plays an important role in country's GDP. Nuts (hazelnuts, almonds, walnuts, chestnuts), citrus fruits, apples, peaches, apricots, grapes and related products like wine are major agri based products.

Art & Culture

Georgian culture is highly influenced by Classical Empires of Greece, Roman Empire, Byzantine, Iranian etc. Ethnic Georgians forms the majority population. Georgian ecclesiastic art, Georgian polyphony music, Chakrulo folk song,

INDONESIA	
Capital:	Jakarta
Geographical location (Coordinates):	The Country extends between 0.79° S, 113.92° E
Area:	1,904,569 sq. km
Currency:	Rupiah (IDR)
System of Governance:	Unitary Presidential Constitutional Republic
Independence:	17 August 1945

Agriculture

Major agriculture products include Palm Oil, Palm Kernel, Rubber, Cocoa, Coffee, Tea, Tobacco, and Sugarcane. Rice, Maize, Cassava, Tropical Fruits, Spices, Poultry, Fisheries are also produced for local consumption and export purposes.

Art & Culture

Indonesia is an ethnically diverse country; with various native ethnic groups and Javanese is the largest among them. Dances (Javanese, Sundanese, Minang, Balinese, Saman), Dance drama (Ludruk, Ketoprak, Sandiwara, Lenong, Balinese) Theatre and shadow puppetry based on Ramayana and Mahabharata. Menari, Gawai Dayak, Pacu jawi, Tiwah are some of the major festivals.

IRAN	
Capital:	Tehran
Geographical location (Coordinates):	The Country extends between 32.43° N, 53.69° E
Area:	1,648,195 sq. km
Currency:	Rial (IRR)
System of Governance:	Unitary Presidential Islamic Republic
Independence:	1 April 1979 (Republic)

Agriculture

Main agricultural products include wheat, rice, barley, potatoes, dates, figs, pistachios, walnuts, almonds, sugar-beets, fruits, nuts. Major cash crops are cotton and tobacco. Animal derived products like Wool, meat, fisheries, Milk and dairy products are also contribute to country's economy.

Art & Culture:

Prominent Iranian art and culture reflects in its distinct Persian architecture, literature, music (Sasanian), Intricate style of painting, weaving, pottery, calligraphy, stonemasonry and metalworks. Ballet, Theatre & puppetry like Arusak-bāzi, Siāh-bāzi , Baqqāl-bāzi , Ruhowzi, Sāye-bāzi are quite popular.

ISRAEL	
Capital:	Jerusalem
Geographical location (Coordinates):	The Country extends between 31.04° N, 34.85° E
Area:	22,072 sq. km
Currency:	New Shekel
System of Governance:	Unitary Parliamentary Republic
Independence	14 May 1948

Agriculture

Despite abundant in saline, arid and semi-arid soil, Israel manages to produce a majority of its own food requirements. Fruit, vegetables and other horticultural products are major products. Oranges, grapefruits, lemons, apples, apricots, grapes, peaches, mangoes, plums, and pears are important fruits while greenhouse grown vegetables like tomatoes, cherry tomatoes, peppers, herbs, melons are a major chunk.

Art & Culture

Israeli culture reflects various Jewish characteristics in art, music, sculpture festivals and other cultural features. In addition it reflects a blend of other cultures due to immigration of jews. The prominent among these are Israel Philharmonic Orchestra, Israeli Opera, trances and related electronic music styles, Caananite sculpture etc. Judaism is the major religion and Rosh Hashanah the major festival.

IRAQ			
Capital:	Baghdad	Capital:	Baghdad
Geographical location (Coordinates):	The Country extends between 33.22° N, 43.68° E	System of Governance:	Federal Parliamentary Constitutional Republic
Area:	437,072 sq. km	Independence:	3 October 1932
Currency:	Iraqi Dinar (IQD)		

Agriculture

Wheat and barley are Iraq's main crops while Dates are a major cash and food crop. Tomatoes and potatoes are important Vegetables. Livestock rearing, Poultry and inland fisheries.

Art & Culture

Music forms like maqam-al-Iraqi, Iraqi Symphony Orchestra, Iraqi architecture patterns (with shanashol, bad girs etc.), Arabesque geometry and calligraphy with specific Iraqi features.

JAPAN	
Capital:	Tokyo
Geographical location (Coordinates):	The Country extends between 36.20° N, 138.25° E
Area:	377,973 sq. km
Currency:	Yen
System of Governance:	Unitary Parliamentary Constitutional Monarchy
Foundation	11 February 660 BC.

Agriculture

Rice is the main agriculture product of Japan and placed an important part of Japanese dishes. Japan is one of the world's largest fishing destination and accounts for roughly 1/5th of the global catch.

Art & Culture

Shinto is the largest religion in Japan, practiced by the majority and Japanese is the main language. Okinawan, Miyako, and other Ryukyuan languages are also spoken in different parts. Japanese sculpture, painting, architecture, calligraphy, ikebana (flower arranging), bugaku (court dance and music), Noh (dance-drama), kyogen (comic opera), Bunraku (puppet theatre), and Kabuki(dance and singing drama) are quite popular.

JORDAN	
Capital:	Amman
Geographical location (Coordinates):	The Country extends between 30.59° N, 36.23° E
Area:	89,342 sq. km
Currency:	Jordanian Dinar (JOD)
System of overnance:	Unitary Parliamentary Constitutional Monarchy
Independence:	25 May 1946

Agriculture:

Horticulture remains one of the major components of the agriculture sector along with poultry industry, and small-scale herding. Jordan imports majority of food items like from wheat, rice, barley, corn, sugar, tea, coffee etc.

Art & Culture

Islam is the major religion and the country is also home to some of the oldest Christian communities in the world and reflects one of the few Islamic countries with culturally openess. Jordanian Bedouin singing, traditional music, traditional dances like dabke, Jordian paintings, sculptures reflect the Country's religious tradition.

KAZAKHSTAN	
Capital:	Nur-Sultan
Geographical location (Coordinates):	The Country extends between 48.01° N, 66.92° E
Area:	2,724,900 sq. km
Currency:	Tenge (KZT)
System of Governance:	Unitary Presidential Constitutional Republic
Independence:	16 December 1991

Agriculture:
A major part of country's territory is suitable for agricultural production, but only about 1/3rd of land is used for agricultural production. The Wheat is the major crop and also exported outside country. Other important crops are rice, barley, cotton, oilseeds, vegetables, sugar beet, tobacco, melons and forage crops. Livestock products like dairy goods, leather, meat, and wool are also growing.

Art & Culture:
Kazakh art works include decorated yurts, felt products, woolen products, wooden crafts, silverware, needle work, embroidery bone artifacts and accessories are made of gold, silver, jade and semi-precious stones. Musical forms like Kuy is often accompanied by traditional instruments like Kobyz, Sybyzgy, Shankobyz etc. Nomadic culture of central Asia reflects is various folk dances of the country.

KUWAIT

Capital:	Kuwaiti City
Geographical location (Coordinates):	The Country extends between 29.31° N, 47.48° E
Area:	17,818 sq. km
Currency:	Kuwaiti Dinar (KWD)
System of Governance:	Unitary Constitutional Monarchy
Independence:	19 June 1961

Agriculture

Kuwait's desert climate permits limited agricultural activity. It's main agriculture products are were tomatoes, dried onions, melons , dates, cucumbers, eggplants.

Art & Culture

Kuwaitis are ethnically diverse with Arabs and Persians both forms important part of the society. Diwāniyyah gathering is feature of the society, Kuwait popular musical genres like sawt, theatrical tradition, folk arts, Bedouin crafts, soap operas are prominent part of Juwaiti art and culture.

KYRGYZSTAN

Capital:	Bishkek
Geographical location (Coordinates):	The Country extends between 41.20° N, 74.77° E
Area:	199,951 sq. km
Currency:	Som (KGS)
System of Governance:	Unitary Parliamentary Constitutional Republic
Independence	31 August 1991

Agriculture:

Agriculture employs a major percent of the country's labor force and accounts for about 1/5th of the GDP. The main food crops grown are wheat, barley, maize, potatoes, vegetables and fruits. While sugar beet, cotton and tobacco are important cash crops.

Art & Culture:

Boz-ui (house) shirdaks(rugs), kalpak(hat), komuz (musical instrument) are some of the prominent cultural art symbols of Kyrgyzstan.

LAOS

Capital:	Vientiane
Geographical location (Coordinates):	The Country extends between 19.85° N, 102.5° E
Area:	237,955 sq. km
Currency:	Kip (LAK)
System of Governance:	Unitary Marxist– Leninist Single Party Socialist
Independence:	22 October 1953

Agriculture:

Agricultural contributes around 50% of the GDP. majority of farmers are engaged in subsistence agriculture and the basic staple of such farmers is the production of sticky rice for local consumption. Rice, vegetables and beans, sugarcane, starchy roots, and tobacco are major crops. Mung-beans, soybeans, peanuts, tobacco, cotton, sugarcane, coffee, and tea are important cash crops.

Art & Culture:

Multi-ethnic groups are important part of Laos society, where major group is Lao. Other groups are Khmu, Hmong, Phouthai, Makong,Tai etc. The majority follow the Buddhism. Lao, Hmong, Khmu and French are spoken languages.

LEBANON

Capital:	Beirut
Geographical location (Coordinates):	The Country extends between 33.85° N, 35.86° E
Area:	10,452 sq. km
Currency:	Lebanese pound (LBP)
System of Governance:	Unitary Confessionalist Parliamentary Republic
Independence:	22 November 1943

Agriculture:

Agriculture plays only a minor role in Lebanon's economy, contributing about 5 percent of GDP and about 10% percent of the effective labor force. Some of the major agricultural products are sugar beets, potatoes oranges, apples, lemons and limes, bananas, olives, grapefruit, and wheat.

Art & Culture:

Lebanon's diversity population and multiethinicity is due to various groups which occupied during vraius period like Canaanite-Phoenicians, Persians to the Turks and French. Traditional folk music remains along with modern music, the wealth of art, has been very ancient. Some of the greatest poets such as Khalil Gibran who is ranked as the third-best poet of all time is product of this culture.

MALAYSIA

Capital:	Kuala Lumpur
Geographical location (Coordinates):	The Country extends between 4.21° N, 101.98° E
Area:	330,803 sq. km
Currency:	Ringgit
System of Governance:	Federal Parliamentary Elective Constitutional Monarchy
Independence:	31 August 1957

Agriculture:

Rubber, palm oil, and cocoa are major agricultural exports. Bananas, coconuts, durian, pineapples, rice, rambutan and various other exotic fruits and vegetables are also grown extensively. Malaysia grows about 70% of the rice, which is the staple food of the country.

Art & Culture

Among the greater Malaysian society there are different cultures like Malay, Chinese, Indian, Eurasian , along with the cultures of the indigenous groups of the peninsula and north Borneo. The major religion is Islam followed by Buddhism, Christianity, and Hinduism. Hari Merdeka or Independence Day is celebrated along with religion based festivals. Music is an integral part of Malaysian society. Carving, silversmithing Handwoven baskets, Weaving, songket (luxurious textiles), beetle nut sets, kris, wooden masks, etc. are famous Malaysian artworks.

MALDIVES

Capital:	Male
Geographical location (Coordinates):	The Country extends between 3.20° N, 73.22° E
Area:	298 sq. km
Currency:	Rufiyaa (MVR)
System of Governance:	Unitary Presidential Republic
Independence:	26 July 1965.

Agriculture:

Coconut palms and related products, fish are major export products. Millet, corn, pumpkins, sweet potatoes, pineapples, sugarcane, almonds, various tropical vegetables and fruits are also grown alongwiththe staple food of the country, Rice.

Art & Culture:
The culture, traditions and customs of Maldives are influenced by Indian, Sri Lankan, Malaysian, Arab, Persian, Indonesian and even African influences. Dances like Boduberu, kathak and instruments like bulbul tarang, wood carving and lacquer work are quite popular in Maldives.

MONGOLIA	
Capital:	Ulaanbaatar
Geographical location (Coordinates):	The Country extends between 46.86° N, 103.84° E
Area:	1,566,000 sq. km
Currency:	Tögrög (MNT)
System of Governance:	Semi-presidential Representative Democratic Republic
Independence:	29 December 1911

Agriculture:
Only limited area is cultivable with irrigation. pastoralism is one of the key economic activities, employing almost half of the population and accounting for 90 per cent of agricultural output. Over 30 million cattle, horses, yaks, goats, camels etc.are part of animal derived products in the form of meat and milk products, skins & hides, wool, cashmere etc.

Art & Culture:
Buddhism is the major religion followed by a large number of non-religious groups. Mongolia art and culture influenced largely by religion. Bronze sculptures, Thangka and Mongol zurag paintings, urtyn duu and khoomei singing styles, architecture with pyramidal roofs and ger style are some prominent features of Mongolian arts and heritage.

MYANMAR	
Capital:	Naypyitaw
Geographical location (Coordinates):	The Country extends between 21.91° N, 95.95° E
Area:	676,578 sq. km
Currency:	Kyat (MMK)
System of Governance:	Unitary Parliamentary Constitutional Republic
Independence	4 January 1948

Agriculture:
Agriculture sector is the backbone of Myanmar's economy and contributes more than 35% of GDP and employs more than 65% percent of the labour force. Importnat agricultural exports include rice, maize, vegetables & fruits, black gram, green gram, pigeon pea, chick pea, tamarind, sesame, onion and raw rubber.

Art & Culture:

Mon, Pyu, and the Burmese are majot three ethnic groups these also influenced a lot to the country's arts and culture. This culture also is an amalgam of royal and common traditions. Pwe dramatic forms, hsaing waing music,dance form influenced by South India, goldwork, silverwork, Sculpture with Buddhist and mythological images, Wood carving, lacquerwork etc. are some of the prominent Myanmar's art and cultural styles.

NEPAL	
Capital:	Kathmandu
Geographical location (Coordinates):	The Country extends between 28.39° N, 84.12° E
Area:	147,181 sq. km
Currency:	Nepalese Rupee (NPR)
System of Governance:	Federal Parliamentary Republic
Declaration of Kingdom	25 September 1768

Agriculture:

Nepal is an agricultural dependent economy with almost 1/3rd of the land is used for crop-cultivation and related activities. Rice, wheat, maize, millet, barley, and buckwheat are major cereals while major cash crops are sugarcane, jute, cotton, rubber, tobacco.oilseed.

Art & Culture:

Hinduism is the major religion followed by more than 80% of the population, while Buddhism is the second major religion of this mountain kingdom.

NORTH KOREA	
Capital:	Pyongyang
Geographical location (Coordinates):	The Country extends between 40.34° N, 127.51° E
Area:	120,540 sq. km
Currency:	Korean People's Won (KPW)
System of Governance:	Unitary Single Party Republic
Independence:	1 March 1919

Agriculture:

Major agricultural products are rice, corn, potatoes, wheat, soybeans, pulses, beef, pork, egg etc.

Art & Culture

Traditional Korean ch'angguk alongwith Western classical and pop music, distinct graphic arts, ink and oil painting, techniques of western watercolour, mural arts etc. are some of the features of art and culture.

OMAN	
Capital:	Muscat
Geographical location (Coordinates):	The Country extends between 21.47° N, 55.97° E

Area:	309,500 sq. km
Currency:	Rial (OMR)
System of Governance:	Unitary Parliamentary Absolute Monarchy
Independence:	1951

Agriculture:
Date is the most important agricultural product. Other products include bananas, mangoes, coconuts, limes, nuts, melons, bananas, coconuts, alfalfa, tobacco tomatoes, cabbages, eggplant, okra, cucumbers etc.

Art & Culture:
Intricate floral and geometric designs are integral part of Omani jewellery, woodwork, metal, leatherwork, pottery, weaving, textiles-design etc. Omani architecture pattern include vaulted arches, carved wooden ceilings, and roof beams with colourful floral and geometric designs, mashrabiya. Dances styles like Al-Bar'ah, shallat al-baura, nazag sheraa, yarah mashumah are popular.

Name:	Pakistan
Capital:	Islamabad
Geographical location (Coordinates):	The Country extends between 30.37° N, 69.34° E
Area:	881,913 sq. km
Currency:	Pakistani Rupee (PKR)
System of Governance:	Federal Parliamentary Constitutional Republic
Independence	14 August 1947

Agriculture

Agriculture contributes largely to the Pakistan's economy and a major contributor of country's GDP and labour force. Major agricultural products are cotton, wheat, rice, sugarcane, fruits, vegetables. Meat, eggs and dairy products are other agricultural produce.

Art & Culture

Pakistan shares its ancient culture with undivided India and a broader sense the Indian sub-continent and thus have rich art and heritage. It is reflected in paintings,architecture, sculpture, calligraphy, Naqashi, performing arts, theaters, drama etc.

PHILIPPINES	
Capital:	Manila
Geographical location (Coordinates):	The Country extends between 12.88° N, 121.77° E
Area:	300,000 sq. km
Currency:	Peso (PHP)
System of Governance:	Unitary Presidential Constitutional Republic
Independence:	4 July 1946

Agriculture

Agriculture contributes about 20 % to the GDP of country. Rice, coconuts, corn, sugarcane, bananas, pineapples, mangoes are part of the major agricultural products.

Art & Culture

Diverse cultural influences, art and traditions are reflection of Philippines'

multi-ethnic society. Symphonies, sonatas, concertos, Tagalogs, talindaw, kumintang, kundiman, panambitan are various music and song forms. Wood-carving, textile weaving, bamboo, rattan weaving, metal-smithing are some of the traditional art forms.

QATAR	
Capital:	Doha
Geographical location (Coordinates):	The Country extends between 25.35° N, 51.18° E
Area:	11,581 sq. km
Currency:	Riyal (QAR)
System of Governance:	Hereditary Monarchy
Independence:	3 September 1971

Agriculture

Due to limited arable land agriculture currently plays only a minor role in the country's economy. Date palms, carrots, potatoes, onions fodder beets are some of the major crops. Meat and dairy products are other agricultural produce.

Art & Culture

Ardah, al-moradah, al-ashori are famous dance forms. Famous art styles are based on surrealism, realism, expressionism, abstract art, calligraphy. Qatari music is influenced by Bedouin music styles.

SAUDI ARABIA	
Capital:	Riyadh
Geographical location (Coordinates):	The Country extends between 23.88° N, 45.07° E
Area:	2,149,690 sq. km
Currency:	Saudi riyal (SAR)
System of Governance:	Unitary Islamic Absolute Monarchy
Foundation of ingdom	23 September 1932

Agriculture:
Major agricultural products are dates, wheat, fruits, vegetables, Horticulture items, dairy products, eggs, fish, poultry etc.

Art & Culture

Spiriual minaret architecture is distinctive Saudi style of architecture. Dance forms include Saudi ardah, Music and song forms include al-sihba, while art and crafts include calligraphy and motifs with featured intricate patterns of geometric shapes, leaves, crescents and flowers.

SINGAPORE	
Capital:	Singapore
Geographical location (Coordinates):	The Country extends between 1.35° N, 103.81° E
Area:	725.1 sq. km
Currency:	Singapore Dollar (SGD)
System of Governance:	Unitary Dominant-Party Parliamentary Constitutional Republic
Proclamation	9 August 1965

Agriculture:
There is limited agricultural production and the country is dependent upon imports for its food requirements. Limited vegetables, fish and eggs are produced locally.

Art & Culture:
Singaporean society is a multicultural society with glimpses of Chinese, English, Malay and Tamil languages and culture. Human figure, landscape, portraits, still life, urban scenes, and village scenes are important theme of visual arts. Sculpture, architecture and other art forms have colonial and malay influences. Deepvali, Vesak Day, Chinese New Year and Christmas are important festivals.

SOUTH KOREA	
Capital:	Seoul
Geographical location (Coordinates):	The Country extends between 35.90° N, 127.77° E
Area:	100,363 sq. km
Currency:	Korean Republic Won (KRW)
System of Governance:	Unitary Presidential Constitutional Republic
Independence:	15 August 1945

Agriculture:
Rice is the main agricultural commodity and the country produces most of its domestic consumption of rice. Barley, wheat, soybean and fruits like apple, Pear, peach, mandarin and grapes are also grown.

Art & Culture:
Traditional Korean music and other related art forms-Guagak; the popular court music Yeomillak, jeongjae; music forms like jeongak, pansori, sanjo and japga are quite popular. salpurichum, gutchum, hallyangchum, buchaechum, geommu are some of the famous folk dances forms. Famous Pottery styles are Cheongja, Buncheong and Baekja.

<table>
<tr><td colspan="2" align="center">SRI LANKA</td></tr>
<tr><td>Capital:</td><td>Sri Jayawardene-pura Kotte</td></tr>
<tr><td>Geographical location
(Coordinates):</td><td>The Country extends between
7.87° N, 80.77° E</td></tr>
<tr><td>Area:</td><td>65,610 sq. km</td></tr>
<tr><td>Currency:</td><td>Sri Lankan Rupee (LKR)</td></tr>
<tr><td>System of
Governance:</td><td>Unitary Semi-Presidential
Constitutional Republic</td></tr>
<tr><td>Independence:</td><td>4 February 1948</td></tr>
</table>

Agriculture:
Rice, tea, fruit, vegetables, and oilseed crops are cultivated in the country. Fisheries and Livestock farming is also practiced in Sri Lanka and plays an important role in country's economy.

Art & Culture:
Sri Lankan culture like its neighbourhood includes a lot of customs and rituals. It is reflected in its art, architecture, sculptures, festivals, paintings etc. Martial art forms-Cheena di and Angampora; paintings like Frescoes and religious paintings, dances like kandyan and devil dancing are quite famous. Vesak Poya, Kandy Esala Poya Perahera, Deepawali, Eid are famous festivals celebrated in Sri Lanka.

<table>
<tr><td colspan="2" align="center">SYRIA</td></tr>
<tr><td>Capital:</td><td>Damascus</td></tr>
<tr><td>Geographical location
(Coordinates):</td><td>The Country extends between
34.8° N, 38.9° E</td></tr>
<tr><td>Area:</td><td>185,180 sq. km</td></tr>
<tr><td>Currency:</td><td>Syrian Pound (SYP)</td></tr>
<tr><td>System of
Governance:</td><td>Unitary dominant-party semi-presidential republic</td></tr>
<tr><td>Independence:</td><td>17 April 1946</td></tr>
</table>

Agriculture:
The major agricultural products are cotton, olives, wheat, barley, lentils, chickpeas, sugar beets, beef, mutton, eggs, poultry, and milk. Cotton is the main cash crop. Due to devastation of civil war the agriculture is in a severe crisis.

Art & Culture:
Syria have old age cultural heritage. Various art forms evolve dover the years. Famous dance forms are Aleppo, Idlib, Syrian Jazeera, Dabkeh; Poetic forms like muwashshah, and musical forms like Syrian chant are quite popular in Syrian Society.

TAIWAN	
Capital:	Taipei
Geographical location (Coordinates):	The Country extends between 23.69° N, 120.96° E
Area:	36,197 sq. km
Currency:	New Taiwan Dollar (TWD)
System of Governance:	Unitary Semi-Presidential Republic
Proclamation of Republic:	1 January 1912

Agriculture:
Rice, wheat, sweet potatoes, bananas, peanuts, soybeans are major food crops. Sugar, pineapples, citrus fruits, crude tea,asparagus are important exports Oolong tea, cotton, tobacco, jute, Mushroom and sisal are also produced.

Art & Culture:
Blend of traditional and modern art, aboriginal art, and folk art are part of Taiwan's art and culture. The culture influences of various religions like Buddhism, Confucianism, Taoism and Hakka, Holo and other indigenous are quite reflected in culture. Woodcarving, weaving, wickerwork, pottery, flower arrangement, sculpture, ceramics are famous art forms of Taiwan.

TAJIKISTAN	
Capital:	Dushanbe
Geographical location (Coordinates):	The Country extends between 38.86° N, 71.27° E
Area:	143,100 k sq. Km.
Currency:	Somoni (TJS)
System of Governance:	Unitary Dominant-Party Presidential Constitutional Republic
Independence:	9 September 1991

Agriculture:
Economy of Tajikistan is mainly agriculture based as more than 60 % of the labour force is employed in the agricultural sector. The primary food crops are wheat, barley, maize, potatoes, and rice. Cotton is the major cash crop and employs a major part of workforce.

Art & Culture:
The culture of Tajikistan is a mixture of Persian and Mongolian culture. The main Tajik handicrafts are embroidery, weaving and appliqué. Various dances, legends and music linked to the birds specially hawk are distinguishing characteristics of Tajjik culture. Tajik hawk dance, Russian and Persian versions of pop-music. slip painting, gushtingiri (freestyle wrestling) are some of other prominent features.

THAILAND	
Capital:	Bangkok
Geographical location (Coordinates):	The Country extends between15.8° N, 100.9° E

Area:	513,120 sq. km
Currency:	Baht (THB)
System of Governance:	Unitary Parliamentary Constitutional Monarchy
Constitution:	6 April 2017

Agriculture

Agriculture plays an important role in the Thai economy. About 50% of the the labour force is employed in this sector. Rice, Rubber, sugar, pineapples, coconuts, tapioca, tuna, shrimp are major exports. Palm oil and coffee is also grown on a large scale.

Art & Culture

The culture and arts of Thailand is highly influenced by Indian culture and Buddhism. The mythological Garuda holds an important place in Thai arts. Thai folklore, Thai dance forms like khon, Menora; music forms like Mor lam, Piphat, Khrueang sai, Mahori and Ramleela based on Ramakien (Ramayana) are quite popular in Thailand.

TIMOR-LESTE (EAST TIMOR)	
Capital:	Dili
Geographical location (Coordinates):	The Country extends between 8.87° S, 125.72° E
Area:	15,007 sq. km
Currency:	US Dollar (USD)
System of Governance:	Unitary Semi-Presidential Constitutional Republic
Independence	20 May 2002

Agriculture

About 80% of the population is dependent upon Agriculture for their livelihood. Rice, Maize are main staple foods. Sweet potato cassava, peanut, various vegetables, fruits, spices and tree crops are also grown on a large scale.

Art & Culture

Different influences like Portuguese, Indonesian, and Chinese are quite reflected in art and culture of the country. Famous handicrafts are tais, finely woven baskets and mats, paintings, pottery, jewelry, dolls and intricately embroidered bags, musical instruments, metal knives and wood carvings. Soro tais, tebedai, sau batar, foti raba, likurai are dance forms. Instruments like lakadou, kfui, kaiket, babadok, gongs are integral part of country's music.

TURKMENISTAN	
Capital:	Ashgabat
Geographical location (Coordinates):	The Country extends between 38.96° N, 59.55° E
Area:	sq. km

Currency:	Turkmen New Manat (TMT)
System of Governance:	Unitary Presidential Republic
Independence	27 October 1991

Agriculture:
Major crops are wheat, corn, fodder crops along with grapes, almonds, vegetables, melons, pomegranates, figs, olives. Animal produce like wool, meat, milk also part of agriculture economy of the country.

Art & Culture:
Nomadic imprints are part of Turkmenistan art and culture. The various dance and music closely resembles that of Kyrgyz and Kazakh folk music forms. Musical styles like mukamlar, kirklar, navoi etc. accompanied by the dutar is characteristic of Turkmenistan.

UNITED ARAB EMIRATES

Capital:	Abu Dhabi
Geographical location (Coordinates):	The Country extends between 23.42° N, 53.84° E
Area:	83,600 sq. km
Currency:	UAE Dirham (AED)
System of Governance:	Federal Constitutional Monarchy
Independence:	2 December 1971

Agriculture:
Main agricultural Products include tomatoes, melons, and dates. Other produce includes citrus, mangoes, celery, potatoes, cucumbers, lettuce, peppers, fodder crops and other vegetables and fruits.

Art & Culture:
Main dance forms include Al Ayalah, yowalah, Yola, Mated, Hawan. Musical instruments like Al Ras, oud, daf, nai, rababa, tanboura, doumbek often part of typical UAE musical forms. Barjeel and other architectural styles are part of architecture.

UZBEKISTAN

Capital:	Tashkent
Geographical location (Coordinates):	The Country extends between 41.37° N, 64.58° E
Area:	448,978 sq. km
Currency:	Uzbek Som (UZS)
System of Governance:	Unitary Presidential Constitutional Republic
Proclamation of independence:	31 August 1991

Agriculture:
Uzbekistan is one of the world's largest producer and exporter of cotton. Rice, wheat, rye are major cereals. Other significant agricultural products include fruits and vegetables, silk, dairy and meat.

Art & Culture:
Ferghana, Bukhara and Khorezm are famous dance styles; musical genres like Shash-maqam. Uzbek music is often performed with instruments like karnay, surnay and doira.

VIETNAM	
Capital:	Ho Chi Minh City
Geographical location (Coordinates):	The Country extends between 14.05° N, 108.27° E
Area:	331,212 sq. km
Currency:	Dong (VND)
System of Governance:	Unitary Marxist-Leninist Single-Party Socialist Republic
Independence:	2 September 1945

Agriculture:
Major food crops include Rice, Maize, sugarcane, cassava, sweet potatoes and nuts. Tea, Coffe and fruits like banana, coconut, citrus, orange, mango, jackfruit, Kapok are also grown.

Art & Culture:
Vietnamese music has been highly influenced by the m music stylesof China, Korea, US and UK. Traditional music forms include, don ca tai tu, Chau Van etc. while types of musical types include music of the Royal family, Cheo, Tuong, Xam singing, Don ca tai tu, folk songs, Ca Tru etc.

YEMEN	
Capital:	Sana'a
Geographical location (Coordinates):	The Country extends between 15.55° N, 48.51° E
Area:	527,968 sq. km
Currency:	Yemeni Rial (YER)
System of Governance:	Unitary Presidential Constitutional Republic
Proclamation of Republic	30 November 1967

Agriculture:
Limited agriculture production is due to shortage of arable land. The main cash crop is qat Sorghum, maize, millet and pulses are the main food crops. Cultivation of Coffee, vegetables and fishery and livestock farming is also practiced.

Art & Culture
Different poetic and musical genres like zamil, razfah, balah dan, qasidah etc. are part of yemen culture. Dances like bara, la'bah are quite popular while Al-oud and the simsimi-ya are famous Yemeni musical instruments.

RUSSIA	
Capital:	Moscow
Geographical location (Coordinates):	The Country extends between 61.52° N, 105.31° E
Area:	17,098,246 sq. km
Currency:	Ruble (RUB)
System of Governance:	Federal Dominant-Party Semi-Presidential Constitutional Republic
Proclamation of Republic:	14 September 1917

Agriculture:

Wheat is the major crops grown in Russia. Other important crops are barley, sunflower seed, oats, potatoes, pumpkin and rye. Oilseed cake meal, sugar and honey are also produced.

Art & Culture:

The culture of Russia has a long and rich cultural history. It is home to almost 190 ethnic groups. Musical forms like opera,ballet and handicrafts like nesting dolls; colorfully painted onion domes in architecture are some of the disticnctive styles of Russain culture.

NORTH AMERICA COUNTRIES

- **Third largest continent** after Asia and Africa.
- Extends from **7°N to 85°N latitude** and east to west from 20°W to 179°W. Spreads over an area of 24 million sq. km.
- The Tropic of Cancer and the North circle pass through the continent.
- Includes three large countries - USA, Canada, and Mexico.

Climate and Vegetation

- **Tundra :** Arctic Circle, Arctic Ocean and Hudson Bay.
- Summers and Winters are cool and long; Lichens, mosses and Low berry.
- **Taiga :** Winters (long and cold), Summer(short and warm.)
- **Trees:** Pine, Fir, larch.

Mediterranean Climate

Influenced by trade wind in summer which make hot dry summer.

As the climate is unfavourable for plant growth only scrub like vegetations are common here.

ANTIGUA AND BARBUDA	
Capital:	Saint John's
Geographical location (Coordinates):	The Country extends between 17.06° N, 61.79° W
Area:	440 sq. Km
Currency:	East Caribbean Dollar (XCD)

System of Governance:	Unitary Parliamentary Constitutional Monarchy
Independence:	1 November 1981

Agriculture:

The limited agricultural output is due to scarce water supply and shortage of labor. Agricultural exports include cotton, fruits and vegetables like bananas, coconuts, cucumbers, mangoes, sugarcane and pineapples, hot peppers. Livestock farming is also an important sector.

Art & Culture:

Afro-Caribbean music like Calypso and other musical genres like steel-drum, zouk, reggae, benna, quadrille and soca are fairly popular in the country. African constitutes the major ethnic population while Christianity is the predominant religion. Antiguan Creole and English is the major spoken language. The Carribaen culture is also reflected in Painting, sculpture, carving and sculpture.

BAHAMAS

Capital:	Nassau
Geographical location (Coordinates):	The Country extends between 25.03° N, 77.39° W
Area:	13,878 sq. Km
Currency:	Bahamian Dollar (BSD)
System of Governance:	Unitary Parliamentary Constitutional Monarchy
Independence:	10 July 1973

Agriculture:

Agriculture is relatively subsistence in nature and only a very small fraction of land area is used for cultivation of crops. Main agriculture crops are Okra, tomatoes, onions, orange, grapefruit, and cucumber. Some of these are exported.

Art & Culture:

Bahamian culture is a mixture of mostly African, with part of British and American influences. Christianity is the predominant religion and Bahamianese Dialect' is spoken colloquially alongwith official use of English. Goombay, junkanoo and rake 'n' scrape are important part of indigenous forms of music & dance.

BARBADOS

Capital:	Bridgetown
Geographical location (Coordinates):	The Country extends between 13.19° N, 59.54° W
Area:	439 sq. Km
Currency:	Barbadian Dollar (BBD)

System of Governance:	Unitary Parliamentary Constitutional Monarchy
Independence:	30 November 1966

Agriculture:

Sugarcane, yams, sweet potatoes, corn, eddoes, cassava, and several bean varieties are major food crops. Fisheries and livestock rearing are also done on a small scale.

Art & Culture:

Strong African influences are reflected in various types of art forms of Barbados like paintings, murals, sculptures, crafts. The tuk band is indigenous musical tradition of Barbados which is often accompanied by instruments like penny-whistles, snare drums, and bass drums. Calypso, reggae, and steel band music are also popular in the country.

BELIZE

Capital:	Belmopan
Geographical location (Coordinates):	The Country extends between 17.18° N, 88.49° W
Area:	22,966 sq. Km
Currency:	Belize Dollar (BZD)
System of Governance:	Unitary Parliamentary Constitutional Monarchy
Independence:	21 September 1981

Agriculture:

Agriculture is an important part of Belize's economy which is largely due to adequate rainfall and a relatively stable sub-tropical climate round the year. Major food crops include Sugar, citrus, and banana. Food process industries based on the production of cacao, corn, hot pepper sauces, jams, jellies are also growing.

Art & Culture:

Various genre of Afro-Caribbean garifuna music like punta are quite distinctive of the culture of the country. Brukdow, Rap and hip-hop are also quite popular in addition to soca, dancehall, reggae etc.

CANADA

Capital:	Ottawa
Geographical location (Coordinates):	The Country extends between 56.13° N, 106.34° W
Area:	9,984,670 sq. Km
Currency:	Canadian Dollar (CAD)

System of Governance:	Federal Parliamentary Constitutional Monarchy
Independence:	July 1, 1867

Agriculture:

It is one of the largest producers of agricultural products. Some of the major crops are wheat, barley, corn,

canola, oats etc.The Canadian milk and dairy products are also an important part of agricultural economy.

Art & Culture:

Multi-cultural influences can easily be reflected in Canadian music, arts and crafts. Step dance, ballet and other modern dances are very popular form in addition to Canadian folk dances. Château Style, Neo-Gothic styles are some of the prominent canadian architectural styles.

COSTA RICA

Capital:	San José
Geographical location (Coordinates):	The Country extends between 9.74° N, 83.75° W
Area:	51,100 sq. Km
Currency:	Costa Rican Colón (CRC)
System of Governance:	Unitary Presidential Constitutional Republic
Independence	15 September 1821

Agriculture:

Coffee, rice, bananas, sugarcane, beans, Oil palm, fruits and vegetables and other horticulture products are important agriculture products. Animal products like milk & dairy products, egg, meat are other important produce.

Art & Culture:

The culture of costa rica is diverse by virtue of cultural influences of indigenous Costa Rican tribes, Mesoamerican and South Americans. Merengue, Cumbia, Tex-Mex, soca, rock and roll is some of the famous music genres. Dances like salsa, Cabillito Nicoyano, El Torito, and Punto Guanacasteco are also fairly popular.

CUBA

Capital:	Havana
Geographical location (Coordinates):	The Country extends between 21.52° N, 77.78° W
Area:	109,884 sq. Km
Currency:	Cuban Peso (CUP)

System of Governance:	Unitary Marxist–Leninist Single-Party Socialist Republic
Independence:	20 May 1902

Agriculture:

Sugarcane and sugarcane based products, tobacco, rice, potatoes, sweet potatoes, coffee, other vegetables and fruits like oranges, lemons and limes, grapefruit, plantains, bananas, mangoes, pineapples , ginger, potatoes etc.

Art & Culture:

Mulattos constitute more than half of the total Cuban population while Spanish is the official language. Majority of the population follow Roman Catholic Church. The diversity of Cuban culture is reflected in its various art forms. Danzón, Mambo, cha-cha-cha, Salsa, Ballet are some of the most popular dance forms in cuba. Other important musical genres include guaracha, bolero etc.

DOMINICA

Capital:	Roseau
Geographical location (Coordinates):	The Country extends between 15.41° N, 61.37° W
Area:	750 sq. Km
Currency:	East Caribbean Dollar (XCD)
System of Governance:	Unitary Parliamentary Republic
Independence:	3 November 1978

Agriculture:

Main agricultural produce include coffee, cocoa, bananas and citrus fruits. Other important products are coconuts and essential oils. Fishing industry is also quite vast in the country.

Art & Culture:

A mixture of cultural traditions and forms is reflected in the county as influenced by Creole, African and European customs and traditions. Carnival music like Chanté mas, Lapo kabwit,Creole music is fairly popular in this island nation.

DOMINICAN REPUBLIC

Capital:	Santo Domingo
Geographical location (Coordinates):	The Country extends between 18.73° N, 70.16° W
Area:	48,671 sq. Km

Currency:	Peso (DOP)
System of Governance:	Unitary Presidential Republic
Independence:	16 August 1863

Agriculture:

Agriculture's share is more than 10% of the country's GDP. Agriculture is an important sector and about 1/3rd of the total land is suitable for agriculture. Major crops are sugarcane, coffee, Cocoa, tobacco and banana. Rice, coconuts, cassava, tomatoes, pulses, peanuts are other important crops.

Art & Culture:

Art, sculpture etc. have Spanish and French influence. Most popular dances and music genres include merengue, salsa, bachata among others. Potteries, carved basket weaved palm products, coral and seashells jewellery are famous folk arts.

UNITED STATES OF AMERICA

Capital:	Washington, D.C.
Geographical location (Coordinates):	37.0902° N, 95.7129° W
Area:	3,796,742 sq. Km
Currency:	United States Dollar (USD)
System of Governance:	Federal Presidential Constitution Republic
Independence	4 July 1776

Agriculture

Major agricultural products include Corn, wheat, soybeans, cotton and hay. Corn, wheat, and soybeans are grown for both animal feed and human consumption. Although agriculture is practiced in every US state, it is concentrated in the Great Plains of the Midwest. United States is also among the world's top producer nations of cow's milk and dairy products.

Art & Culture

The Art & Culture of United States reflects culture of Native Americans in addition to culture of immigration population from other countries and reflects cosmopolitan culture or multi-ethnic society. More than 70% of Americans identify themselves as Christians. There is no official language of the United States, while almost every language in the world is spoken in the country. The United States also has a vibrant movie industry, centred in Hollywood. American folk art is an artistic style and is identified with quilts and other hand-crafted items. American music is very diverse with styles like jazz, gospel, country and western, bluegrass, rock 'n' roll , hip-hop etc.

GRENADA

Capital:	Saint George's
Geographical location (Coordinates):	The Country extends between 12.11° N, 61.67° W

Area:	348 sq. Km
Currency:	East Caribbean Dollar (XCD)
System of Governance:	Unitary two-party Parliamentary System Constitutional Monarchy
Independence:	7 February 1974

Agriculture:

Agriculture sector accounts for more than 20% of the country's total employment. Bananas, cocoa, beans, nutmeg mace and other fruits and vegetables are important agriculture produce. Other important products are cotton, cloves, limes, cinnamon, coffee, yams, sweet potatoes, corn and peas.

Art & Culture:

Multiethnic groups consisting of descendants of former African slaves, mixed black and white racial strains, people from Asian and European origin. French-African patois is also spoken with English as official language. Majority follow the Roman Catholic.

Distinct canvasses made up of materials like calabash, cutlass, wood, metal, cloth, bamboo etc. are unique. Popular performance arts include Drama, dance, music etc.

GUATEMALA

Capital:	Guatemala City
Geographical location (Coordinates):	The Country extends between 15.78° N, 90.23° W
Area:	108,889 sq. Km
Currency:	Quetzal (GTQ)
System of Governance:	Unitary Presidential Republic
Independence:	15 September 1821

Agriculture:

Agriculture accounts for about 1/4th of Guatemala's total GDP. More than half of the country's labour force is employed in this sector. The principal cash crops are coffee, sugar, bananas, cotton, hemp, essential oils, and cacao. Fisheries industry is also thriving here.

Art & Culture:

The influences of ancient Mayan civilization and the neighbouring Mexican culture are quite reflected in art and culture of Guatemala. Arts and handicrafts like woven textiles, pottery, carvings and ceramics is quite prevalent among the society. Music genres like Garifuna music, fumba music, tejano music, punta, reggae, ranchera music and other folk music forms are popular in Guatemala. Music genres and dances including Ballet, national chorus, and opera are also performed throughout the country.

- ⊰ World's **largest island** and **smallest continent**.
- ⊰ The tropic of **Capricorn** cuts the continent almost into half.
- ⊰ The **Great Barrier Reef** (largest coral reef in the world) is situated in Australia.

  The location of Australia is in between India and Pacific Ocean and it stretches west to east from 114° E longitude to 154° E longitude and from 10°S to 40°S Latitude.

  The island was discovered by **Captain cook** in 1770.

Climate and Vegetation

Natural Vegetation

The Predominant vegetation types are –

Tropical rain forest region with dense cover of coconut and palms, mangrove growing near shoreline

The deciduous forest region with tall and short tree , shrubs, small plants and mosses.

The dry desert and desert scrub: It is the region with vegetation such as cactic.

AUSTRALIA	
Capital:	Canberra
Geographical location (Coordinates):	The Country extends between 25.27° S, 133.77° E
Area:	7,692,024 sq. km
Currency:	Australian dollar (AUD)
System of Governance:	Federal Parliamentary Constitutional Monarchy
Independence:	1 January 1901

Agriculture:
The major crops are wheat, rice, barley, oats, sorghum, maize, triticale. The country also produces oilseeds like canola, sunflowers, soybeans, peanuts, grain legumes (lupins and chick peas), Cash crops (sugarcane, cotton, tobacco), fruits and vegetables. Livestock products are also important part of country's economy. Australia exports meats, and wool in addition to grains.

Art & Culture:
Australia exhibits a diverse range of performing art, music, dance, sculpture etc. Indigenous culture along with culture of the immigrants is inherent to the Australia's cultural identity. Popular music forms are Australian folk, bush ballads accompanied by didgeridoo, country music, pop music etc. Dances like Melbourne Shuffle, New Vogue, corroboree, Ballet are prominent.

<table>
<tr><td colspan="2" align="center">FIJI</td></tr>
<tr><td>Capital:</td><td>Suva</td></tr>
<tr><td>Geographical location (Coordinates):</td><td>The Country xtends between 17.71° S, 178.06° E</td></tr>
<tr><td>Area:</td><td>18,274 sq. km</td></tr>
<tr><td>Currency:</td><td>Fijian dollar (FJD)</td></tr>
<tr><td>System of Governance:</td><td>Unitary Parliamentary Constitutional Republic</td></tr>
<tr><td>Independence:</td><td>10 October 1970</td></tr>
<tr><td colspan="2">Agriculture:
Agriculture (with forestry and fisheries) accounts for around 8% of the GDP of Fiji. Sugarcane is the major crop contributing to the country's economy. Other agricultural products which are grown and exported include coconuts, bananas, rice, maize, pineapples, watermelons, tobacco, ginger and cocoa.</td></tr>
<tr><td colspan="2">Art & Culture:
Fiji exhibits a variety of Polynesian and Melanesian music forms. Qawwali, Bhajans, Thumri and Jazz are also popular and so are the meke, dele, cibi dance forms.</td></tr>
<tr><td colspan="2" align="center">KIRIBATI</td></tr>
<tr><td>Capital:</td><td>Tarawa</td></tr>
<tr><td>Geographical location (Coordinates):</td><td>The Country extends between 3.37° S, 168.73° W</td></tr>
<tr><td>Area:</td><td>811 sq. km</td></tr>
<tr><td>Currency:</td><td>Kiribati Dollar</td></tr>
<tr><td>System of Governance:</td><td>Unitary Parliamentary Republic</td></tr>
<tr><td>Independence:</td><td>12 July 1979</td></tr>
<tr><td colspan="2">Agriculture:
Agriculture (with forestry and fisheries) accounts for around 1/4th of the total GDP of Kiribati. The major agricultural products include coconut (copra), bananas, screw-pine, breadfruit, papaya, taro, sweet potatoes and vegetables.</td></tr>
<tr><td colspan="2">Art & Culture:
Majority of the population belongs to the Micronesian ethnicity, while Gilbertese (Tae-tae ni Kiribati) is the most widely spoken language throughout this country. Buki, Ruoia, Te Kabuti, Tirere, Kaimatoa are original dances from the country, body percussion is integral part of music. Various Handicrafts items are important part of Kiribati arts.</td></tr>
<tr><td colspan="2" align="center">MARSHALL ISLANDS</td></tr>
<tr><td>Capital:</td><td>Majuro</td></tr>
<tr><td>Geographical location (Coordinates):</td><td>The Country extends between 7.1315° N, 171.1845° E</td></tr>
<tr><td>Area:</td><td>181.43 sq. km</td></tr>
</table>

Currency:	US Dollar (USD)
System of Governance:	Unitary Parliamentary Republic
Independence:	21 October 1986

Agriculture:
Coconut (Copra) is the main cash crop. The main food crops are bananas, breadfruit, pandanus, taro and other tropical fruits and vegetables. Livestock farming is also growing alongwith fisheries and poultry.

Art & Culture:
Micronesian culture is quite reflective in the arts and culture of the Island nation. Marshallese dances like beet dance, Jobwa (Jebwa) stick dance and other traditional dances are important part of the culture. The musical chant, roro is typical of Marshall Islands although the lyrics vary by island, but the style remains the same.

FEDERATED STATES OF MICRONESIA

Capital:	Palikir
Geographical location (Coordinates):	The Country extends between 7.42° N, 150.55° E
Area:	702 sq. km
Currency:	US Dollar (USD)
System of Governance:	Federal Parliamentary Republic
Independence:	3 November 1986

Agriculture:
Major agricultural products include Coconuts, Copra, sweet potatoes, bananas, cassavas, taros, yams and breadfruit. The agriculture is mainly for subsistence. Other vegetables and fruits like cucumbers, eggplant, cabbage, bell peppers, tomatoes, pineapples, papayas, pandanus, lemon, limes, oranges and tangerines are also produced.

Art & Culture:
Stick dancing, Moonlight Dance are among the main traditional dances. Architecture is a mixture of indigenous designs, colonial influences, including western models. Once a highly valued art form like finely carved wooden crafts, canoe carving have limited presence now.

NAURU

Capital:	Yaren
Geographical location (Coordinates):	The Country extends between 0.52° S, 166.93° E
Area:	21 sq. km
Currency:	Australian Dollar (AUD)

System of Governance:	Unitary Parliamentary Republic
Independence:	31 January 1968

Agriculture:
Limited agricultural activities in Nauru as only 20 percent of land is suitable for agricultural use and about 90 percent of the food products are imported. Coconut remains the only small and viable crop in the island nation and fishing is one among the limited fresh food available to the people.

Art & Culture:
Traditional culture is a mix of Micronesian, Melanesian and Polynesian cultures. Rhythmic singing, dancing, reigen music are performed on special occasions. Materials like kokospalme wood, kokosfasern fans and screw tree sheets are main part of traditional arts and crafts.

NEW ZEALAND	
Capital:	Wellington
Geographical location (Coordinates):	The Country extends between 40.90° S, 174.88° E
Area:	268,021 sq. km
Currency:	New Zealand Dollar (NZD)
System of Governance:	Unitary Parliamentary Constitutional Monarchy
Independence:	26 September 1907

Agriculture:
Agriculture (with forestry, fisheries and allied sector) accounts for more than 40% of total export. It also employs over 6% of total workforce of the country. New Zealand is one of the world's largest exporters of dairy products and sheep meat. Various vegetables and fruits like kiwifruit, avocado, apples, pears, peaches, nectarines, plums, apricots and cherries are also produced on a larger scale.

Art & Culture:
The art and culture of New Zealand reflects both the Indigenous Maori culture and the culture of immigrants. Dances like Haka, Poi Balls, art forms like parekha, landscape art, carving, tattooing, weaving, painting are quite distinct style of the culture.

PALAU	
Capital:	Ngerulmud
Geographical location (Coordinates):	The Country extends between 7.51° N, 134.58° E

Area:	459 sq. km
Currency:	US dollar (USD)
System of Governance:	Unitary Presidential Constitutional Republic
Independence	18 July 1947

Agriculture:

Taro, tapioca and other tropical fruits and vegetables forms the major crops. Other activities dependent on livestock like meat products, poultry along with fisheries is also practiced

Art & Culture:

The graphic arts are highly developed in Palau. Carved wooden storyboards, shell-jewelry making, weaving are main art forms while dance forms include styles of stick dances and war stances. Traditional music along with the modern pop music have important place in the society.

PAPUA NEW GUINEA

Capital:	Port Moresby
Geographical location (Coordinates):	The Country extends between 6.31°S, 143.95° E
Area:	462,840 sq. km
Currency:	kina
System of Governance:	Unitary Parliamentary Constitutional Monarchy
Independence:	1 July 1949

Agriculture:

Agriculture accounts a major part of country's GDP. Main staple crops are Yam, taro, banana and sweet potato. Coffee, oil, cocoa, copra, tea, sugar and rubber are main cash crops. Other products include Sugarcane and vegetables like spinach, cauliflower, broccoli, broad beans and cucumber. The country has also valuable fisheries resources.

Art & Culture:

The country diversity is reflected in its 800 recorded distinct tribal groups that speak at least 750 different languages. Tok Pisin is the most spoken language while Hiri Motu is the trade language.

SAMOA

Capital:	Apia
Geographical location (Coordinates):	The Country extends between 13.75° S, 172.10° W
Area:	2,842 sq. Km

Currency:	Tala (WST)
System of Governance:	Unitary Dominant-Party Parliamentary Democracy
Independence:	14 June 1889

Agriculture:

Agriculture along with fisheries and forestry is an important part of Samoan GDP. Coconuts & derived products, bananas, taro, yams, cocoa and coffee are the main agriculture produce. Sugarcane and various other fruits and vegetables like taamu, breadfruit, and manioc are also grown.

Art & Culture:

Samoan society is governed by the Samoan Way known as Fa'a Samoa. Tatau or tattoo is the main spiritual and cultural heritage of Samoans. Tapa is one of the art form which is also used traditionally as clothing and is an important part of traditional ceremonies. Dance and music is central to the Samoan culture. Some of the Samoan dance forms include Fa'ataupati, Sasa and Siva tau.

SOLOMON ISLANDS

Capital:	Honiara
Geographical location (Coordinates):	The Country extends between 9.64° S, 160.15° E
Area:	28,400 sq. Km
Currency:	Solomon Islands Dollar (SBD)
System of Governance:	Unitary Parliamentary Constitutional Monarchy
Independence:	7 July 1978

Agriculture:

Major cash crops coconut and derived products, betel nut, oil palm and cocoa beans and coffee. Other important crops include pineapple, potato, onion, Ngali-nuts and various spices. Sweet potato, cassava, banana, taro, yam, beans, cabbage, watercress, watermelon, breadfruits, Gnetum are important subsistence crops.

Art & Culture:

Culture of the country is unique due to its old age traditional forms of art and heritage. Traditional Melanesian music in Solomon Islands includes vocals accompanied by pan-pipe, slit-drum and other musical instruments with unique tunings.

TONGA

Capital:	Nuku'alofa
Geographical location (Coordinates):	The Country extends between 21.17° S, 175.19° W
Area:	748 sq. Km

Currency:	Pa'anga (TOP)
System of Governance:	Unitary Parliamentary Constitutional Monarchy
Independence:	4 June 1970

Agriculture:

Agriculture and fishing activities in Tonga is mainly for subsistence also for exports. Major export crops include yams, taro, cassava, sweet potatoes, kava, breadfruit, papaya, pineapple, banana and watermelon. Other vegetables like tomatoes, asparagus, gourds, cabbages, capsicum, cauliflower, cucumbers, squash and beans are also cultivated.

Art & Culture:

Like arts and cultural heritage of other nations the Tongans arts and handicrafts, including bone carving, wood carving, basket making and fine weaving techniques passed down through generations. Famous traditional forms like tapa, keepsakes are unique to the cultural identity, so is the traditional dancing forms.

TUVALU	
Capital:	Funafuti
Geographical location (Coordinates):	The Country extends between 7.10° S, 177.64° E
Area:	26 sq. Km
Currency:	Tuvaluan Dollar
System of Governance:	Unitary Non-Partisan Parliamentary Constitutional Monarchy
Independence	1 October 1978

Agriculture:

Major crops include coconut (Copra), swamp taro,Sugarcane. Other important products are bananas, breadfruit are supplemental crops. Livestock products are very little but fisheries products are utilized fro local consumption.

Art & Culture:

Kolose , Fala leaves clothing, decorated mats, dancing skirts, and fans with dyed fibers are some of the famous art forms of Tuvalu. Action songs such as faatele are popular along with Western-style dancing, and pop music.

VANUATU	
Capital:	Port Vila
Geographical location (Coordinates):	The Country extends between 15.37° S, 166.95° E
Area:	12,189 sq. Km

Currency:	Vatu (VUV)
System of Governance:	Unitary Parliamentary Republic
Independence	30 July 1980

Agriculture:
Limited land is available for agriculture and the majority of farming is for subsistence. Major food crops are coconut, taro, yams, kumara, and banana. Other important crops include different fruits and vegetables.

Art & Culture:
Majority of the population follow Christianity,while Bislama is the national language. Several other indigenous languages are spoken in this small republic. Musical instruments like stamping tubes, rattles, slit gongs are important part of traditional Vanuatun music. Modern music forms like zouk, reggaeton are quite popular in the country.

SOUTH AMERICA COUNTRIES

- ◄ South America is a long triangular shaped continent. It is **4th largest** continent.
- ◄ Stretches from 12°N to 55°S latitude.
- ◄ **Mountains- The Andes** (longest mountain range in the world.), Aconcagua, Ojendal Salado, Chimborazo, Cotopaxi,
- ◄ **Lakes- Titicaca** (highest navigable lake in world), Poopo, Argentino, Junin, Buenos Aires,Nahuel Huapi.

ARGENTINA

Capital:	Buenos Aires
Geographical location (Coordinates):	The Country extends between 38.41° S, 63.61° W
Area:	2,780,400 sq. Km
Currency:	Argentine Peso (ARS)
System of Governance:	Federal Presidential Constitutional Republic
Independence:	9 July 1816,

Agriculture:
The main crops of Argentina include Rice, wheat, corn, soy, sorghum and sunflower. Argentina is one of the top countries with the highest land area for organic farming. Major organic exports include pears, apples, oranges, lemons, garlic, onions, beans, oilseeds, corn, wheat, soy and sunflower.

Art & Culture:
The unique mixture of European and Latin American influences is reflected in country's music, lifestyle and other art forms. Dance is an essential part of the culture; the famous dances are Argentine Tango, Chamame, Cuarteto etc. Music accompanied by typical instruments like quena, charango etc. are integral to Argentina's music. Some of the famous art forms are Pottery, woven goods and clothes like poncho.

<table>
<tr><td colspan="2" align="center">BOLIVIA</td></tr>
<tr><td>Capital:</td><td>Sucre (judicial) and La Paz (legislative)</td></tr>
<tr><td>Geographical location (Coordinates):</td><td>The Country extends between 16.29° S, 63.59° W</td></tr>
<tr><td>Area:</td><td>1,098,581 sq. Km</td></tr>
<tr><td>Currency:</td><td>Boliviano (BOB)</td></tr>
<tr><td>System of Governance:</td><td>Plurinational Legislative Assembly</td></tr>
<tr><td>Independence</td><td>6 August 1825</td></tr>
</table>

Agriculture:

Agriculture sector plays an important role in Bolivian economy. Major agricultural products include quinoa, coffee, cocoa, corn,potato, sugarcane, rice, tropical and temperate climate fruits. Major export items also include sweaters and textiles of alpaca wool.

Art & Culture:

This South American country has a multitude of different cultures. Mestizo Baroque is the unique Bolivia style of art and architecture. High pitched singing like Huayno accompanied by instruments like harp, accordion, charango, guitar, saxophone, etc. is one typical musical form. Painting, sculpture and pottery are other famous art forms.

<table>
<tr><td colspan="2" align="center">BRAZIL</td></tr>
<tr><td>Capital:</td><td>Brasilia</td></tr>
<tr><td>Geographical location (Coordinates):</td><td>The Country extends between 14.23° S, 51.92°W</td></tr>
<tr><td>Area:</td><td>8,515,767 sq. Km</td></tr>
<tr><td>Currency:</td><td>Real (BRL)</td></tr>
<tr><td>System of Governance:</td><td>Federal Presidential Constitutional Republic</td></tr>
<tr><td>Independence:</td><td>7 September 1822</td></tr>
</table>

Agriculture:

The major agricultural products are coffee, sugarcane, soy, cotton, corn, rice, wheat, tobacco, beans. Other horticulture products also play an important role in economy. Main export items include sugar cane, ethanol, frozen chickens, beef products in addition to coffee and soybeans.

Art & Culture:

Brazilian culture is amalgamation of the cultures of indigenous Indians, Portuguese and Africans. Musical styles like Jazz, Pop, ballad, opera sertanejo, axé, Pagode and dance forms like samba, Bumba Meu Boi, Carioca Funk are most popular in Brazil.

<table>
<tr><td colspan="2" align="center">CHILE</td></tr>
<tr><td>Capital:</td><td>Santiago</td></tr>
<tr><td>Geographical location (Coordinates):</td><td>The Country extends between 35.67° S, 71.54° W</td></tr>
<tr><td>Area:</td><td>756,096 sq. Km</td></tr>
<tr><td>Currency:</td><td>Peso (CLP)</td></tr>
<tr><td>System of Governance:</td><td>Unitary Presidential Constitutional Republic</td></tr>
<tr><td>Independence</td><td>18 September 1810</td></tr>
</table>

Agriculture:

Agriculture accounts for about 10% of total GDP of the country and provides almost 1/5th of the total employment. Major products include grapes, apples, onions, wheat, corn, oats, peaches, garlic, asparagus, beans, beef, poultry, wool and fisheries. Timber is also an important component of Chile's export.

Art & Culture:

Unlike their neighbours the culture and ethnicities of Chile are relatively homogenous throughout. Catholic traditions have been thoroughly mixed with native religious traditions of the country. Chilean graphic arts have been dominated by paintings. Traditional folk music and other music genres like Nueva Canción Chilena represent the best of Chile's performance arts.

<table>
<tr><td colspan="2" align="center">COLOMBIA</td></tr>
<tr><td>Capital:</td><td>Bogota</td></tr>
<tr><td>Geographical location (Coordinates):</td><td>The Country extends between 4.57° N, 74.29° W</td></tr>
<tr><td>Area:</td><td>1,141,748 sq. Km</td></tr>
<tr><td>Currency:</td><td>Peso (COP)</td></tr>
<tr><td>System of Governance:</td><td>Unitary Presidential Constitutional Republic</td></tr>
<tr><td>Independence</td><td>20 July 1810</td></tr>
</table>

Agriculture:

Some of the major agricultural products of Colombia include coffee, banana, plantains, rice, tobacco, corn, sugarcane, cocoa beans, oilseed, and vegetables, flowers and fisheries product.

Art & Culture:

Colombian music has diverse musical environment which blends style of European and indigenous population. Some of the popular music styles include mapalé, vallenato, cumbia and porro. Traditional chants and dances of Colombia are among the UNESCO intangible cultural heritage lists.

<table>
<tr><td colspan="2" align="center">ECUADOR</td></tr>
<tr><td>Capital:</td><td>Quito</td></tr>
<tr><td>Geographical location (Coordinates):</td><td>The Country extends between 1.83° S, 78.18° W</td></tr>
<tr><td>Area:</td><td>283,561 sq. Km</td></tr>
<tr><td>Currency:</td><td>US Dollar (USD)</td></tr>
<tr><td>System ofGovernance:</td><td>Unitary Presidential Constitutional Republic</td></tr>
<tr><td>Independence:</td><td>10 August 1809</td></tr>
<tr><td colspan="2">Agriculture:
Bananas, coffee, tea, rice, corn, barley, sugar, beans, corn, potatoes and other tropical fruits and vegetables are main agricultural products. Horticulture products like roses and carnations are also thriving in the country.</td></tr>
<tr><td colspan="2">Art & Culture:
Various cultures including indigenous groups, Spanish have influenced Ecuadorian culture. These are reflected in music, literature, architecture, and various other art forms.</td></tr>
<tr><td colspan="2" align="center">GUYANA</td></tr>
<tr><td>Capital:</td><td>Georgetown</td></tr>
<tr><td>Geographical location (Coordinates):</td><td>The Country extends between
4.86° N, 58.93° W</td></tr>
<tr><td>Area:</td><td>214,970 sq. Km</td></tr>
<tr><td>Currency:</td><td>Guyanese Dollar (GYD)</td></tr>
<tr><td>System of Governance:</td><td>Unitary Presidential Constitutional</td></tr>
<tr><td>Independence:</td><td>26 May 1966</td></tr>
<tr><td colspan="2">Agriculture:
The major agriculture crops of Guyana include Rice, sugar, coffee, cocoa, coconuts, edible oils, copra, fruit, vegetables, and tobacco. Others allied sector are Fisheries and Livestock farming including cattle, sheep, pigs, goats, and poultry products.</td></tr>
<tr><td colspan="2">Art & Culture:
Rich heritage of folk music, dance, drama and other art forms of main ethnic (Indigenous Amerindian, African, Indian and other multi-racial) groups reflected in culture. Some of the prominent Guyanese Architecture contains wooden buildings with jalousies, high ceilings, large-wooden verandas while abstract expressionism is one of the most popular art styles in Guyana. Calypso music and Indian instrument based Chutney-Soca music genres are fairly popular.</td></tr>
<tr><td colspan="2" align="center">PARAGUAY</td></tr>
<tr><td>Capital:</td><td>Asunción</td></tr>
<tr><td>Geographical location (Coordinates):</td><td>The Country extends between 23.44° S, 58.44° W</td></tr>
</table>

Area:	406,752 sq. Km
Currency:	Guaraní (PYG)
System of Governance:	Unitary Dominant-Party Presidential Republic
Independence:	14 May 1811

Agriculture:
Cotton and Soybean are the major agriculture products used for export. Other crops include coffee, corn, rice, wheat, citrus fruits, sugarcane, and peanuts. Timber, meat, dairy products, and hides are used both for local consumption and for export. Timber is another important export.

Art & Culture:
The country's art and culture is influenced by African, Indian, European and Latin groups. Prominent musical genres are calypso, chutney, Soca, local Guyanese soca-chutney, Bachata, Salsa etc. Folklore is similar to the Caribbean folklores, mixed with African, Indian, Amerindian and others form the typical folklore of the country. Lively Polka and bottle dances are some distinct dance forms.

PERU

Capital:	Lima
Geographical location (Coordinates):	The Country extends between 9.19° S, 75.01° W
Area:	1,285,216 sq. Km
Currency:	Sol (PEN)
System of Governance:	Unitary Presidential Republic
Independence:	28 July 1821

Agriculture:
Quinoa, potatoes, sugarcane, cotton, maize, rice, coffee, asparagus are main agricultural products of Peru. Varieties of fine wool derived from the Andean animals including llamas, alpacas and guanacos are also an important part of agriculture and allied sector.

Art & Culture:
Peruvian art reflects the Cupisnique and Chavín cultures in the form of gold, silver and ceramic works. Decorative architecture elements in both design and building construction is characteristic of Peruvian architecture.

SURINAME

Capital:	Paramaribo
Geographical location (Coordinates):	The Country extends between 3.91° N, 56.02° W
Area:	163,821 sq. Km
Currency:	Surinamese Dollar (SRD)
System of Governance:	Unitary Republic

Independence:	25 November 1975

Agriculture:
Rice, sugar, plantains, bananas, citrus fruits, coffee, coconuts, and palm oil are main agricultural crops.

Art & Culture:
Asian, African and European influences are readily visible in culture of Suriname. Forms of music like kaseko and dances like awassa are important cultural elements.

URUGUAY

Capital:	Montevideo
Geographical location (Coordinates):	The Country extends between 32.52° S, 55.76° W
Area:	176,215 sq. Km
Currency:	Uruguayan peso (UYU)
System of Governance:	Unitary Presidential Constitutional Republic
Independence:	25 August 1825

Agriculture:
The major agricultural crops are rice, wheat, soybeans, sunflower seeds and grapes. Other main animal products are milk, meat, and poultry products.

Art & Culture:
Gaucho lifestyle depicts in various Uruguay's art like crafted leather goods and other art forms. Other important aspect of culture reflects in impressive architecture, other performance and visual arts. Tango, milonga and candombe are important traditional dances of the country.

VENEZUELA

Capital:	Caracas
Geographical location (Coordinates):	The Country extends between 6.42° N, 66.58° W
Area:	916,445 sq. Km
Currency:	Bolívar Soberano (VES)
System of Governance:	Federal Presidential Constitutional Republic
Independence:	13 January 1830

Agriculture:
Agriculture is very limited in this oil-rich country. Crops like coffee and cocoa are produced along with some food crops.

Art & Culture:
Mestizos, white, black and Amerindians are the major ethnic groups that add diversity to the culture of the country. The colonial Spanish influence is greatly depicted in various forms. Important traditional music styles include Gaita, while dances like Salsa, Joropo are quite popular in this country.

- ◁ It is the **second** smallest continent.
- ◁ Stretches from 35°N to 80°N latitude and from 10°W to 60°E longitude.
- ◁ Separated from Asia by Russia's **Ural** mountains and the Caspian and Black sea.
- ◁ **Highest point-** Mt. Elbrus.
- ◁ **Lowest point-** Caspian sea (28 m below sea level).

ALBANIA

Capital:	Tirana
Geographical location:	41°19′N 19°49′E
Area:	28,748 sq. Km
Currency:	Lek (ALL)
System of Governance:	Unitary parliamentary constitutional republic
Independence:	28 November 1912

Agriculture:

Agriculture in Albania is a significant sector of the economy of Albania, which contributes to 22.5% of the country's GDP. The main agricultural products in the country are tobacco, figs, olives, wheat, maize, potatoes, vegetables, fruits, sugar beets, grapes, meat, honey, dairy products, and traditional medicine and aromatic plants. Aquaculture and Viticulture are import agricultural activities of Albania.

Art & Culture:

Albanians are a native Balkan people who live in Southern Europe. They call themselves Shqiptarë. Albanians live in ethnically compact settlements in large areas, primarily in Albania, Kosovo and Macedonia, but also in Montenegro and Greece. There are two cultural groups in Albanian territories: the Ghegs and Tosks. Ghegs live in the northern part while Tosks live in the southern part.

ANDORRA

Capital:	Andorra la Vella
Geographical location:	42°30′N 1°31′E
Area:	467.63 sq. Km
Currency:	Euro (EUR)
System of Governance:	Unitary parliamentary semi-elective diarchy
Independence:	8 September 1278

Agriculture:

Only about 2% of the land is suitable for crops. Tobacco, the most distinctive Andorran crop. Other farm products include cereals, potatoes, and garden vegetables. Grapes are used mainly for raisins and for the making of anisette. Most food is imported.

Art & Culture:
Andorra's most valued cultural assets are 50 Romanesque churches and their interior murals and frescos. An essential part of Andorran culture is its folk dances, performed with pride and enthusiasm at festivals and other events. The varied and rich Catalan folklore is a part of everyday life. Dances such as the contrapas and marraxta are Catalan in character, and have been passed down through the ages with little change. Music is also a strong part of Andorran culture.

ARMENIA

Capital:	Yerevan
Geographical location:	40°11′N 44°31′E
Area:	29,743 sq. Km
Currency:	Dram (AMD)
System of Governance:	Unitary parliamentary republic
Independence:	21 September 1991

Agriculture:
Fertile volcanic soil of Armenia allows cultivation of wheat and barley as well as pasturage for sheep, goats and horses. Armenia also produces peaches, walnuts and quince, and it's brandy enjoys a worldwide reputation. The principal agricultural products are wheat, barley, potatoes, vegetables, grapes and fruits.

Art & Culture:
Bordering Europe, Asia and the Mediterranean, Armenia has adopted cultural traits from these regions. Classical music is very popular and Armenian musicians are highly accomplished. Jazz also plays a prominent role with many summer performances taking place in outdoor venues like parks. Examples of Armenian architecture can be seen all over the country in a myriad of religious buildings.

AUSTRIA

Capital:	Vienna
Geographical location:	48°12′N 16°21′E
Area:	83,879 sq. Km
Currency:	Euro (EUR)
System of Governance:	Federal parliamentary republic
Independence:	27 July 1955

Agriculture:
Although small, the agricultural sector is highly diversified and efficient. Most production is oriented toward local consumption. Chief crops are wheat, rye, oats, barley, potatoes, and sugar beets. Austria is near self-sufficiency in wheat, oats, rye, fruits, vegetables, sugar and a number of other items including wines.

Art & Culture:

Vienna has long been considered the music capital of Europe, and is home to world-class music schools. Vienna is also home to some of the best venues on the planet, such as the Golden Hall, the Vienna State Opera and the Musikverein, to name a few. Austrians are open to a diverse range of cultures, religions, and languages. Although German is the official language, most Austrians are multilingual.

AZERBAIJAN

Capital:	Baku
Geographical location:	40°25′N 49°50′E
Area:	86,600 sq. Km
Currency:	Manat (AZN)
System of Governance:	Unitary semi-presidential republic
Independence:	30 August 1991

Agriculture:

Agriculture is an important part of the economy of Azerbaijan. It contributes only 6% of the GDP. Majority of Azerbaijan's cultivated land is irrigated. The primary crops produced in Azerbaijan are agricultural cash crops, grapes, cotton, tobacco, citrus fruits, and vegetables. Livestock, dairy products, and wine and spirits are also important farm products.

Art & Culture:

The Culture of Azerbaijan developed under the influence of Iranian, Turkic and Caucasian heritage as well as Russian influences. Azerbaijan is home to many ethnicities, most of them belonging to the Azeris group. Every year a cultural festival is held in Goychay, Azerbaijan known as Pomegranate

Festival. Abayi is an example of numerous Azerbaijani folk dances. These dances are old and extremely melodious.

BELARUS

Capital:	Minsk
Geographical location:	53°55′N 27°33′E
Area:	207,595 sq. Km
Currency:	Belarusian ruble (BYN)
System of Governance:	Unitary presidential republic
Independence:	27 July 1990

Agriculture:

Agriculture is a shrinking sector of the Belarusian economy. Its main agricultural products are barley, rye, oats and wheat, as well as potatoes, flax, rapeseed and sugarbeets. Products of animal origin are mainly pork, beef and poultry. Much of its agricultural produce is exported to neighbouring states, with Russia a major market.

Art & Culture:

Modern-day Belarus began to form a unique cultural identity independent from neighboring Ukraine and Russia, around the turn of the 18th century, after separating from the Polish-Lithuanian Grand Duchy. The most celebrated Belarusian, Marc Chagall, is recognized as one of the most inspirational artists of the 20th century. Belarus has four World Heritage Sites, with two of them being shared between Belarus and its neighboring countries.

BELGIUM

Capital:	Brussels
Geographical location:	50°51′N 4°21′E
Area:	30,688 sq. Km
Currency:	Euro (EUR)
System of Governance:	Federal parliamentary constitutional monarchy
Independence:	4 October 1830

Agriculture:

Agriculture in Belgium is mainly divided between crop production and raising livestock. The nation's main crops include barley, corn, potatoes, sugar beets, wheat, and assorted fruits and vegetables. Sugar beets, potatoes, and barley are the main staples. Livestock production dominates Belgian agriculture. It accounts for 65 percent of the nation's farms.

Art & Culture:

About one third of the inhabitants speak the old tongue of Walloon and a variant of Dutch, Flemish is spoken by at least 60 percent. Belgium's incredibly rich artistic tradition extends from its artworks to architecture, music, literature, and traditionally authentic folkloric festivals. Museum and art gallery visits are very popular, and many medieval old towns are a great source of pride.

BOSNIA AND HERZEGOVINA

Capital:	Sarajevo
Geographical location:	43°52′N 18°25′E
Area:	51,129 sq. Km
Currency:	Convertible mark (BAM)
System of Governance:	Federal parliamentary constitutional republic
Independence:	1 March 1992

Agriculture:

The most productive natural resources sectors are fruits and vegetables, livestock and poultry. Principal crop is corn followed by wheat and barley. Agricultural products only represent approximately 9 percent of exports, but account for 17 percent of total imports. Primary imported food products include beverages (alcoholic and non-alcoholic), grains, tobacco products and meat and dairy products.

Art & Culture:

Majority of population comprises Bosnians, Serbs, and Croats, people of Jewish, Albanian, Romanian and Turkish descent. Their diversity is also evident in social norms, religious and cultural festivities, music, art, and cuisine. Regional dances and folk costumes are a treat to watch during festivals. There is strong religious influence in the art and architecture of the country. Among its many attractions are medieval tombstones that can be traced back to the Bosnian Kingdom.

BULGARIA

Capital:	Sofia
Geographical location:	42°41′N 23°19′E
Area:	110,993.6 sq. Km
Currency:	Lev (BGN)
System of Governance:	Unitary parliamentary republic
Independence:	5 October 1908

Agriculture:

Agriculture in Bulgaria accounts for about one-fifth of the total national income of Bulgaria. Cereal crops are grown on almost three-fifths of the sown land. Wheat is by far the most important, followed by corn (maize) and barley; rye, oats, soybeans and rice also are grown. Tobacco, which is of a good-quality oriental type and is grown mainly in the south, is an especially important industrial crop.

Art & Culture:

The culture of Bulgaria is based on an interesting blend of Thracian, Slavic and Bulgar traditions, along with the influence of the Eastern Orthodox Church. Many ancient customs remain, such as Thracian fire dancing, which is recognized by UNESCO as an Intangible Cultural Heritage. Bulgaria also has a strong folkloric tradition that pervades many aspects of art, literature, music, celebrations and daily life.

CROATIA

Capital:	Zagreb
Geographical location:	45°48′N 16°0′E
Area:	56,594 sq. Km
Currency:	Kuna (HRK)
System of Governance:	Unitary parliamentary constitutional republic
Independence:	25 June 1991

Agriculture:

Farming in croatia is characterized by capital-intensive, market-oriented production and larger landholdings. The major crops of the region are sugar beets, corn (maize), wheat, potatoes, barley, soybeans, sunflowers and tobacco. Oats, rye, millet, rice, beans, peas, and chicory are also grown. Pigs, cattle, and poultry are important to the economy of the region. Fruit growing, viticulture and cattle and pig breeding are typical agricultural occupations.

Art & Culture:

The rich culture of Croatia is a mix of past traditions seasoned with remnants of the earlier Greek, Roman civilizations. Expressed in early times in music, dance, art and Catholicism's magnificent architecture, its visual elements were also influenced by the Venetian Renaissance period. Village customs, national costume, folk dances, music and song have been powerful tools to help preserve the heritage of the land.

CYPRUS

Capital:	Nicosia
Geographical location:	35°10′N 33°22′E
Area:	9,251 sq. Km
Currency:	Euro (EUR)
System of Governance:	Unitary presidential constitutional republic
Independence:	1 October 1960

Agriculture:

Most farmers raise a variety of subsistence crops, ranging from grains and vegetables to fruits. Citrus fruits and potatoes along with grapes, kiwi and avocados are grown both for the domestic market and as exports to EU nations. Principal crops included barley, potatoes, grapes, grapefruit, oranges, lemons, and wheat. Tomatoes, carrots, olives and other fruits and vegetables are also grown.

Art & Culture:

The Greek Cypriots and Turkish Cypriots, the two main ethnic communities of Cyprus, share many cultural aspects together but also have several differences. The Greek Cypriots are mostly Orthodox Christians while the Turkish Cypriots are traditionally Sunni Muslims. Music, dancing, songs and poetry are integral to the culture of Cyprus. The folk music scene of the island is influenced by Greek, Turkish and Arabic Music.

CZECH REPUBLIC

Capital:	Prague
Geographical location:	50°05′N 14°28′E
Area:	78,866 sq. Km
Currency:	Czech koruna (CZK)
System of Governance:	Unitary parliamentary constitutional republic
Independence:	1 January 1993

Agriculture:

Agriculture is a small but important sector of the economy. The principal crops are grains (wheat, rye, barley, oats, and corn), which support the Czech Republic's dozens of small breweries. There is a long tradition of brewing in the Czech Republic; some of the world's oldest brands were invented there. Czech Republic is Europe's second largest producer of hops. Other important crops include oilseeds, sugar beets, potatoes, and apples.

Art & Culture:

The Czech nation possesses a distinctive culture. The culture of a nation encompasses the set of norms, behaviors, beliefs, and customs that exist within its population. National culture has specific characteristics such as language, religion, ethnic and racial identity, history, and traditions.

DENMARK	
Capital:	Copenhagen
Geographical location:	55°43′N 12°34′E
Area:	42,933 sq. Km
Currency:	Danish krone (DKK)
System of Governance:	Unitary parliamentary constitutional monarchy
Independence:	5 June 1849

Agriculture:

Denmark produces 3 times the amount of food it needs for itself. Arable land, moderate climate along with extremely advanced technology and infrastructure have made agriculture so productive in the country. Denmark is home to various types of agricultural production from animal products such as pork, beef, poultry and dairy to vegetable products including potato starch and grass seeds, as well as traditional grain and vegetable crops.

Art & Culture:

The culture of Denmark has a rich intellectual and artistic heritage. "Hygge" is a fundamental aspect of Danish culture. Hygge, meaning 'snug'; is a concept that evokes "coziness", particularly when relaxing with good friends or loved ones and while enjoying good food. Danish folklore is made up of folk tales, legends, songs, music, dancing, popular beliefs and traditions, mostly communicated by the inhabitants across the country.

ESTONIA	
Capital:	Tallinna
Geographical location:	59°25′N 24°45′E
Area:	45,227 sq. Km
Currency:	Euro (EUR)
System of Governance:	Unitary parliamentary republic
Independence:	24 February 1918

Agriculture:
Estonia's climate and natural environment are ideal for animal husbandry and grain-growing, and thus the country is most self-sufficient in dairy and grain farming. Its dairy sector is large, generating more than a quarter of Estonia's agricultural revenue. The foods produced include animal products, cereals, potatoes, fruits and vegetables, and fish.

Art & Culture:

Estonian culture is evident in various aspects of everyday life. Their festivities are artistic, as well as expressive of Christian and Protestant beliefs. Many visual artists have their place in the country, evident in the numerous collections of masterpieces in various museums. Theater and music are also important elements of Estonian culture, with numerous festivals dedicated to different theatrical genres.

FINLAND

Capital:	Helsinki
Geographical location:	60°10′N 24°56′E
Area:	338,424 sq. Km
Currency:	Euro (EUR)
System of Governance:	Unitary parliamentary republic
Independence:	6 December 1917

Agriculture:

Due to the severe climatic conditions and a relatively short growing season, Finland relies heavily on imported food and agricultural products. Forests play a key role in the country's economy, making it one of the world's leading wood producers and providing raw materials for the crucial wood-processing industries.

Art & Culture:

The Finnish culture is a mix of indigenous heritage, Nordic and European influences. This can be observed in festivals, literature, visual arts, music, cinema, and even cuisine. Finnish artists and architects have made major contributions to industrial design and sculpture. Finns are also very musical people, with rich folk traditions, such as Sami Music, often used to express beliefs and myths. Festivities and traditions in Finland are closely tied to the Christian Calendar.

FRANCE

Capital:	Paris
Geographical location:	48°51′N 2°21′E
Area:	640,679 sq. Km
Currency:	Euro (EUR); CFP franc (XPF)
System of Governance:	Unitary semi-presidential republic
Independence:	14 July 1789

Agriculture:

France has been one of the most dominant agricultural centers of Europe for centuries. The major agricultural products that place France among the top producers in the world market are sugar beets, wine, milk, beef and veal, cereals, and oilseeds. France leads the EU in sugar beet production. It takes second place in the world in the production of highly popular wine varieties.

Art & Culture:
The culture of France has been influenced over the centuries by the country's turbulent history and its long-standing contacts with neighboring countries, as well as its colonies. In the 19th century, Paris became the cultural hub of the world for its decorative Art Nouveau style. Cultural events such as opera, ballet, classical concerts, theater performances and other traditional events are valued highly, as is the French natural ability for art.

GEORGIA

Capital:	Tbilisi
Geographical location:	41°43′N 44°47′E
Area:	69,700 sq. Km
Currency:	Georgian lari (GEL)
System of Governance:	Unitary parliamentary constitutional republic
Independence:	26 May 1918

Agriculture:
Georgia's fertile soil and favorable climate support production of a wide variety of high-value agricultural products including grapes and wine, nuts (hazelnuts, almonds, walnuts, and chestnuts), citrus fruits, apples, peaches and apricots. It also grows an increasing quantity of crops, including vegetables and corn, for domestic consumption. Georgia relies on imported powdered milk, meat products, and wheat imports.

Art & Culture:
Georgia's monumental architecture, unique traditional music and colorful dances, world-renowned cinema, theater and art combine to give the country a unique position in europe. Georgians are separated into smaller regional provincial ethno-cultural entities, each with its own unique cultural flavor in terms of their peculiar traditions, customs, folklore, dress, cuisine and language.

GERMANY

Capital:	Berlin
Geographical location:	52°31′N 13°23′E
Area:	357,386 sq. Km
Currency:	Euro (EUR)
System of Governance:	Federal parliamentary republic
Independence:	3 October 1990

Agriculture:
Agricultural products of Germany vary from region to region. Chief agricultural products include milk, pork, beef, poultry, cereals, potatoes, wheat, barley, cabbages, and sugar beets. In some regions wine, fruits, and vegetables, and other horticultural products play an important role. In the flat terrain of northern Germany, cereals and sugar beets are grown.

Art & Culture:

Known as the "Land of Poets and Thinkers," German culture has been heavily influenced by religion, composers, writers, and philosophers. Architectural contributions from Germany include the Carolingian and Ottonian styles, important precursors of Romanesque. German art has a long and distinguished tradition in the visual arts. Important German Renaissance painters include Albrecht Altdorfer, Lucas Cranach the Elder etc.

GREECE

Capital:	Athens
Geographical location:	37°58′N 23°43′E
Area:	131,957 sq. Km
Currency:	Euro (EUR)
System of Governance:	Unitary parliamentary republic
Independence:	25 March 1821

Agriculture:

Agriculture is centered in the plains of Thessaly, Macedonia, and Thrace, where corn, wheat, barley, sugar beets, cotton, and tobacco are harvested. Greece is a major EU producer of cotton and tobacco. Greece's olive are the country's most renowned export crop. Grapes, melons, tomatoes, peaches and oranges are also popular exports.

Art & Culture:

Greece is considered to be the cradle of Western culture and democracy. The ancient Greeks pioneered in many fields

fields including biology, geometry, history, philosophy and physics. They introduced such important literary forms as epic and lyric poetry, history, tragedy and comedy. In their pursuit of order and proportion, the Greeks created an ideal of beauty that strongly influenced Western art.

HUNGARY

Capital:	Budapest
Geographical location:	47°26′N 19°15′E
Area:	93,030 sq. Km
Currency:	Forint (HUF)
System of Governance:	Unitary dominant-party parliamentary republic
Independence:	23 October 1989

Agriculture:

Hungary's most important crops include corn, wheat, sugar beets, barley, potatoes, and sunflower seeds. It also produces grapes and wine, including several famous wines. Livestock production is also important in Hungary, including cattle, pigs, sheep, horses, and poultry. Important livestock products include milk, meat, butter, eggs, and wool. Hungary has some important freshwater fisheries.

Art & Culture:

The rich culture of Hungary is strong in folk traditions and has its own distinctive style, influenced by the various ethnic groups including the Roma people. Music of all kinds, from classical to folk, is an important part of everyday life, as is the country's rich literary heritage. Crafts such as ceramics and embroidery, Hungary's distinct, traditional cuisine, strong fruit brandies, dance and the ever-popular spa treatments all reflect the heritage of this fascinating country.

ICELAND

Capital:	Reykjavík
Geographical location:	64°08′N 21°56′W
Area:	102,775 sq. Km
Currency:	Icelandic króna (ISK)
System of Governance:	Unitary parliamentary republic
Independence:	17 June 1944

Agriculture:

About 78% of Iceland is agriculturally unproductive, and only about 1% of the land area is actually used for cultivation. Of this amount, 99% is used to cultivate hay and other fodder crops, with the remaining 1% used for potato and fodder root production. Hay is the principal crop; other crops are potatoes, turnips, oats and garden vegetables. In hot-spring areas, vegetables, flowers and even tropical fruits are cultivated for domestic consumption in greenhouses heated with hot water from the springs.

Art & Culture:

The culture of Iceland is rich and varied as well as being known for its literary heritage which began in the 12th century. Other Icelandic traditional arts include weaving, silversmithing, and wood carving. The Reykjavík area has several professional theatres, a symphony orchestra, an opera and many art galleries, bookstores, cinemas and museums. There are also four active folk dance ensembles in Iceland.

IRELAND

Capital:	Dublin
Geographical location:	53.14°N, 7.69°W
Area:	84,421 sq. Km
Currency:	Euro (EUR)
System of Governance:	Parliamentary democratic republic
Independence:	21 January 1919

Agriculture:

A major livestock producer, Ireland has very limited horticultural and grain production on account of its topography and climate. Much of its beef and dairy products are exported. Ireland imports around 80 percent of its animal feed, food and beverage needs. Principal crops include barley, sugar beets, potatoes, wheat and oats.

Art & Culture:

Irish dance, gypsy music, great literature and links to tragic, romantic, Arthurian legends such as Tristan and Isolde are all part of Ireland's rich and colorful cultural heritage. Legends, folk tales and beliefs in supernatural beings such as Leprechauns are commonplace, and the lucky three-leaf shamrock is a much-loved symbol. The pot of gold at the end of the rainbow originated in Irish mythology and Halloween is a favorite holiday. 'Wearing of the green', the traditional costume, is done with pride.

ITALY

Capital:	Rome
Geographical location:	41°54′N 12°29′E
Area:	301,340 sq. Km
Currency:	Euro (EUR)
System of Governance:	Unitary parliamentary republic
Independence:	25 April 1946

Agriculture:

Agriculture is one of Italy's key economic sectors, accounting for around 2.1% of GDP. Italy's agriculture is typical of the northern and southern division found within the European Union (EU). The northern part of Italy produces primarily grains, soybeans, meat, and dairy products, while the south specializes in fruits, vegetables, olive oil, wine and durum wheat. Italy is one of the largest agricultural producers and food processors in the EU.

Art & Culture:

Italian culture is best represented in art, music, fashion and cuisine, many of which are now a UNESCO World Heritage. Music, whether classical or modern, is an integral part of life. Country has invented the musical stave, and the piano and opera have given birth to many of the world's greatest composers, conductors and singers. Theater performances have a long heritage here, based on the tradition of traveling players and their Canovaccio comedies.

KOSOVO

Capital:	Pristina
Geographical location:	42°40′N 21°10′E
Area:	10,887 sq. Km
Currency:	Euro (EUR)
System of Governance:	Unitary parliamentary constitutional republic
Independence:	17 February 2008

Agriculture:

About half of the nation's area is agricultural land. The arable land is mostly used for corn, wheat, pastures, meadows and vineyards. It contributes almost to 35% of GDP including the forestry sector. Wine has historically been produced in Kosovo. The main heartland of Kosovo's wine industry is in Orahovac, where millions of litres of wine are produced.

Art & Culture:

Ethnic Albanians form the majority of Kosovo's population, with Albanian the country's official language and Islam the major religion. Village life, with its extensive family networks ruled by a patriarch, still exist in the rural areas. Music, dance and art are highly valued, forming a major part of the cultural events and celebrations in the country, especially the elaborate wedding ceremonies with their elaborate costumes and make-up.

LATVIA

Capital:	Riga
Geographical location:	56°57′N 24°6′E
Area:	64,589 sq. Km
Currency:	Euro (EUR)
System of Governance:	Unitary parliamentary constitutional republic
Independence:	18 November 1918

Agriculture:

Agriculture is focused on cereals, potatoes, forage crops, and dairy production. Cereal production takes up the highest share in agricultural output, followed by milk, fodder crops, oilseeds, pigs, potatoes, cattle, and eggs. Organic farming plays an important role in the agricultural production of the country. Latvia ranks among five EU member states with the highest ratio of organic agriculture against the total area of agricultural land in the country.

Art & Culture:

Majority of Latvians are part of the Lutheran Church with large Catholic and Orthodox Christian minorities. Traditional Latvian folklore, especially the dance of the folk songs, dates back well over a thousand years. Many folk songs, dances and music that was influenced by Baltic Germans between the 13th and 19th centuries were reborn. Choir traditions are very strong in Latvia.

LIECHTENSTEIN

Capital:	Vaduz
Geographical location:	47°10′N 9°30′E
Area:	160 sq. Km
Currency:	Swiss franc (CHF)
System of Governance:	Unitary parliamentary semi-constitutional monarchy
Independence:	23 January 1719

Agriculture:

About one fourth of Liechtenstein's territory consists of arable land. Animal husbandry and dairy farming are among the principal agricultural activities. Livestock graze in the alpine meadows during the summer. The fertile soil of the Rhine valley is used mostly for market vegetable gardening. Local agriculture products include wheat, barley, corn, potatoes, and grapes.

Art & Culture:
Much of Liechtenstein's culture is directly derived from surrounding European influences. This includes the language, spirituality and art. The country is a tremendously religious state. Catholicism is the main practice.

LITHUANIA

Capital:	Vilnius
Geographical location:	54°41′N 25°19′E
Area:	65,300 sq. Km
Currency:	Euro (EUR)
System of Governance:	Unitary semi-presidential republic
Independence:	16 February 1918

Agriculture:
Lithuania is historically an agricultural country. About half of its land area is devoted to crops and pastures. The favourable climatic conditions make it possible to cultivate potatoes, barley, wheat, rye, legumes, and rapeseed. Grain form a significant part of the crop structure.

Art & Culture:
The culture of Lithuania combines an indigenous heritage, represented by the unique Lithuanian language, with Nordic cultural aspects and Christian traditions resulting from historical ties with Poland. Lithuania has a long history of folk, popular and classical musical development. Its folk music is based primarily around polyphonic music played on flutes, zithers (kanklės) and other instruments.

LUXEMBOURG

Capital:	Luxembourg City
Geographical location:	49°48′N 06°07′E
Area:	2,586 sq. Km
Currency:	Euro (EUR)
System of Governance:	Unitary parliamentary constitutional monarchy
Independence:	15 March 1815

Agriculture:
The main agricultural areas are situated around the floodplain of the Moselle River. While the climate is conducive to several crops, poor or marginal soil limits production in many areas. Extensive livestock production accounts for 80 percent of agricultural profits, resulting in many farmers raising crops and livestock.

Art & Culture:
Although the small country's culture has naturally been heavily influenced by its large neighboring countries and previous rulers, Luxembourg maintains many of its rural folk traditions, while producing some of the region's finest artists. The capital, Luxembourg City, has twice been named European Capital of Culture and is a UNESCO World Heritage site due to its historical significance.

MALTA

Capital:	Valletta
Geographical location:	35°54′N 14°31′E
Area:	316 sq. Km
Currency:	Euro (EUR)
System of Governance:	Unitary parliamentary constitutional republic
Independence:	21 September 1964

Agriculture:

Most of the crops and foodstuffs produced are consumed domestically. The main crops are potatoes, cauliflower, grapes, wheat, barley, tomatoes, citrus, and green peppers. Potatoes are by far the main crop. Livestock production includes beef, chicken, lamb, pork, rabbit, and turkey.

Art & Culture:

The Maltese are a Mediterranean people whose nation has variously been ruled by the Romans, Moors, Germans, Sicilians, French, and British. Each invading faction brought new ideas, words, foods, art and architecture to enrich the island culture. Most of the people speak both English and Maltese. One of Malta's more unique elements is the folk music known as għana, which is a form of spirited debate improvised to a background of guitar.

MOLDOVA

Capital:	Chişinău
Geographical location:	47°0′N 28°55′E
Area:	33,846 sq. Km
Currency:	Leu (MDL)
System of Governance:	Unitary parliamentary constitutional republic
Independence:	27 August 1991

Agriculture:

Moldova's proximity to the Black Sea gives it a mild and sunny climate. The fertile soil supports wheat, corn, barley, tobacco, sugar beet, and soybeans. Beef and dairy cattle are raised, and beekeeping is widespread. Moldova's best-known product comes from its extensive and well-developed vineyards concentrated in the central and southern regions.

Art & Culture:

Moldova's elements of folk culture, such as wood carving and embroidery, are shared with other Balkan countries, but many aspects, such as pottery decoration and the 2,000-year old Doina lyrical songs, are unique to Moldova. The country's folk traditions and costumes are highly valued. The Colinda Christmas tradition of masked and costumed singers, musicians and dancers going from door to door to give performances and receive gifts bears a resemblance to the Christian tradition of carolling.

MONACO

Capital:	Monaco city
Geographical location:	43°44′N 7°25′E`

Area:	2.2 sq. Km
Currency:	Euro (EUR)
System of Governance:	Unitary parliamentary constitutional monarchy
Independence:	17 May 1814

Agriculture:

There are no arable lands or other agriculturally suited areas in the principality; virtually 100 percent of the Monaco territory is heavily urbanized. Accordingly, there is no commercial agriculture in the country. All foods are imported and some of them are further processed and exported.

Art & Culture:

Monaco's culture has strong influences from its neighbors, France, Italy and Spain. French make up the largest group at 28 percent. The Roman Catholic Church makes up the largest proportion. An amazing array of world-class galleries and music performances throughout the year are distinct feature of its culture.

MONTENEGRO

Capital:	Podgorica
Geographical location:	42°47′N 19°28′E
Area:	13,812 sq. Km
Currency:	Euro (EUR)
System of Governance:	Unitary dominant-party parliamentary constitutional republic
Independence:	3 June 2006

Agriculture:

Agricultural land covers about one third of the country's territory. Agriculture in Montenegro is very diverse, from the cultivation of olives and citruses, vegetables, and viticulture, to extensive livestock breeding. Agricultural land is dominated by pastures and meadows. Major crops include corn, wheat, sugar beets, potatoes, and grapes.

Art & Culture:

The Montenegrin love of traditional dance, music, epic songs, and poems and its social culture revolves around clans. Its historic cities and famous medieval murals reflect the development of architecture and art in the country. Religion is an important aspect, with the majority of Orthodox Christian. Traditional festivals are highly regarded, as most take place to preserve and protect the ancient customs, legends, music and dance forms of the land.

NETHERLANDS

Capital:	Amsterdam
Geographical location:	52°22′N 4°53′E

Area:	41,543 sq. Km
Currency:	Euro; US dollar
System of Governance:	Unitary parliamentary constitutional monarchy
Independence:	26 July 1581

Agriculture:
More than one fourth of the total land area of the Netherlands is under seasonal or permanent crop production. Most farms are effectively managed and worked intensively with mechanical equipment. Principal crops are sugar beets, potatoes, wheat, barley, rye and triticale. The Netherlands is famous for its bulbs grown for export, principally tulip, hyacinth, daffodils, narcissus and crocus.

Art & Culture:
The culture of the Netherlands is diverse, reflecting regional differences as well as the foreign influences. The Netherlands and its people have long played an important role as a centre of cultural liberalism and tolerance. The official language of the Netherlands is Dutch, spoken by almost all people in the Netherlands. The Dutch Golden Age is popularly regarded as its zenith. Dutch Golden Age painting was among the most acclaimed in the world.

NORTH MACEDONIA (FORMERLY MACEDONIA)

Capital:	Skopje
Geographical location:	42°0′N 21°26′E
Area:	25,713 sq. Km
Currency:	Macedonian denar (MKD)
System of Governance:	Unitary parliamentary republic
Independence:	8 September 1991

Agriculture:
Land use for agriculture in the form of cropland and pastures is substantial in Macedonia and occupies approximately half of the surface area of the country. The main crops are tobacco, fruits (including apples and grapes), vegetables, wheat, rice, and corn (maize). Viticulture and dairy farming are also important.

Art & Culture:
Roman, Byzantine, Bulgarian, Greek, Ottoman and Serbian cultures all play a part in the rich heritage of literature, arts, music, cuisine, and architecture of the country. Architecture plays a strong part, with urban single-story houses built around a central courtyard. Folk music and folk dancing are popular, and rock and pop music are ubiquitous. Icon painting and wood carving both have long histories in North Macedonia.

NORWAY

Capital:	Oslo
Geographical location:	59°56′N 10°41′E

Area:	385,207 sq. Km
Currency:	Norwegian krone (NOK)
System of Governance:	Unitary parliamentary constitutional monarchy
Independence:	17 May 1814

Agriculture:
Given the adverse climate and soil condition, only 3 percent of the land is cultivated. Grains are grown only in the south while western Norway has some livestock raising and dairy farming. The leading crops are cereals—particularly barley, wheat, and oats and potatoes. Norway is a major fishing nation and is self-sufficient in many agricultural products, but fruits, vegetables, and most grains are all imported.

Art & Culture:
Much of the culture of Norway can be traced back to the Vikings, a group of Scandinavian seafaring pirates, traders, and pioneers that settled in Northern Europe in the eighth century. People of this country have always identified with rural culture, which can be seen in its traditional costumes and folk music. Jante Law is an essential part of modern Norwegian culture and emphasizes humility, equality, respect, and simplicity.

POLAND

Capital:	Warsaw
Geographical location:	52°13′N 21°02′E
Area:	312,696 sq. Km
Currency:	Polish złoty (PLN)
System of Governance:	Unitary semi-presidential constitutional republic
Independence:	11 November 1918

Agriculture:
Poland's agricultural sector is vital for European and Global market. The most important crops are grains, of which the highest yields came from rye, wheat, barley and oats. Other major crops are potatoes, sugar beets, fodder crops, flax, hops, tobacco, and fruits.

Farms all over Poland raise dairy cows, beef cattle, pigs, poultry, and cultivate fruit.

Art & Culture:
Polish culture has a historical context, but it continues to evolve, incorporating old traditions with modern life. Poland has a lively music scene with the roots of the country's music being traced as far back as the 13th century. Polish folk dance has a long and rich tradition and is associated with several historical or religious events of the country. Christianity is the dominant religion in Poland with about 92.2% of Poles being Roman Catholics.

PORTUGAL

Capital:	Lisbon
Geographical location:	38°46′N 9°9′W

Area:	92,212 sq. Km
Currency:	Euro (EUR)
System of Governance:	Unitary semi-presidential constitutional republic
Independence:	1 December 1640

Agriculture:
Portugal's climatic and topographic conditions allow for a large number of crops, including olives, figs, citrus, mushrooms, sunflower, tomatoes, cereals, bananas and pineapples. Here, wine, table grapes, leaf vegetables, dairy, tomatoes for processing, rice, sugar beets, mushrooms, cork and olives are competitive. Portugal is one of the world's largest exporters of tomato paste and a leading exporter of wines.

Art & Culture:
Portugal is home to several ancient architectural structures, as well as typical art, furniture and literary collections. It has a large number of cultural landmarks ranging from

museums to ancient church buildings to medieval castles. Fado is the best known musical genre, which is melancholy guitar. Centuries of talented Portuguese artists are displayed not only in the galleries, but also in walls, buildings and streets. There is even a National Tile Museum in Lisbon to see this unique art form.

ROMANIA

Capital:	Bucharest
Geographical location:	44°25′N 26°06′E
Area:	238,397 sq. Km
Currency:	Romanian Leu (RON)
System of Governance:	Unitary semi-presidential republic
Independence:	9 May 1877

Agriculture:
The climate and relief are most favourable to the development of cereal crops. Wheat and corn (maize) are most important, followed by barley, rye, and oats. Vegetables and legumes–peas, beans, and lentils—are planted on relatively small plots. Peas are the predominant crop. Dairy products are also an important component of Romanian agriculture, as are wool, eggs and honey.

Art & Culture:
The unique culture of Romania is the result of its position at the heart of Europe which historically enjoyed distinct cultures and histories. Traditional arts include weaving, embroidery, ceramics and wood carvings, and dance styles and folk music are treasured. The small, formerly nomadic, Roma population has its own strong cultural identity, language and rituals.

<table>
<tr><td colspan="2" align="center">SAN MARINO</td></tr>
<tr><td>Capital:</td><td>San Marino</td></tr>
<tr><td>Geographical location:</td><td>43°56′N 12°26′E</td></tr>
<tr><td>Area:</td><td>61.2 sq. Km</td></tr>
<tr><td>Currency:</td><td>Euro (EUR)</td></tr>
<tr><td>System of Governance:</td><td>Unitary parliamentary diarchic directorial epublic</td></tr>
<tr><td>Independence:</td><td>3 September 301</td></tr>
</table>

Agriculture:
Arable land comprises some 17 percent of San Marino's rugged territory, and agricultural products include wheat, grapes, corn, olives, cattle, pigs, horses, beef, cheese and hides. Italy supplies much of the republic's food, while the main export products are wine and cheeses

Art & Culture:
San Marino is comprised of native Sammarinese and Italian citizens. Although Italian-speaking and heavily influenced by the surrounding Italian culture, the Sammarinese have maintained their individuality through the centuries. Traditional cuisine is famous especially local wines and cheeses are renowned in Italy and abroad.

<table>
<tr><td colspan="2" align="center">SERBIA</td></tr>
<tr><td>Capital:</td><td>Belgrade</td></tr>
<tr><td>Geographical location:</td><td>44°48′N 20°28′E</td></tr>
<tr><td>Area:</td><td>88,361 sq. Km</td></tr>
<tr><td>Currency:</td><td>Serbian dinar (RSD)</td></tr>
<tr><td>System of Governance:</td><td>Unitary parliamentary constitutional republic</td></tr>
<tr><td>Independence:</td><td>5 June 2006</td></tr>
</table>

Agriculture:
Serbia produces various agricultural products, mostly grains, fruits and vegetables. Approximately 60 percent of agricultural land is used for cereal crop production including corn, wheat, barley, sunflowers, soya, and sugar beets. Serbia is among the top five producers in the world of raspberries and plums. It is also a significant producer of maize and wheat.

Art & Culture:
The Byzantine Empire had a great influence on the culture. Orthodox Christianity is Serbia's most dominant religion. Serbs have many traditions. The Slava is exclusive custom of the Serbs, each family has one patron saint that they venerate on their feast day. The most distinct Serbian musical instrument, the one-stringed gusle. Today, many of Serbia's best-known pop acts incorporate traditional Serbian sounds into their music.

<table>
<tr><td colspan="2" align="center">SLOVAKIA</td></tr>
<tr><td>Capital:</td><td>Bratislava</td></tr>
<tr><td>Geographical location:</td><td>48°09′N 17°07′E</td></tr>
<tr><td>Area:</td><td>49,035 sq. Km</td></tr>
<tr><td>Currency:</td><td>Euro (EUR)</td></tr>
<tr><td>System of Governance:</td><td>Unitary parliamentary republic</td></tr>
<tr><td>Independence:</td><td>1 January 1993</td></tr>
</table>

Agriculture:
More than one-third of Slovakia's territory is cultivated, and the primary agricultural products are sugar beets, potatoes, wheat, barley, fruit, forest products, corn, pigs, cattle, poultry, and sheep. Grapes (for wine production) and tobacco are also cultivated here. Animal products, including oils, represent over 80 percent of all agricultural receipts.

Art & Culture:
Slavic, Austrian, Hungarian, and German influences all figure heavily into the Slovak Republic's culture. Many ancient Slovak folk traditions remain intact to this day. Fabric weaving, woodcarving and the glass
windows found in the Slovak Republic's many wooden houses and churches are the country's best known folk arts. Bratislava contains philharmonic, symphonic and chamber orchestras.

<table>
<tr><td colspan="2" align="center">SLOVENIA</td></tr>
<tr><td>Capital:</td><td>Ljubljana</td></tr>
<tr><td>Geographical location:</td><td>46°03′N 14°30′E</td></tr>
<tr><td>Area:</td><td>20,273 sq. Km</td></tr>
<tr><td>Currency:</td><td>Euro (EUR)</td></tr>
<tr><td>System of Governance:</td><td>Unitary parliamentary constitutional republic</td></tr>
<tr><td>Independence:</td><td>25 June 1991</td></tr>
</table>

Agriculture:
Slovenia's mountainous terrain, with forests account for more than 50 percent of the territory. Agriculture contributes just about 4 percent of GDP, with dairy farming and livestock (cattle, sheep and poultry) dominating this sector. Major crops include cereals such as corn and wheat, potatoes, sugar beets, and fruits (particularly grapes). The country exports some beverages, particularly wine, and food, mainly to EU markets.

Art & Culture:

Slovenia has produced a significant number of poets, writers, artists, and musicians, many of whom created work which has strongly influenced the cultural landscape. Occupation by Roman, Germanic, and Eastern bloc forces has helped shape everything from architecture to cuisine. Age-old handicrafts such as glassware and lace are still admired, and many traditional buildings have been lovingly preserved and are still in use.

TURKEY	
Capital:	Madrid
Geographical location:	40°26′N 3°42′W
Area:	505,990 sq. Km
Currency:	Euro (EUR)
System of Governance:	Unitary parliamentary constitutional monarchy
Independence:	20 January 1479

Agriculture:

Barley, wheat, rice, Corn (maize) are major cereals grown in Spain. Other crops include cotton; tobacco; sugar beets; olives, and legumes (beans, lentils, and chickpeas). Fruit growing is also significant, with citrus fruits, especially oranges. Other fruit crops include apples, apricots, bananas, pears, peaches and plums. Spain also produces vegetables (especially tomatoes, onions, and potatoes) and nuts (almonds).

Art & Culture:

The rich culture of Spain can be seen in every aspect of its culture from language, cuisine, music, art, literature, folk traditions to Catholicism and in the diverse ethnic communities. Spain's Christian and Moorish architectural contributions are monumental and its distinct regional cultures are strong. Flamenco music, dance and the controversial bullfights are easily recognizable elements of Spanish heritage.

SWEDEN	
Capital:	Stockholm
Geographical location:	59°21′N 18°4′E
Area:	450,295 sq. Km
Currency:	Swedish krona (SEK)
System of Governance:	Unitary parliamentary constitutional monarchy
Independence:	6 June 1916

Agriculture:

Grains (particularly oats, wheat, barley, and rye), potatoes and other root crops, vegetables, and fruits are the chief agricultural products. Sugar beet cultivation in Skåne is important and produces almost enough sugar to make Sweden self-sufficient. Dairy farming is the largest sector. Pork and poultry production is also relatively large, while sheep and lamb production is quite small.

Art & Culture:

Sweden is known for Nordic culture, one that was once dominated by Viking traders. Even though modern Sweden is a very industrialized country, there are still pockets of vintage Scandinavia found throughout the country. Plenty of museums are located throughout the capital, and major conurbations like Malmo and Gothenburg boast a range of cultural sites that depict their reliance on the sea and trade.

SWITZERLAND	
Capital:	Bern
Geographical location:	46°57′N 7°27′E
Area:	41,285 sq. Km
Currency:	Swiss franc (CHF)
System of Governance:	Federal semi-direct democracy under a multi-party parliamentary directorial republic
Independence:	1 August 1291

Agriculture:

The Swiss soils, terrain, and climate do not favor agriculture particularly and farms are usually family enterprises, mostly small in size. They produce cereals such as wheat and barley, root crops such as sugar beets and potatoes, and fruits such as apples and grapes. Dairy products, such as cow's milk and world-renowned Swiss cheeses, make up a significant portion of the agricultural revenue.

Art & Culture:

Switzerland's culture has been strongly influenced by its neighbors, Germany, Italy, France, Liechtenstein, and Austria. There are many different festivals in Switzerland, one of these is the Fastnacht or carnival. An unusual custom is the mask festival. In February, men and boys roam the streets wearing hand carved masks and goat skin tunics. Many customs also revolve around agriculture. One of these is the "burning of the Boeoegg" that marks the start of spring.

TURKEY	
Capital:	Ankara
Geographical location:	40°N 33°E
Area:	783,356 sq. Km
Currency:	Turkish lira (TRY)

System of Governance:	Unitary presidential constitutional republic
Independence:	29 October 1923

Agriculture:

Turkey's agricultural economy is among the top ten in the world. Turkey is a major producer of wheat, sugar beets, milk, poultry, cotton, tomatoes and other fruits and vegetables, and is a top producer in the world for apricots and hazelnuts. Turkey import oilseeds, including soybeans and meals, as well as grain products and cotton.

Art & Culture:

The early Roman times, Ottoman Empirical control and immigration from the Balkans, Greece and other European destinations have all helped shape the culture of Turkey. Several locations of cultural significance have been designated a UNESCO World Heritage sites, including historic areas around Istanbul. A majority of locals are Muslims, but variations and levels of Islam are found across the region. Football is almost as important when it comes to local culture.

UKRAINE	
Capital:	Kiev
Geographical location:	50°27′N 30°30′E
Area:	603,628 sq. Km
Currency:	Ukrainian hryvnia (UAH)
System of Governance:	Unitary semi-presidential constitutional republic
Independence:	24 August 1991

Agriculture:

The climate of Ukraine suits for both spring and winter crops. The leading role in the agriculture belongs to the grain production. The main crops are spring barley, winter wheat and corn. Ukraine occupies the third place in the world in the corn export, fifth place in the wheat export. The main industrial or technical crops are sugar beets and sunflowers. Most of grain crops are exported to North Africa and the Middle East.

Art & Culture:

Ukrainian customs are heavily influenced by Orthodox Christianity, the dominant religion in the country.

The tradition of the Easter egg, known as pysanky, has long roots in Ukraine. Artisan textile arts play an important role in Ukrainian culture especially in wedding traditions. Embroidery, weaving and lace-making are used in traditional folk dress and in traditional celebrations.

<table>
<tr><td colspan="2" align="center">UNITED KINGDOM (UK)</td></tr>
<tr><td>Capital:</td><td>London</td></tr>
<tr><td>Geographical location:</td><td>51°30′N 0°7′W</td></tr>
<tr><td>Area:</td><td>242,495 sq. Km</td></tr>
<tr><td>Currency:</td><td>Pound sterling (GBP)</td></tr>
<tr><td>System of Governance:</td><td>Unitary parliamentary constitutional monarchy</td></tr>
<tr><td>Independence:</td><td>NA</td></tr>
</table>

Agriculture:

Agriculture in the United Kingdom uses 69% of the country's land area. The UK produces less than 60% of the food it eats. Crops commonly grown in the United Kingdom include cereals, chiefly wheat, oats and barley; root vegetables, chiefly potatoes and sugar beet; pulse crops such as beans or peas; forage crops such as cabbages, vetches, rape and kale; fruit, particularly apples and pears; and hay for animal feed.

Art & Culture:

The four nations which make up the UK each have their own distinctive cultures, folk tales, legends and a strong sense of nationalism and identity towards their own definitive heritage. The present-day culture in the UK rests mainly on its artistic achievements in the fields of dance, the visual arts, and music. London's theater district is second only to Broadway, and its orchestras, opera and dance companies are among the best in the world.

<table>
<tr><td colspan="2" align="center">VATICAN CITY (HOLY SEE)</td></tr>
<tr><td>Capital:</td><td>Vatican City</td></tr>
<tr><td>Geographical location:</td><td>41°54′N 12°27′E</td></tr>
<tr><td>Area:</td><td>0.44 sq. Km</td></tr>
<tr><td>Currency:</td><td>Euro (EUR)</td></tr>
<tr><td>System of Governance:</td><td>Unitary absolute monarchy</td></tr>
<tr><td>Independence:</td><td>11 February 1929</td></tr>
</table>

Agriculture:

Being the smallest country in the world in terms of land area, the whole county is an urban centre with no agricultural activities.

Art & Culture:

Vatican City is itself of great cultural significance. With its museums and basilica housing items of immense cultural importance, it is no wonder the Vatican City has been declared a UNESCO World Heritage site. Indeed, it contains some of the globe's most prized artworks. Additionally, the Vatican Library protects hundreds of works of historical, cultural, and scientific importance.

- Second largest continent.
- Stretches from 37°N to 35°S latitude.
- The Equator passes through almost the middle of the continent.
- Special feature is its **Great Rift Valley**.

Climate

As a large continent, Africa experiences a variety of climate. They are tropical monsoon, humid and sub humid tropical climate, mediterranean hot summer, hot desert climate, tropical wet/dry climate.

ALGERIA	
Capital:	Algiers
Geographical location:	36°42′N 3°13′E
Area:	2,381,741 sq. Km
Currency:	Dinar (DZD)
System of Governance:	Unitary Semi-presidential republic
Independence:	3 July 1962

Agriculture:

Agricultural production is a moderate contributor to the Algerian economy, accounting for 11-12 percent of GDP and 22 percent of total employment in 1997. Algeria's main crops are cereals (mainly wheat and barley), citrus fruit, vegetables, and grapes. Fresh dates exports is the second-largest export after hydrocarbons. Algerian dates are mainly exported to France, Russia, Senegal, and Belgium.

Art & Culture:

The culture, traditions, and customs of the country are influenced by the communities that have contributed to the history of Algeria such as Berbers, Byzantines, French etc. It's tradition and culture is influenced by early sea voyagers such as Spain, Turks, Italian, and Arabs. However, most Algerians identify with Arabian culture. The most common genres of music are Rai and Shaabi.

ANGOLA	
Capital:	Luanda
Geographical location:	8°50′S 13°20′E
Area:	1,246,700 sq. Km
Currency:	Kwanza (AOA)
System of Governance:	Unitary dominant-party presidential constitutional republic
Independence:	11 November 1975

Agriculture:
Subsistence agriculture provides the main livelihood for most of Angola's population, but more than half of the country's food is still imported. Angola's main agricultural crops include cassava, corn, beans, potatoes, sweet potatoes, soy, bananas, coffee, rice, vegetables and fruits.
Art & Culture:
Portuguese, African and ethnic influences are evident in many aspects of Angolan culture such as language, music, food, and art. Despite their history of civil unrest, Angolans are very spirited people with an obvious love for festivals and merriment. Folk music is important and well preserved, particularly the semba genre, which is a fusion of African styles. Other dominant musical styles are rebita, kabetulam, kazukuta and kizomba. Angolan artisans are very skilled in sculpture and craft-making. Each ethnic group has its own distinctive style.

BENIN

Capital:	Porto-Novo
Geographical location:	9°18'N 2°19'E
Area:	1,14,763 sq. Km
Currency:	West African CFA franc (XOF)
System of Governance:	Unitary presidential republic
Independence:	1 August 1960

Agriculture:
The economy of Benin is dependent on subsistence agriculture, cotton production, and regional trade. Cotton accounts for 40% of the GDP and roughly 80% of official export. Maize (corn), beans, rice, peanuts, cashews, pineapples, cassava, yams and other various tubers are grown for local consumption.
Art & Culture:
French colonial rule and subsequent close ties with France have left a deep impact on all aspects of cultural life of Benin. Each ethnic group also has its own centuries-old tradition, which itself often mixes with the French influence. These cultural traditions are clustered in two distinct regions, the Muslim north and Christian south. Plastic art is the most prominent, as carved wooden masks representing images and spirits of the departed are made and used in traditional ceremonies.

BOTSWANA

Capital:	Gaborone
Geographical location:	24°40'S 25°55'E
Area:	5,81,730 sq. Km
Currency:	Botswana pula (BWP)
System of Governance:	Unitary parliamentary constitutional republic
Independence:	30 September 1966

Agriculture:

Agriculture only comprises approximately 2% of GDP, but it is vital to livelihood for many citizens of Botswana who operate farms for subsistence. The principal crops for domestic use are sorghum, corn, and millet. Livestock production, especially cattle, contributes an estimated 80% to the agricultural GDP.

Art & Culture:

Every ethnic culture in Botswana has its own heritage of myths, legends, rituals, values and traditional artistic norms. However, the overlapping similarities between the different components create a homogenous culture, giving a rich and colorful diverse whole. Setswana, originally the tongue of the Tswana group, is the official language of Botswana, with English the main business language. A large number of people belong to a religion called Zionism, which is based on a fusion of African traditions and the Christian faith.

BURKINA FASO

Capital:	Ouagadougou
Geographical location:	12°20′N 1°40′W
Area:	2,74,200 sq. Km
Currency:	West African CFA franc (XOF)
System of Governance:	Unitary Semi-presidential republic
Independence:	5 August 1960

Agriculture:

Agriculture represents 32% of its GDP and occupies 80% of the working population. It consists mostly of rearing livestock. The people grow crops of sorghum, pearl millet, maize (corn), peanuts, rice and cotton, with surpluses to be sold.

Art & Culture:

Culture is quite visible in all facets of life in the country. Art is also very close to the hearts of the locals. Mossi people are prominent ethnic group. Other groups include Bobo, Senufo, Mande, Lobi, Gurunsi, and the Fulani people. Most of the people work as farmers. Approximately 45% of the country's population adheres to traditional beliefs. Another 43% practices Islam. A small population practices Christianity.

BURUNDI

Capital:	Gitega
Geographical location:	3°30′S 30°00′E
Area:	27,834 sq. Km
Currency:	Burundian franc (BIF)
System of Governance:	Unitary presidential republic
Independence:	1 July 1962

Agriculture:

Burundi's agricultural sector benefits from a mild climate due to high elevation of the land and regular rainfall. The economy is predominantly agricultural, accounting for about 50% of GDP. Primary exports are coffee and tea. Other agricultural products include cotton, tea, maize, sorghum, sweet potatoes, bananas, manioc (tapioca); beef, milk and hides.

Art & Culture:

Burundi has linguistic homogeneous people. all speak the same national language: Kirundi. French is the first foreign language and English is progressively becoming more important. Swahili is also spoken in urban areas. The vast majority of Burundi citizens are Christian. Others follow African religions and Islam. The major ethnic groups are Hutu and Tutsi. The culture of Burundi includes mainly songs, dances, stories and legends. Poetry is sometimes recited during social gatherings.

CAPE VERDE

Capital:	Praia
Geographical location:	14°55′N 23°31′W
Area:	4,033 sq. Km
Currency:	Cape Verdean escudo (CVE)
System of Governance:	Unitary Semi-presidential republic
Independence:	5 July 1975

Agriculture:

Only five of the ten main islands normally support significant agricultural production. The most widespread agricultural activity is gardening for domestic consumption. Garden crops include corn, cassava, sweet potatoes, and bananas. Bananas, almost the only agricultural export, are grown on irrigated land. Sugarcane, another cash crop, is used on the islands to produce rum.

Art & Culture:

Cape Verdean social and cultural patterns are similar to those of rural Portugal. Football games and church activities are typical sources of social interaction and entertainment. Its culture is heavily influenced by its unique music, such as the 'morna', a melancholy sound harking back to the days of slavery, 'batuko', a more jovial genre which gets everybody dancing and 'funana', an intriguing vocal tune which vibrates throughout the islands.

CAMEROON

Capital:	Yaoundé
Geographical location:	3°52′N 11°31′E
Area:	4,75,442 sq. Km
Currency:	Central African CFA franc (XAF)

System of Governance:	Unitary dominant-party presidential republic
Independence:	1 January 1960

Agriculture:

Cameroon is well known for its organic farming because of its climatic, geographic and ecological diversity, which enables farmers to grow a wide variety of crops. The most frequently cultivated export crops on Cameroonian organic farms are bananas, pineapples, avocados, mangoes, papayas, coffee and cocoa. Its primary export crops are cocoa, cotton, coffee, bananas, rubber and palm oil.

Art & Culture:

Cameroon is home to a large number of distinct ethnic groups, the country has developed a diverse, but rich culture. Each group celebrates its own contributions through festivals, literature and handicrafts. Its culture consists of numerous religions including Christianity, Islam, and many other indigenous religions.

CENTRAL AFRICAN REPUBLIC (CAR)

Capital:	Bangui
Geographical location:	4°22′N 18°35′E
Area:	6,22,984 sq. Km
Currency:	Central African CFA franc (XAF)
System of Governance:	Unitary Semi-presidential constitutional republic
Independence:	13 August 1960

Agriculture:

Subsistence agriculture, together with forestry, is the backbone of the economy of the Central African Republic (CAR). Principal food crops include cassava, peanuts, sorghum, millet, maize, sesame, and plantains. Principal cash crops for export include cotton, coffee, and tobacco.

Art & Culture

The people of the Central African Republic are composed of several groups, mainly the Bwaka, Madjia, Baya, and Banda. 25% of the population is Protestant. 25% is Roman Catholic. There is a small Islamic minority of 15% and 35% of the population have indigeneous beliefs. Music is a hodgepodge of influences, with sanza being the popular instrument. Genres like soukous, Afrobeat, pop music, and Western rock are all favorites, but the Pygmies have their own folk traditions.

CHAD

Capital:	N'Djamena
Geographical location:	12°06′N 16°02′E

Area:	12,84,000 sq. Km
Currency:	Central African CFA franc (XAF)
System of Governance:	Unitary dominant-party presidential republic
Independence:	11 August 1960

Agriculture

Chad's subsistence farmers practice traditional slash-and-burn agriculture in tandem with crop rotation. Sorghum is the most important food crop, followed by millet and berebere. Less prevalent grains are corn, rice, and wheat. Other secondary crops include peanuts, sesame, legumes, and tubers, as well as a variety of garden vegetables.

Art & Culture:

Chad is an ethnically diverse nation. The Colonial French rule has influenced their contemporary society, but about 200 ethnic groups still live in the country. These groups are divided along geographic lines. The southern region is primarily settled by the Sara people who are Christian. The northern region is inhabited primarily by nomadic tribal groups, who are Muslim. The center of the country–the Sahel region–is a blending of nomadic and sedentary people. Performing arts are generally nonexistent, though religious rituals are common.

COMOROS	
Capital:	Moroni
Geographical location:	11°41′S 43°16′E
Area:	1,659 sq. Km
Currency:	Comorian franc (KMF)
System of Governance:	Federal presidential republic
Independence:	6 July 1975

Agriculture:

The economy of the Comoros is primarily agricultural, with arable land comprising 45 percent of the total land area. Chief crops are manioc, coconuts, bananas, sweet potatoes, rice, corn, and cloves. Other crops include sugarcane, sisal, peppers, spices, coffee, and various perfume plants such as ylang-ylang, abelmosk, lemon grass, jasmine, and citronella.

Art & Culture:

Comorians are followers of Islam, and religious celebrations are widely observed. The local culture is a hodgepodge of Arab, French and African influences. People have a strong regard for music and other performance arts and local artisans are skilled in sculpture, pottery, embroidery, and basketry. Diversity is also evident in the many prevalent languages used on the islands, including French, Comorian, Arabic, and Swahili.

DEMOCRATIC REPUBLIC OF THE CONGO (DRC)	
Capital:	Kinshasa
Geographical location:	4°19′S 15°19′E
Area:	23,45,409 sq. Km
Currency:	Congolese franc (CDF)
System of Governance:	Kleptocracy Semi-presidential republic
Independence:	30 June 1960

Agriculture:

Agriculture is an industry in the country and has plenty of potential. Subsistence farmers produce mainly manioc, corn, tubers, and sorghum. DRC's principal cash crops are coffee, rubber, palm oil, cocoa, tea. Coffee is the DRC's most important and leading agricultural export.

Art & Culture:

The culture of the Democratic Republic of the Congo reflects the diversity of its hundreds of ethnic groups and their differing ways of life throughout the country. Another feature in Congo culture is its music. The DRC has blended its ethnic musical sources with Cuban rumba, and merengue to give birth to soukous. Internationally, the country is famous for its professional basketball NBA and football players.

REPUBLIC OF THE CONGO	
Capital:	Brazzaville
Geographical location:	4°16′S 15°17′E
Area:	3,42,000 sq. Km
Currency:	Central African CFA franc (XAF)
System of Governance:	Unitary dominant-party semi-presidential republic
Independence:	15 August 1960

Agriculture:

Agriculture in the Republic of the Congo is mostly at the subsistence level. Cassava (manioc) is the basic food crop everywhere in the country except in the southern region, where bananas and plantains are prevalent. Among the cash crops, the most important are sugarcane and tobacco, though palm kernels, cacao, and coffee are also cultivated to some extent.sunflowers. Mst of grain crops are exported to North Africa and the Middle East.

Art & Culture:

Culture is most evident in the well-preserved tribal and ethnic traditions of the Congolese, as well as in the music they play, infused with French, Arab and African roots. The people follow a variety of religious beliefs, but a majority of the population is either Catholic or Protestant. There are also Muslims, Animists and Baha'i. The music of Congo-Brazzaville is very similar to that of the DRC or Congo-Kinshasa. Congolese also have high regard for art and are very skilled painters and crafts makers.

CÔTE D'IVOIRE	
Capital:	Yamoussoukro
Geographical location:	6°51′N 5°18′W
Area:	3,22,463 sq. Km
Currency:	West African CFA franc (XOF)
System of Governance:	Unitary presidential republic under a parliamentary system
Independence:	7 August 1960

Agriculture:

In Ivory Coast about two-thirds of the land is agricultural and therefore their economy's foundation is mostly based on their agriculture. Fifty-five percent of their income comes from exports of cocoa and coffee. The Ivory Coast is not yet self-sufficient in food production and imports substantial quantities of rice, wheat, fish, and red meat for domestic consumption.

Art & Culture:

The diversity of culture in Ivory Coast is truly remarkable, with over 60 indigenous ethnic groups each with their own unique traditions. Music is also a big part of life in the Ivory Coast. Different instruments including the talking drum, kpalogo, djembe, shekere, cleavers and akombe are used to express various emotions. These are handcrafted from indigenous materials like animal skins, gourds and horns. The most iconic Ivoirian art is the mask. The intricacy and variety of designs are truly impressive.

DJIBOUTI	
Capital:	Djibouti
Geographical location:	11°36′N 43°10′E
Area:	23,200 sq. Km
Currency:	Djiboutian francs (DJF)
System of Governance:	Unitary dominant-party presidential republic under an authoritarian dictatorship
Independence:	27 June 1977

Agriculture:

Agriculture makes up minimal 3 percent of the economic activities of Djibouti. It depends on imports in most foods. Climatic conditions and poor soils limit farm output and domestic food production meets about 15% of demand.

Art & Culture:

Djibouti enjoys a rich culture based on tribal traditions. In addition to Afars and Issas, sub-clans like Gadabuursi also inhabit the country. Population speaks Somali and Afar as their mother tongues, but the official languages are Arabic and French. Music plays an important part in Djiboutian life and the two main ethnic groups both have their own traditions. Afar music is similar to the folk songs of the countries in the Horn of Africa like Ethiopia, but has distinct Arabic influences.

EGYPT	
Capital:	Cairo
Geographical location:	30°2′N 31°13′E
Area:	10,10,408 sq. Km
Currency:	Egyptian pound (EGP)
System of Governance:	Unitary Semi-presidential republic
Independence:	28 February 1922

Agriculture:

The Egyptians grew a variety of crops for consumption, including grains, vegetables and fruits. However, their diets revolve around several staple crops, especially cereals and barley. Other major grains grown included einkorn wheat and emmer wheat, grown to make bread. Other staples for the majority of the population included beans, lentils, and chickpeas and fava beans. Root crops, such as onions, garlic and radishes were grown, along with salad crops, such as lettuce and parsley.

Art & Culture:

Egypt has a rich culture which spans thousands of years and was one of the earliest and greatest civilizations the world has ever seen. The Egyptians pioneered many things, including written language. Egypt was also one of the first civilizations to introduce design into its art. The religion of Islam, practiced by 90 percent of the country's population, profoundly influences the culture of today. Egyptian music is a rich mixture of indigenous, Mediterranean, African and Western elements.

EQUATORIAL GUINEA	
Capital:	Malabo
Geographical location:	3°45′N 8°47′E
Area:	28,050 sq. Km
Currency:	Central African CFA franc (XAF)

System of Governance:	Unitary dominant-party presidential republic (de jure)
Independence:	12 October 1968

Agriculture:

Agriculture is the main economic activity in Equatorial Guinea. Agriculture (including forestry and fishing) accounts for about 55 percent of GDP and 60 percent of exports. The main food crop is cassava, sweet potatoes and bananas. Guinean cocoa, of excellent quality and Coffee grown is of comparatively poor quality.

Art & Culture:

The mainland's culture is heavily influenced by ancient rituals and songs, while Bioko Island is ruled by colonial Spanish traditions. Music and dance is at the core of Equatorial Guinea, and they are treated by the natives as religiously significant. People are mostly Roman Catholic, while a small percentage of the population practicing animism. Many ancient customs have been preserved by the Bubi. Traditional dances like balélé can be seen throughout the year and on special occasions like Christmas.

ERITREA	
Capital:	Asmara
Geographical location:	15°20′N 38°55′E
Area:	1,17,600 sq. Km
Currency:	Nakfa (ERN)
System of Governance:	Unitary one-party presidential republic under a totalitarian dictatorship
Independence:	24 May 1991

Agriculture:

Agriculture is the main economic activity in Eritrea. It makes up 11 percent of the wider economy's value. Eritrea has 5,65,000 hectares of arable land and permanent crops. Eritrea's main agricultural products include sorghum, millet, barley, wheat, legumes, vegetables, fruits, sesame, linseed, cattle, sheep, goats and camels.

Art & Culture:

Art is expressed through both music and crafts. Drumming is common in many communities. The Tigray-Tigrinya group is known for its popular musical genre called guaila. Majority of the population practices either the Christian or the Muslim faith. The rest adhere to indigenous religions and other sects like Roman Catholicism, Protestantism, etc. One of the most interesting aspects of the Eritrean culture is the traditional coffee ceremony, which can be seen during festivities.

<table>
<tr><td colspan="2" align="center">ESWATINI (FORMERLY SWAZILAND)</td></tr>
<tr><td>Capital:</td><td>Mbabane (executive); Lobamba (legislative)</td></tr>
<tr><td>Geographical location:</td><td>26°30′S 31°30′E</td></tr>
<tr><td>Area:</td><td>17,364 sq. Km</td></tr>
<tr><td>Currency:</td><td>Swazi lilangeni (SZL); South African rand (ZAR)</td></tr>
<tr><td>System of Governance:</td><td>Unitary parliamentary absolute diarchy</td></tr>
<tr><td>Independence:</td><td>6 September 1968</td></tr>
</table>

Agriculture:

Eswatini's agricultural sector is the second largest contributor to the economy. Commercial agriculture is dominated by sugar, forestry, citrus fruits and beef production for export. People practice subsistence farming, primarily maize cultivation. The country is historically a net importer of maize, animal feed, vegetable, and other products. The top five import products are wheat, yellow maize, rice, whole maize, and fruits and vegetables.

Art & Culture:

Despite being surrounded by much larger South Africa, Swaziland has its own distinct culture that remains very much intact. Many men still carry traditional battle axes, many women still sport traditional beehive hairstyles, and both sexes still wear the same colorful outfits they have sported for centuries. Songs accompany all Swazi rituals, from weddings to coming-of-age ceremonies. The most popular Swazi dance, sibhaca, is performed barefoot in colorful tasseled costumes.

<table>
<tr><td colspan="2" align="center">ETHIOPIA</td></tr>
<tr><td>Capital:</td><td>Addis Ababa</td></tr>
<tr><td>Geographical location:</td><td>9°1′N 38°45′E</td></tr>
<tr><td>Area:</td><td>11,04,300 sq. Km</td></tr>
<tr><td>Currency:</td><td>Birr (ETB)</td></tr>
<tr><td>System of Governance:</td><td>Federal dominant-party parliamentary republic</td></tr>
<tr><td>Independence:</td><td>5 May 1941</td></tr>
</table>

Agriculture:

Ethiopia's agriculture is plagued by periodic drought, soil degradation caused by overgrazing, deforestation, high levels of taxation and poor infrastructure. Yet agriculture is the country's most promising resource. Principal crops include coffee, pulses, oilseeds, cereals, potatoes, sugarcane, and vegetables. Exports are almost entirely agricultural commodities. Coffee is the largest foreign exchange earner. Ethiopia is also Africa's second biggest maize producer.

Art & Culture:

Ethiopians have one of the richest, most well-preserved cultures in the world. Christianity is the predominant religion, followed by Islam and other traditional animist beliefs. Ethiopian music is extremely diverse and modern influences come from folk music from all over the Horn of Africa, particularly Somalia. Hand woven fabrics (often decorated with intricate patterns) are used to create elegant garments.

GABON	
Capital:	Libreville
Geographical location:	0°23′N 9°27′E
Area:	2,67,667 sq. Km
Currency:	Central African franc (XAF)
System of Governance:	Unitary dominant-party presidential republic
Independence:	17 August 1960

Agriculture:

The Gabonese agricultural sector includes food crops, rubber, and palm oil. Main agricultural produce include manioc, bananas, corn, rice, taro, and yams. Gabon relies heavily on other African states and Europe for much of its food and other agricultural needs.

Art & Culture:

The Gabonese are very spiritual people. In fact, their traditions are mostly centered around worship and the afterlife. Gabonese considered music, instruments, masks, sculptures, and tribal dances as rites and acts of worship. Each of the Gabonese ethnic groups has its own specific traditions involving masks, sculptures, music, songs and dances, or a combination of these elements.

GAMBIA	
Capital:	Banjul
Geographical location:	13°28′N 16°36′W
Area:	10,689 sq. Km
Currency:	Dalasi (GMD)
System of Governance:	Unitary presidential republic
Independence:	18 February 1965

Agriculture:

Agriculture is a major driver of growth in The Gambia. It accounts for approximately one quarter of GDP. The main agricultural products grown locally are peanuts, rice, millet and sorghum. The main fruits produced include mangoes and cashews. These are also the major cash crops, while rice is the staple crop.

Art & Culture:

Gambia is home to multi-cultural people with several ethnic groups. People are generally bi-lingual and able to speak English. More than 90 percent of the population is Muslim, while the rest are either animists or Christians. The music of the Gambia is closely linked musically with that of its neighbour, Senegal. It fuses popular Western music and dance, with sabar, the traditional drumming and dance music of the Wolof and Serer people.

GHANA

Capital:	Accra
Geographical location:	5°33′N 0°12′W
Area:	2,39,567 sq. Km
Currency:	Ghanaian cedi (GHS)
System of Governance:	Unitary presidential constitutional republic
Independence:	6 March 1957

Agriculture:

Agriculture in Ghana consists of a variety of agricultural products andis an established economic sector.

Agricultural crops, including yams, grains, cocoa, oil palms, kola nuts, and timber, form the base of agriculture in Ghana's economy. Cocoa is Ghana's principal agricultural export.

Art & Culture:

Ghana's culture is diverse because of its number of ethnicities from the Akans of Akanland to the Dagombas of the Dagbon region, the Ashantis of Kumasi, and many other minorities. Music is an important part of the Ghanaian tradition. There are three distinct types of local sounds: ethnic music; highlife music, and choral music. Dancing is also distinct, with certain moves depicting different acts of celebration, praise, worship, and storytelling.

GUINEA

Capital:	Conakry
Geographical location:	9°31′N 13°42′W
Area:	2,45,857 sq. Km
Currency:	Guinean francs (GNF)

System of Governance:	Unitary presidential republic
Independence:	2 October 1958

Agriculture:

Only 2.6% of Guinea's arable land area is cultivated. Agriculture accounts for 24% of GDP. The principal subsistence crops are manioc, rice, sweet potatoes, yams, and corn. Cash crops are peanuts, palm kernels, bananas, pineapples, coffee, coconut, sugarcane, and citrus fruits.

Art & Culture:

Guinea inhibits a wide range of ethnic groups, which have their own beliefs and ways of life. In addition to the Indigenous ethnic groups, the French influenced the culture heavily during colonial times. Some of the ethnic groups living in the country include the likes of the Maninka, the Fula/Peuhl, the Susus, and many more. Three religions viz Islam, Christianity, and traditional beliefs dominate in the country.

GUINEA-BISSAU

Capital:	Bissau
Geographical location:	11°52′N 15°36′W
Area:	36,125 sq. Km
Currency:	West African CFA franc (XOF)
System of Governance:	Unitary Semi-presidential republic
Independence:	24 September 1973

Agriculture:

The economy of Guinea-Bissau is mostly agricultural but also includes forestry and fishing. Guinea-Bissau produces its own food, and farming is largely based on local subsistence. Some of the most common crops grown in the country are rice, vegetables, beans, cassava, peanuts, potatoes and palm oil. They also raise livestock and catch fish and shrimp, which are used locally as well as exported.

Art & Culture:

Guineans are predominantly Muslim, adhering to the teachings and religious observances of Islam. Among the major ethnic groups in the country are Peuhl or Fula, the Maninka, Susus. Music is one of the biggest aspects of Guinea-Bissau culture, and locals celebrate a lot of festivals to commemorate this prevalent art form. Guineans play a wide range of string and percussion instruments, including the ngoni, balafon, kora and the guitar.

KENYA

Capital:	Nairobi
Geographical location:	1°16′ S , 36°48′ E
Area:	5,80,367 sq. Km
Currency:	Kenyan shilling (KES)

System of Governance:	Unitary presidential constitutional republic
Independence:	12 December 1963

Agriculture:

Agriculture is the second largest contributor to Kenya's economy. The principal cash crops are tea, horticultural produce, and coffee. Horticultural produce and tea are the main growth sectors and the two most valuable of all of Kenya's exports. The production of major food staples such as corn is subject to sharp weather-related fluctuations. About 50% of the population lives below the poverty line, a significant portion of the population regularly starves and is heavily dependent on food aid.

Art & Culture:

The culture of Kenya consists of multiple traditions. Notable populations include the Swahili; Bantu communities; and Nilotic communities. The Maasai culture is well known to tourism, despite constituting a relatively small part of Kenya's population. Kenya has an extensive music, television and theater scene. The drums are the most dominant instrument in popular Kenyan music. The isukuti is a vigorous dance performed during the birth of a child, marriage and funerals. Other traditional dances include the Ohangl, Nzele, and Mugithi.

LESOTHO

Capital:	Maseru
Geographical location:	29°28′S 27°56′E
Area:	30,355 sq. Km
Currency:	Lesotho loti (LSL), South African rand (ZAR)
System of Governance:	Unitary parliamentary constitutional monarchy
Independence:	4 October 1966

Agriculture:

Lesotho's primary crops are corn (maize), beans, wheat, sorghum, and peas. Droughts have had a devastating effect and destroyed many summer harvests and livestock. The mountainous terrain means that only 10% of the land can be cultivated. Despite this, Lesotho's economy is largely dependent on agriculture. Terracing is a regular agricultural practice in Lesotho.

Art & Culture:

Although the country is 99 percent Christian, even the religious practices contain strong influences taken from traditional customs and beliefs such as burying the dead facing east in a sitting position so they can rise at dawn when needed by their descendents. Traditional tribal music and dance linked to the seasons and the agricultural lifestyle form an important part of the culture here, and traditional handicrafts are produced for actual use as well as souvenirs.

<table>
<tr><td colspan="2" align="center">LIBERIA</td></tr>
<tr><td>Capital:</td><td>Monrovia</td></tr>
<tr><td>Geographical location:</td><td>6°19′N 10°48′W</td></tr>
<tr><td>Area:</td><td>1,11,369 sq. Km</td></tr>
<tr><td>Currency:</td><td>Liberian dollar (LRD)</td></tr>
<tr><td>System of Governance:</td><td>Unitary presidential constitutional republic</td></tr>
<tr><td>Independence:</td><td>26 July 1847</td></tr>
</table>

Agriculture:

Agriculture provides sustenance for many households engaged in cassava, rubber, rice, oil palm, cocoa, or sugarcane production. More households engage in cassava production than any other crop. Cassava and rice are the primary staple food crops. The main cash crops and foreign exchange earners are rubber, cocoa, and timber. Rubber is one of the dominant generators of state revenues.

Art & Culture:

The diverse tribal ethnicities making up the population of Liberia have added richness to the cultural life in the country. Christian music is popular, with hymns sung a-capella in the iconic African style. Spirituality and the region's ancient rituals are reflected in the unusually intricate carving style, and modern Liberian artists are finding fame outside the country. Dance is a valued heritage, with the Liberian National Culture Group giving performances both in the country and overseas based on traditional themes.

<table>
<tr><td colspan="2" align="center">LIBYA</td></tr>
<tr><td>Capital:</td><td>Tripoli</td></tr>
<tr><td>Geographical location:</td><td>32°52′N 13°11′E</td></tr>
<tr><td>Area:</td><td>17,59,541 sq. Km</td></tr>
<tr><td>Currency:</td><td>Libyan dinars (LYD)</td></tr>
<tr><td>System of Governance:</td><td>Unitary provisional government</td></tr>
<tr><td>Independence:</td><td>24 December 1951</td></tr>
</table>

Agriculture:

Apart from a limited production of barley and wheat, major agricultural products of Libya are mostly fruits and vegetables such as dates, almonds, grapes, citrus fruits, watermelon, olives, and tomatoes, which constitute about 80 percent of annual agricultural production. Agricultural activities take place mainly along the coastline. Inland farming is very limited because of water shortages.

Art & Culture:	
Libya's rich culture began with the Berber tribes and their pastoral lifestyle, but influences the Phoenician, Carthaginian, Ancient Greek and Roman empires are visible. The most destructive element in the country's history was that of the Gaddafi decades, when he destroyed the ancient Berber culture, language and way of life. Although Arabic is still Libya's official language, Berber tongues are thriving again and desert hospitality is shown to all. The nomadic Bedouin are the majority here, with their own iconic crafts, dances, rituals, and music.	

MADAGASCAR

Capital:	Antananarivo
Geographical location:	18°55′S 47°31′E
Area:	5,87,041 sq. Km
Currency:	Malagasy ariary (MGA)
System of Governance:	Unitary Semi-presidential constitutional republic
Independence:	26 June 1960

Agriculture:
Rice is the main produce and main export crop of Madagascar. It is mainly planted in a terraced paddy system in the central highlands. Other major subsistence crops include cassava, corn and sweet potato, while coffee, cloves, vanilla and other cash crops are exported. The traditional slash-and-burn agriculture (tavy) is still followed which put pressure on the native and very diverse flora of Madagascar.

Art & Culture:
Islam and Christianity are the dominant religions. Traditional music and dance originating from Indonesia and Africa are a vital part of all ceremonies and festivals, and reinforce the links to the archipelago's long history. Fady, taboos are still respected in many regions and govern daily lives.

MALAWI

Capital:	Lilongwe
Geographical location:	13°57′S 33°42′E
Area:	1,18,484 sq. Km
Currency:	Kwacha (D) (MWK)
System of Governance:	Unitary presidential constitutional republic
Independence:	6 July 1964

Agriculture:
The main economic products of Malawi are tobacco, tea, cotton, groundnuts, sugar and coffee. The main food crops are maize, cassava, sweet potatoes, sorghum, bananas, rice,and Irish potatoes and cattle, sheep and goats are raised. The main industries deal with agricultural processing of tobacco, tea and sugar and timber products.

Art & Culture:
In Malawi, housing, languages, dress, song, dance and beliefs are as varied as the tribes themselves. The style and decoration of clothing denotes the individual's tribe, with the most important garment the chitenge, a wrap-around skirt worn by women over

a regular skirt to be used as a baby-carrier, apron, basket and more. Music and dance are an essential part of cultural life, both urban and rural communities, with 'a-capella gospel' songs and 'reggae' the most-loved ones.

	MALI
Capital:	Bamako
Geographical location:	12°39′N 8°0′W
Area:	12,40,192 sq. Km
Currency:	West African CFA franc (XOF)
System of Governance:	Unitary Semi-presidential republic
Independence:	20 June 1960

Agriculture:
Agricultural production in Mali is largely dominated by cotton and cereals including rice, millet, sorghum, and wheat. The most productive agricultural area lies along the banks of the Niger River. Rice is grown extensively along the banks of the Niger. Sorghum is planted extensively in the drier parts of the country.

Art & Culture:
From the nomadic Tuareg, Fulani, Bozo fishers, Bambara, and Dogon farmers, each of Mali's dozens of ethnic groups have their own unique languages and history. Malian music and literature have both been heavily influenced by longtime oral storytelling. Traditional storytellers called griots often perform at weddings and other special events. The colorful flowing robes many locals wear are called boubout, but handmade cotton mud cloth fabric also plays an important role in Mali's culture and economy.

	MAURITANIA
Capital:	Nouakchott
Geographical location:	18°09′N 15°58′W
Area:	10,30,000 sq. Km
Currency:	Ouguiya (MRU)

System of Governance:	Unitary semi-presidential Islamic republic
Independence:	28 November 1960

Agriculture:
Most farmers are engaged in subsistence agriculture and never buy food outside their households. Farms produce dates, millet, sorghum, and root crops, while herders raise cattle and sheep. Fishing is the second largest foreign revenue source after mining.

Art & Culture:
Mauritania's culture is a mixture of many influences, both indigenous and external from the ancient Berber people, the Moors and the French, especially visible in both music and cuisine. Mauritanian music is a tradition carried down by the Moors when musicians formed the lowest rung of society and performed for anyone who paid them.

MAURITIUS

Capital:	Port Louis
Geographical location:	20.2°S 57.5°E
Area:	2,040 sq. Km
Currency:	Mauritian rupee (MUR)
System of Governance:	Unitary parliamentary republic
Independence:	12 March 1968

Agriculture:
About 40 percent of the island's surface is being used for cultivation, of which roughly 90 percent is sugar cane, the balance being tea, tobacco and food crops. Historically, sugar cane cultivation was the main agricultural activity in Mauritius. It relies on imports for 70 percent of the country's food requirements.

Art & Culture:
Mauritius has a diverse population made up of people who came or were brought to the island during its history. Many have blended African, European, Indian, or Chinese heritage and follow faiths as diverse as Christianity, Islam, Hinduism, and Buddhism. This has produced a culture with diverse beliefs, rich cuisine and colorful festivals.

MOROCCO

Capital:	Rabat
Geographical location:	34°02′N 6°51′W
Area:	7,10,850 sq. Km
Currency:	Moroccan dirham (MAD)
System of Governance:	Unitary parliamentary constitutional monarchy
Independence:	7 April 1956

Agriculture:

About 22% of the total land area is arable. Main agricultural produce are cereals, plantation crops (olives, almonds, citrus, grapes, dates), pulses, forage, vegetables, industrial crops (sugar beets, sugar cane, cotton) and oilseeds. The bulk of the indigenous population carries out traditional subsistence farming.

Art & Culture:

Moroccan culture is a mixture of Arabic, Roman, French, Spanish and South African influences. Moroccan cuisine differs from region to region. The Berber influences are most prominent in the range of spices used. The great love of grains like couscous is an indication of the country's African roots, while the use of fresh fruits and vegetables comes directly from the country's proximity to the Mediterranean. Moroccan music is a delightful amalgamation with many traditional instruments bearing the mark of other regions.

MOZAMBIQUE

Capital:	Maputo
Geographical location:	25°57′S 32°35′E
Area:	8,01,590 sq. Km
Currency:	Mozambican metical (MZN)
System of Governance:	Unitary dominant-party semi-presidential constitutional republic
Independence:	25 June 1975

Agriculture:

Mozambique's major agricultural products include cotton, cashew nuts, sugarcane, tea, cassava, corn, rice, tropical fruits, beef, and poultry. Agricultural exports include prawns, cashews, cotton, sugar, copra (a coconut product), citrus, coconuts and timber. Cashews and cotton play an essential role in the economy.

Art & Culture:

The country holds seven main tribal ethnicities with each having its own distinct culture. Tribal music is all-important, both for traditional ceremonies and religious occasions, with the instruments handmade and largely unchanged over the centuries. Notable for their excellence in music and dance are the Chopi tribe, also famed for their animal-skin costumed battle dances, while the Makonde are known for their wood-carving, especially in the elaborate masks.

NAMIBIA

Capital:	Windhoek
Geographical location:	22°34′S 17°5′E
Area:	8,25,615 sq. Km
Currency:	Namibian dollars (NAD); South African rand (ZAR)

System of Governance:	Unitary dominant-party semi-presidential republic
Independence:	21 March 1990

Agriculture:

Agriculture in Namibia contributes around 5% of the national GDP. Namibians depend on subsistence agriculture and herding. Primary products included livestock and meat products, crop farming and forestry. Only 2% of Namibia's land receives sufficient rainfall to grow crops. As all inland rivers are ephemeral, irrigation is only possible in the valleys of the border rivers Oranje, Kunene, and Okavango.

Art & Culture:

Around 50 percent of Namibians belong to the Ovambos, most of whom live in the northern regions of the country. Although Finnish missionaries turned most of the Ovambo into practicing Christians, specifically Lutherans, many still follow traditional customs. In central and southern Namibia, the major ethnic group is the Herero. The women don Victorian-style dresses, albeit with a very loud and colorful African flare, while large horn-shaped headgear completes the apparel.

NIGER

Capital:	Niamey
Geographical location:	13°32′N 2°05′E
Area:	12,67,000 sq. Km
Currency:	West African CFA franc (XOF)
System of Governance:	Unitary semi-presidential republic
Independence:	3 August 1960

Agriculture:

The agricultural economy is based largely upon internal markets, subsistence agriculture, and the export of raw commodities: food stuffs and cattle to neighbors. Economic activity centres on subsistence agriculture, animal husbandry, re-export trade. Exports of cattle to neighboring Nigeria, as well as Groundnuts and their oil remain the primary non-mineral exports.

Art & Culture:

Around 90 percent of the population are Muslim. The rest of the population follows the Baha'i faith, Christianity, and Animism. Modern Niger culture is steeped in tradition, either following the Islamic doctrine, or reflecting the indigenous, typically African traditions. French colonialism has also had an influence in the Niger of today, although the country has found it difficult to join the modern global culture of the 21st century.

NIGERIA

Capital:	Abuja
Geographical location:	9°4′N 7°29′E
Area:	9,23,768 sq. Km
Currency:	Naira (NGN)

System of Governance:	Federal presidential constitutional republic
Independence:	1 October 1960

Agriculture:

Major crops of Nigeria include beans rice, sesame, cashew nuts, cassava, cocoa beans, groundnuts, gum arabic, kolanut, maize (corn), melon, millet, palm kernels, palm oil, plantains, rice, rubber, sorghum, soybeans, bananas and yams. Its major exports include groundnuts, cashew nuts, sesame seeds, moringa seeds, ginger, cocoa etc. Cocoa and oil palm are the leading non-oil foreign exchange earner.

Art & Culture:

In modern culture, Nigerians are revered throughout Africa and the world. As a result of Femi Kuti's global musical success and social commentary, he has been dubbed the 'Bob Marley of Africa". This music is known as 'Afrobeat' and influences many modern dance music styles. Nigeria has also had a growing success on the international stage with sport. Soccer is the national sport of Nigeria, and their national team is one of the best in Africa.

RWANDA

Capital:	Kigali
Geographical location:	1°56.633′S 30°3.567′E
Area:	26,338 sq. Km
Currency:	Rwandan franc (RWF)
System of Governance:	Unitary dominant-party presidential constitutional republic
Independence:	1 July 1962

Agriculture:

Agriculture has served historically as a mainstay of Rwanda's economy. Principal agricultural exports are coffee, tea and some value-added agricultural products such as canned tomatoes, honey, French beans, passion fruit, macadamia and mushrooms. Rwanda exports a large number of live animals, unprocessed meat and dairy products across the border to eastern DRC.

Art & Culture:

Despite the country's turbulent political past, Rwanda boasts a rich and diverse culture which spans centuries. Rwandan music is an integral part of both daily life and traditional ceremonies, with different regional groups contributing different sounds, instruments and dances to the national culture. Intore is one of the most famous musical performances which consists of ballet-style dancing, more traditional African dancing and a highly impressive drumming routine.

SÃO TOMÉ AND PRÍNCIPE

Capital:	São Tomé
Geographical location:	0°20′N 6°44′E
Area:	1,001 sq. Km
Currency:	Dobra (STN)

System of Governance:	Unitary semi-presidential republic
Independence:	12 July 1975
Agriculture:	

Plantation agriculture has long dominated the economy of the islands. Climate enables the cultivation of diverse tropical crops, but soils are especially suited for cocoa , which is the major export crop. About half of all cultivated land is used for cocoa production. Copra, palm kernels, bananas, cassava, and coconut are the other important crops.

Art & Culture:
The main cultural influences are Portuguese – as a result of the country's long colonial ties with the European

and West African nations. Both of these influences can be seen clearly in cultural markers as music and cuisine. The country's music is a wonderful amalgamation of African rhythms and Portuguese styles. São Toméan cuisine is based in equal parts on African traditions and Portuguese influence.

SENEGAL

Capital:	Dakar
Geographical location:	14°40′N 17°25′W
Area:	1,96,712 sq. Km
Currency:	West African CFA franc (XOF)
System of Governance:	Unitary presidential republic
Independence:	4 April 1960

Agriculture:

Senegal lies within the drought-prone Sahel region, with irregular rainfall and generally poor soils. Production is subject to drought and threats of pests. Millet, rice, corn, and sorghum are the primary food crops grown. Peanuts, sugarcane, and cotton are important cash crops, and a wide variety of fruits and vegetables are grown for local and export markets.

Art & Culture:

Senegal's dominant ethnic groups share Muslim religion and teranga culture. Music is an important part of all gatherings and storytelling sessions. Senegalese music is played with stringed instruments called kora and xalem accompanied by djembe, tabala, tama, sabar, and other traditional drums. The balafon, a wooden instrument similar to a xylophone, is hit with mallets to play its melodic music.

SEYCHELLES

Capital:	Victoria
Geographical location:	4°37′S 55°27′E

Area:	459 sq. Km
Currency:	Seychellois rupee (SCR)
System of Governance:	Unitary presidential republic
Independence:	29 June 1976

Agriculture:

Agricultural activities include coconuts, bananas, and Tea plantation. Other crops produced for export are cinnamon bark, vanilla, cloves and patchouli (an essence used in soap and perfume). Sweet potatoes, yams, breadfruit and cassava are grown in small quantities but are not sufficient to satisfy the local demand. Oranges, lemons, grapefruit, bananas and mangoes meet the local requirement only in season.

Art & Culture:

Most of the people are descendants of African slaves, West Indian Creole, Asian traders, and a mix of British and French settlers. The language is a unique offshoot of Creole and they have developed intriguing music that features lots of drumming, dance and dress, which are best seen during one of the main festivals, such as the Creole Festival. Arts and crafts are prominent, too, with painted silk fabrics popular items.

SIERRA LEONE

Capital:	Freetown
Geographical location:	8°29′N 13°14′W
Area:	71,740 sq. Km
Currency:	Leone (SLL)
System of Governance:	Unitary presidential constitutional republic
Independence:	27 April 1961

Agriculture:

Rice is the most important staple crop in Sierra Leone. The second staple food grown across the country is cassava. Other major annual food crops include sorghum, maize, millet, sweet potato and groundnut. The main tree crop is the oil palm, used for its perennial fruit. The other main perennial crops are citrus, sugarcane, cocoa, coffee, and coconut.

Art & Culture:

The different local and international influences are clearly evident in the country's cuisine, sports, and music. Sierra Leone's cuisine is heavily rooted in the culture and geography of West Africa. Music is Sierra Leone is perhaps the most eclectic part of the country's culture, as it is a lovely mixture of indigenous, British, and French varieties. Popular genres include Palm Wine asd Gumbe.

SOMALIA	
Capital:	Mogadishu
Geographical location:	2°2′N 45°21′E
Area:	6,37,657 sq. Km
Currency:	Somali shilling (SOS)
System of Governance:	Federal parliamentary republic
Independence:	1 July 1960

Agriculture:

Only 1.6% of Somalia's total land area is cultivated. Corn, sorghum, beans, rice, vegetables, cotton and sesame are grown. The commercial crops, bananas and sugarcane, are grown on irrigated land. Bananas constitute the nation's major commercial crop. Somalia is the world's leading producer of frankincense.

Art & Culture:

Migratory and colonial influence can be noticed in everything, including Somali cuisine, music, and art. Somalis also have a great tradition of creating art, be it visual, written, or spoken. Poetry is an important part of Somali culture. Henna body art is another strong tradition of Somalia. Such body art is worn on special occasions, usually to mark a marriage or the birth of a child.

SOUTH AFRICA	
Capital:	Pretoria (executive); Cape Town (legislative)
Geographical location:	30.56°S, 22.94°E
Area:	12,21,037 sq. Km
Currency:	South African rand (ZAR)

System of Governance:	Unitary dominant-party parliamentary constitutional republic
Independence:	31 May 1910

Agriculture:

South Africa's agricultural economy is highly diversified and includes the production of all the major grains (except rice), oilseeds, deciduous and subtropical fruits, sugar, citrus, wine and most vegetables. Livestock production includes cattle, dairy, hogs, sheep, and poultry. Citrus, wine, table grapes, corn and wool account for the largest exports. South Africa also exports nuts, sugar, mohair, apples and pears.

Art & Culture:

South Africa's indigenous culture suffered during the years of apartheid even native African singers began using English or Afrikaans. Bantu and its various dialects are undergoing a minor renaissance and musicians are

adopting their native tongues once again. Kwaito is a fusion of old and contemporary African beats. Dance is popular in all echelons of South African society. Gumboot, Zulu are the example of traditional dance forms of South Africa.

SOUTH SUDAN

Capital:	Juba
Geographical location:	4°51′ N , 31°36′ E
Area:	619,745 sq. Km
Currency:	South Sudanese Pound (SSP)
System of Governance:	Federal presidential constitutional republic
Independence:	9 July 2011

Agriculture:

Agriculture is the backbone of the economy of South Sudan. Cereals, primarily sorghum and maize, millet and rice are the dominant staple crops in South Sudan. Sorghum is the main staple food in all states, in few states local diet is also based on maize flour. Earlier, the country was a net exporter of agricultural products to regional markets; due to war-related destruction, poor infrastructure and lack of investment in the agriculture sector, South Sudan is now a net importer of food.

Art & Culture:

Most South Sudanese value knowing one's tribal origin, its traditional culture and dialect even while in exile and diaspora. Although the common languages spoken are Juba Arabic and English, Swahili is being introduced to the population to improve the country's relations with its East African neighbours. Many music artists from South Sudan use English, Swahili, Arabi Juba, their dialect or a mix of all.

SUDAN	
Capital:	Khartoum
Geographical location:	15°38′N 032°32′E
Area:	18,86,068 sq. Km
Currency:	Sudanese pound (SDG)
System of Governance:	Federal parliamentary republic
Independence:	1 January 1956

Agriculture:

About one-third of the total area of the country is suitable for agriculture. Abundant rainfall in the south permits both agriculture and grazing grounds. Principal cash crops are cotton, sesame, peanuts, sugarcane, dates, citrus fruits, mangoes, coffee, and tobacco; the principal subsistence crops are sorghum, millet, wheat, beans, cowpeas, pulses, corn, and barley. Cotton is the principal export crop and an integral part of the country's economy.

Art & Culture:

Sudan is an extremely heterogeneous country, being home to over 500 different tribes. Each tribe has its own distinctive ethnicity and many even have their own language. Many diverse influences can be noticed in music, clothing, and cuisine on the country. Sudan has a great tradition of music. Country's music is an eclectic mix of indigenous sounds and languages developed into western style hip-hop and folk music.

TANZANIA	
Capital:	Dodoma
Geographical location:	6.37°S, 34.89°E
Area:	9,47,303 sq. Km
Currency:	Tanzanian shilling (TZS)

System of Governance:	Unitary dominant party presidential constitutional republic
Independence:	9 December 1961

Agriculture:

Agriculture is the main part of Tanzania's economy. Main food crops in Tanzania are maize, sorghum, millet, rice, wheat, beans, cassava, potatoes, and bananas. The agricultural industry makes a large contribution to the country's foreign exchange earnings.

Art & Culture:

Tanzanian culture is a delightful mix of influences with over 120 tribes. Each of these tribes have their own distinct ways of life. Over 120 languages are spoken in Tanzania, most of them from the Bantu family. A slew of festivals go on throughout the year, featuring traditional dress and dance, such as the Wanyambo Festival in Dar es Salaam and the Mwaka Kogwa Festival in Zanzibar.

TOGO	
Capital:	Lomé
Geographical location:	6°8′N 1°13′E
Area:	56,785 sq. Km
Currency:	West African CFA franc (XOF)
System of Governance:	Unitary dominant-party presidential republic
Independence:	27 April 1960

Agriculture:

The majority of the Togolese population depends on subsistence agriculture. Its agricultural products include coffee, cocoa, cotton, yams, cassava (tapioca), corn, beans, rice, pearl millet, sorghum and livestock such as fish. Coffee and cocoa are traditionally the major cash crops for export, but cotton cultivation increased rapidly in recent times.

Art & Culture:

Togo has a rich culture which is reflected in its 37 tribal ethnic groups, which include the Ewe, Mina, and Kabre. French is the official language, although several other languages are spoken. Native tribal influences are still strong in Togo since the majority of the population follows traditional animist beliefs. Recent culture has seen Togo put onto the world stage by its national soccer team which reached the FIFA World Cup in 2006.

TUNISIA	
Capital:	Tunis
Geographical location:	36°49′N 10°11′E
Area:	1,63,610 sq. Km
Currency:	Tunisian dinars (TND)
System of Governance:	Unitary semi-presidential republic
Independence:	20 March 1956

Agriculture:

Tunisia's agricultural sector is of vital importance, contributing 12.6 % of GDP. The main cereal crops are wheat and barley. Tunisian farmers grow olives, dates and fresh fruits for both export and domestic consumption. The main agricultural export is olive oil. Though, organic agriculture is relatively new in Tunisia has one of the most developed organic sectors in Africa.

Art & Culture:

European, Middle Eastern, and African influences all play important parts in Tunisia's national identity. Arabic, Andalusian and Turkish rhythms can be heard in Tunisian music, and many buildings in Tunis feature brightly painted doors and windows next to their European-style beautiful gates. Alloucha, the most famous of Tunisia's high quality carpets, are made in Kairouan. The Cap Bon area is well known for its clay crafts.

UGANDA	
Capital:	Kampala
Geographical location:	1.37°N, 32.29°E
Area:	2,41,038 sq. Km
Currency:	Ugandan shilling (UGX)
System of Governance:	Unitary dominant-party presidential republic
Independence:	9 October 1962

Agriculture

Uganda's favorable soil conditions and climate have contributed to the country's agricultural success. Most areas usually receive plenty of rain. Uganda's main food crops have been plantains, cassava, sweet potatoes, millet, sorghum, corn, beans, and groundnuts. Major cash crops have been coffee, cotton, tea and tobacco.

Art & Culture

The prominent tribes of Uganda are Lango, Acholi, Karamojong, and Pygmies. The traditional kanzu that the Buganda people introduced to Uganda is still the national dress for men, while women are clad in gomesi, which are colorful floor-length dresses tied with a sash. Although all tribes have their own indigenous music. Buganda music is predominantly uses drums and other percussion instruments and is usually accompanied by some complex dances.

ZAMBIA	
Capital:	Lusaka
Geographical location:	15°25′S 28°17′E
Area:	7,52,618 sq. Km
Currency:	Zambian kwacha (ZMW)
System of Governance:	Unitary presidential constitutional republic
Independence:	24 October 1964

Agriculture

The Zambian agriculture sector comprises crops, livestock, and fisheries. Most Zambians are subsistence farmers. Domestic production is comprised of crops such as maize, sorghum, millet, and cassava while exports are driven by sugar, soybeans, coffee, groundnuts, rice, and cotton as well as horticultural produce.

Art & Culture

The Bantu people have done a great job of preserving their indigenous culture in everyday Zambian life. Arts and crafts can still be seen in the form of baskets, textiles, mats, wood carvings, ivory and copper. The Likumbi Lya Mize has been declared "Masterpiece of the Oral and Intangible Heritage of Humanity" by UNESCO. This traditional ceremony is the best way to get a taste of Zambian life.

<table>
<tr><td colspan="2" align="center">ZIMBABWE</td></tr>
<tr><td>Capital:</td><td>Harare</td></tr>
<tr><td>Geographical location:</td><td>17°50′S 31°3′E</td></tr>
<tr><td>Area:</td><td>3,90,757 sq. Km</td></tr>
<tr><td>Currency:</td><td>RTGS Dollar</td></tr>
<tr><td>System of Governance:</td><td>Unitary presidential republic</td></tr>
<tr><td>Independence:</td><td>11 November 1965</td></tr>
</table>

Agriculture:
Zimbabwe produces much of its own food, except in years where drought affects maize and wheat production. The staple food crop is maize, and other cereal crops include barley, millet, sorghum, and wheat. Tobacco is the largest export crop and Zimbabwe is among the world's biggest exporters. Horticulture is growing rapidly and Zimbabwe is now the world's third-largest exporter of roses.

Art & Culture:
Shona is the largest ethnic group, there are several other groups which have influenced the culture of Zimbabwe. Traditional art in Zimbabwe is made up of several different skills, including weaving, pottery, sewing, and carving. The Shona people are renowned for their ornate wooden carvings of idols and ancient gods, while the Ndebele are known for their colorful textiles and hand-painted materials. Music is also a large part of the Zimbabwean culture.

ANTARCTICA

The continent of Antarctica makes up most of the Antarctic region. The Antarctic is a cold, remote area in the Southern Hemisphere encompassed by the Antarctic Convergence. The Antarctic Convergence is an uneven line of latitude where cold, northward-flowing Antarctic waters meet the warmer waters of the world's oceans.

Antarctica is the fifth-largest continent in terms of total area. (It is larger than both Oceania and Europe.) Antarctica is a unique continent in that it does not have a native population. There are no countries in Antarctica, although seven nations claim different parts of it: New Zealand, Australia, France, Norway, the United Kingdom, Chile, and Argentina.

WORLD MAP

N
Arctic OCEAN
Arctic OCEAN
Arctic OCEAN
North Pacific OCEAN
North Pacific OCEAN
North Atlantic OCEAN
South Pacific OCEAN
South Atlantic OCEAN
INDIAN OCEAN
Antarctica
GREENLAND (DENMARK)
SVALBARD (NORWAY)
ALASKA (USA)
CANADA
UNITED STATES OF AMERICA
MEXICO
HAWAIIAN ISLANDS (USA)
CUBA
ICELAND
FAROE ISLANDS
SWEDEN
NORWAY
FINLAND
ESTONIA
LATVIA
LITHUANIA
BELARUS
IRELAND
UNITED KINGDOM
PORTUGAL
RUSSIA
KAZAKHSTAN
MONGOLIA
UZBEKISTAN
TURKMENISTAN
CHINA
NORTH KOREA
SOUTH KOREA
JAPAN
TURKEY
IRAN
AFGHANISTAN
KASHMIR
AZORES (PORTUGAL)
MADEIRA ISLAND (PORTUGAL)
MOROCCO
CANARY ISLANDS (SPAIN)
ALGERIA
LIBYA
EGYPT
SAUDI ARABIA
OMAN
INDIA
MYANMAR (BURMA)
LAOS
THAILAND
CAMBODIA
BANGLADESH
SRI LANKA
MAURITANIA
MALI
NIGER
CHAD
SUDAN
YEMEN
SENEGAL
BURKINA FASO
CAPE VERDE
THE GAMBIA
GUINEA
SIERRA LEONE
LIBERIA
COTE D'IVOIRE
GHANA
BENIN
NIGERIA
SAO TOME
ERITREA
ETHIOPIA
UGANDA
KENYA
SOMALIA
TANZANIA
SEYCHELLES
GABON
DEMOCRATIC REPUBLIC OF THE CONGO
CONGO
ANGOLA
ZAMBIA
NAMIBIA
BOTSWANA
SWAZILAND
LESOTHO
SOUTH AFRICA
COMOROS
MAYOTTE (FRANCE)
MADAGASCAR
MAURITIUS
REUNION
BOLIVIA
PARAGUAY
CHILE
URUGUAY
ARGENTINA
GALAPAGOS
ECUADOR
PERU
AUSTRALIA
NEW ZEALAND
GUAM
PHILIPPINES
FALKLAND ISLANDS (UK)
SOUTH GEORGIA (UK)

Families of Countries

The Balkans is a peninsula in Europe. The region has a combined area of 550,000 km² and an approximate population of 55 million people. The region takes its name from the Balkan Mountains, which run through the centre of Bulgaria into eastern Serbia and then continue to Slovenia as the Dinaric Alps.

The Balkans are bordered by water on three sides: the Black Sea to the east and branches of the Mediterranean Sea to the south and west (including the Adriatic, Ionian, Aegean and Marmara seas). The Balkan Peninsula is bordered on the north by the Danube, Sava, and Krča rivers.

Member Countries

Countries in the Balkan region are:

Albania, Kosovo, Bosnia and Herzegovina, Bulgaria, Croatia, Greece, Montenegro, North Macedonia, Romania (sometimes), Serbia, Slovenia (sometimes), Turkey (sometimes)

Related Countries

Other countries that are not in the Balkan region but that are close to it and/or play or have played an important role in the region's politics, culture and history:

- Austria (see also Austria-Hungary, Assassination of Archduke Franz Ferdinand of Austria)
- Cyprus (see also Cyprus dispute)
- Hungary (see also Austria-Hungary)
- Italy (see Trieste and History of the Republic of Venice)
- Russia (see History of Serbia)

The most common religions in the Balkans are:

Eastern Orthodox and Catholic Christianity and Islam (mostly Sunni or non-denominational). Many different specific kinds of each faith are practiced, with each of the Eastern Orthodox countries having its own national church with its own patriarch.

Eastern Orthodoxy is the Principal Religion in the Following Countries:

- Bulgaria (Bulgarian Orthodox Church)
- Greece (Greek Orthodox Church)
- Montenegro (Serbian Orthodox Church or uncanonical Montenegrin Orthodox Church)

◁   North Macedonia (Serbian Orthodox Church or uncanonical Macedonian Orthodox Church)

◁   Romania (Romanian Orthodox Church)

◁   Serbia (Serbian Orthodox Church)

◁   Roman Catholicism is the principal religion in the following countries:

◁   Croatia

◁   Slovenia

◁   Islam is the principal religion in the following countries:

◁   Albania

◁   Turkey

Bosnia and Herzegovina is a special case - 50% are Muslim Bosniaks, 31% are Serbian Orthodox, and 15% are Catholic Croats (therefore 46% are Christian). The remaining 4% adhere to other denominations of Christianity, other religions, or are irreligious.

CENTRAL AMERICA

Joining North and South America is a narrow strip of land known as Central America. Technically part of North America, this strip of land contains seven countries:

Costa Rica, El Salvador, Guatemala, Belize, Nicaragua, Panama and Honduras.

This part of the world is mostly rain forest. It is rich in natural resources, but many people here are very poor. The Central American countries have seen many wars. There are about 42 million people living in Central America.

Central America is covered with volcanoes, which create rich, fertile soil for farmland. Many people fish here too. The most central part of Central America is 125 miles from the ocean.

To the east of Central America lie hundreds of islands known as the Caribbean Islands. Most of the native people were killed by disease or taken as slaves when the Spanish arrived. The Spaniards brought thousands of slaves from Africa to work on farms in this area. Most people living here are descendants of those slaves.

Facts about Central America

◁   Spanish is the primary language spoken in Central America

◁   Covers 202,000 square miles of land

◁   Population of almost 42 million people

◁   Contains the Pan-American Highway, which is listed in the Guinness World Records as the world's longest "motorable road".

◁   Crops of coffee, bananas and beans grow in the fertile valleys

◁   Honduras, Panama and Costa Rica are often called the "banana republics" because of the importance bananas have to their economies

◁   Most of the population are mestizo, or of indigenous and Spanish decent

◁   Most people are Roman Catholic

◁   The Panama Canal, in Panama, is a man-made short-cut for ships sailing between the Atlantic and Pacific Oceans

Latin America is a region of the Americas. People do not completely agree which countries are in Latin America, but normally, it is the parts where Spanish and Portuguese are spoken (South America, Central America, and Mexico). Sometimes the Caribbean Islands are also included. Other people call all American countries where people speak Spanish, Portuguese, and French Latin America.

The words Latin America come from the use of languages that came from Latin. The Spanish, Portuguese, and French languages, spoken by many people in Latin America, are Romance languages.

Romance languages are derived from Latin. Not all people in Latin America speak Romance languages, some Latin American people speak English like Guyana, Trinidad and Tobago or Belize. Suriname speaks Dutch and many countries have a large population that speaks Native American languages. Paraguay is the only country that has a native language as its official language, which is the Guarany language.

North and Central America

- Belize, Costa Rica,El Salvador,Guatemala,,Honduras,Mexico,Nicaragua,Panama

South America

- Argentina, Bolivia, Brazil, Chile, Colombia, Ecuador, French Guiana

Département of France

- Guyana, Paraguay, Peru, Suriname, Uruguay, Venezuela

Caribbean countries

- Cuba, Dominican Republic, Haiti

Dependencies and constituent entities

- Guadeloupe, Martinique, Puerto Rico, Saint-Barthélemy, Saint-Martin

Important Facts

- Angel Falls in Venezuela is one of the largest waterfalls in the world with a height of almost 1 kilometre.
- Colombia produces more than 90% of the world's emeralds.
- Mexico is sinking by around 10 inches every year.
- Bolivia was the first country to get rid of McDonalds.
- Latin America is the most urbanized continent in the world with almost 80% of its citizens living in cities.
- Mambo, salsa, cha-cha-cha, rumba and tango dances all come from Latin America.
- It has the shortest coastline, compared to its size, of any continent.
- The official name of for Mexico is the United Mexican States.
- The oldest university in North America is the National University of Mexico.
- Costa Rica translated to 'rich coast'.
- The Amazon spans eight countries – Ecuador, Peru, Colombia, Peru, Bolivia, Brazil, Venezuela and Guyana.
- Rio de Janeiro carnival is the world's largest street festival.

- ◁ 20% of the world's oxygen is created from the Amazon jungle.
- ◁ There are 77 uncontacted tribes living in the Amazon Jungle.
- ◁ There are over 20 million inhabitants in Sao Paulo making it one of the world's largest cities.
- ◁ The highest mountain in South America is Argentina's Aconcagua and stands at over 6,961metres high.
- ◁ The world's most southerly city is located at the tip of Argentina and is called Ushuaia. It has around 55,000 inhabitants.
- ◁ Lake Titicaca is the largest lake in South America and straddles both Peru and Bolivia.
- ◁ Costa Rica has been ranked as the happiest country in the world.
- ◁ Asia is Latin America's second largest trading partner after the United States.
- ◁ Ecuador was the first country in the world to give nature constitutional rights and can be defended in court.
- ◁ After the Antarctic, the Atacama Desert in the north of Chile is considered the world's driest.
- ◁ Bolivia was the first country to have a ski resort with a rope tow.
- ◁ Darwin came up with his theory of evolution while visiting the Galapagos Islands.
- ◁ The Uyuni in Bolivia is the world's largest salt flats.

MIDDLE EAST

Middle East, the lands around the southern and eastern shores of the Mediterranean Sea, encompassing at least the Arabian Peninsula and, by some definitions, Iran, North Africa, and sometimes beyond.

The central part of this general area was formerly called the Near East, a name given to it by some of the first modern Western geographers and historians, who tended to divide what they called the Orient into three regions.

Near East applied to the region nearest Europe, extending from the Mediterranean Sea to the Persian Gulf; Middle East, from the Persian Gulf to Southeast Asia; and Far East, those regions facing the Pacific Ocean.

The change in usage began to evolve prior to World War II and tended to be confirmed during that war, when the term Middle East was given to the British military command in Egypt. By the mid-20th century a common definition of the Middle East encompassed the states or territories of Turkey, Cyprus, Syria, Lebanon, Iraq, Iran, Israel, the West Bank, the Gaza Strip, Jordan, Egypt, Sudan, Libya, and the various states and territories of Arabia proper (Saudi Arabia, Kuwait, Yemen, Oman, Bahrain, Qatar, and the Trucial States, or Trucial Oman [now United Arab Emirates]).

Subsequent events have tended, in loose usage, to enlarge the number of lands included in the definition. The three North African countries of Tunisia, Algeria, and Morocco are closely connected in sentiment and foreign policy with the Arab states. In addition, geographic factors often require statesmen and others to take account of Afghanistan and Pakistan in connection with the affairs of the Middle East.

Occasionally, Greece is included in the compass of the Middle East because the Middle Eastern (then Near Eastern) question in its modern form first became apparent when the Greeks rose in rebellion to assert their independence of the Ottoman Empire in 1821 (*see* Eastern Question). Turkey and Greece, together with the predominantly Arabic-speaking lands around the eastern end of the Mediterranean, were also formerly known as the Levant.

Use of the term Middle East nonetheless remains unsettled, and some agencies (notably the United States State Department and certain bodies of the United Nations) still employ the term Near East.

Countries of Middle East (18 countries):

Bahrain, Cyprus, Egypt, Iran, Iraq, Israel, Jordan, Kuwait, Lebanon, Oman, Palestine, Qatar, Saudi Arabia, the Syrian Arab Republic, Turkey, the United Arab Emirates and Yemen.

Bordering Bodies of Water: Mediterranean Sea, Red Sea, Gulf of Aden, Arabian Sea, Persian Gulf, Caspian Sea, Black Sea, Indian Ocean

Major Rivers and Lakes: Tigris River, Euphrates River, Nile River, Dead Sea, Lake Urmia, Lake Van, Suez Canal

Major Geographical Features: Arabian Desert, Kara Kum Desert, Zagros Mountains, Hindu Kush Mountains, Taurus Mountains, Anatolian Plateau

Fun Facts about the Middle East for Kids

- The Middle East is also called the Near East, especially when talking about history.

- 18 separate countries make up this region: Bahrain, Cyprus, Egypt, Iran, Iraq, Israel, Jordan, Kuwait, Lebanon, Northern Cyprus, Oman, Palestine, Qatar, Saudi Arabia, Syria, Turkey, United Arab Emirates and Yemen.

- The most widely spoken languages in the Middle East are Arabic, Persian, Turkish, Berber and Kurdish.

- The largest cities in the Middle East are Cairo, Tehran, Istanbul, Baghdad, Riyadh, Jeddah and Ankara.

- The largest ethnic group in the Middle East are Arabs.

POLYNESIA

Polynesia is a group of over one thousand islands located within a triangle over the central and southern Pacific Ocean. The triangle's corners are at the Hawaiian Islands, New Zealand, and Easter Island. "Polynesia" comes from the Greek words meaning "many islands."

- The word Polynesia is derived from two Greek words: poly which means "many" and nesos which means "islands".

◄   Polynesia literally means "many islands".

◄   In 1756, a French writer named Charles Brosses was the first person to use the word "Polynesia". But, contrary to its modern definition, Brosses used it to refer to all the islands of the Pacific.

◄   In 1831, a French explorer and naval officer who happened to have sailed through the south and western Pacific, named Jules Dumont d'Urville, proposed a restriction on its use to the Geographical Society of Paris.

Polynesia consists of six independent nations, two political units that are parts of larger nations, two self-governing entities, and five territories. Hawaii, of the fifty US states, is one of the two political units included in Polynesia and American Samoa, one of the territories, is administered by the United States.

The six countries in Polynesia are:

- New Zealand
- Solomon Islands
- Tonga
- Tuvalu
- Vanuatu
- Samoa

New Zealand is the largest of the Polynesian countries in terms of both population and area. New Zealand is home to over 4.9 million people and spans over 103,483 square miles (268,021 square kilometers). Of the over 4 million people in New Zealand, only 260,000 identify themselves as Polynesian. New Zealand was previously a colony of the United Kingdom but was granted full autonomy in 1947 with the Statute of Westminster.

Geographic Area

◄   Polynesia is a cultural term referring to one of the three main parts of Oceania.

◄   Polynesian islands in general are contained or located within the Polynesian Triangle.

◄   Geographically, the three main points of this triangle is drawn by the connecting points of Hawaii, New Zealand, and Easter Island.

◄   Other islands inhabited by Polynesian people do not lie within the Triangle.

◄   The other main island groups situating within the Polynesian triangle are Samoa, Tonga, the Cook Islands, Tuvalu, Tokelau, Niue, Wallis and Futuna, and French Polynesia.

◄   Small Polynesian settlements are also located at Papua New Guinea, the Solomon Islands, the Caroline Islands, and Vanuatu.

◄   Outside the Polynesian Triangle, nearby island groups have strong Polynesian traits, such as Rotuma, located at the north of Fiji.

◄   The Lau Islands at the southeast of Fiji possess strong cultural and historic links with Tonga.

◄   People in these island groups speak non-Polynesian languages.

Southeast Asia or Southeastern Asia is a subregion of Asia, consisting of the regions that are geographically south of China, east of the Indian subcontinent and north-west of Australia. Southeast Asia is bordered to the north by East Asia, to the west by South Asia and the Bay of Bengal, to the east by Oceania and the Pacific Ocean, and to the south by Australia and the Indian Ocean.

Countries of Southeast Asia: Brunei, Burma (Myanmar), Cambodia, Timor-Leste, Indonesia, Laos, Malaysia, the Philippines, Singapore, Thailand and Vietnam.

The region is the only part of Asia that lies partly within the Southern Hemisphere, although the majority of it is in the Northern Hemisphere. In contemporary definition, Southeast Asia consists of two geographic regions:

1. Mainland Southeast Asia, also known historically as Indochina, comprising Myanmar, Thailand, Peninsular Malaysia, Laos, Cambodia, and Vietnam.

2. Maritime Southeast Asia, also known historically as Nusantara, the East Indies, or the Malay Archipelago, comprising the Andaman and Nicobar Islands of India, Indonesia (except Western New Guinea, which is considered part of the Australian continent), East Malaysia, Brunei, Singapore, the Philippines, East Timor, Christmas Island, and the Cocos (Keeling) Islands.

- Indonesia is the largest country in Southeast Asia and it also the largest archipelago in the world by size (according to the CIA World Factbook). Geologically, the Indonesian archipelago is one of the most volcanically active regions in the world. Geological uplifts in the region have also produced some impressive mountains, culminating in Puncak Jaya in Papua, Indonesia at 5,030 metres (16,500 feet), on the island of New Guinea; it is the only place where ice glaciers can be found in Southeast Asia. The highest mountain in Southeast Asia is Hkakabo Razi at 5,967 meters and can be found in northern Burma sharing the same range of its parent peak, Mount Everest.

- The South China Sea is the major body of water within Southeast Asia. The Philippines, Vietnam, Malaysia, Brunei, Indonesia, and Singapore, have integral rivers that flow into the South China Sea.

- Mayon Volcano, despite being dangerously active, holds the record of the world's most perfect cone which is built from past and continuous eruption.

- Southeast Asia is bounded to the southeast by the Australian continent, a boundary which runs through Indonesia. But a cultural touch point lies between Papua New Guinea and the Indonesian region of the Papua and West Papua, which shares the island of New Guinea with Papua New Guinea.

Bordering Bodies of Water: Pacific Ocean, Indian Ocean, South China Sea, Gulf of Thailand, Gulf of Tonkin, Java Sea, Philippine Sea, Celebes Sea.

Major Rivers and Lakes: Tonle Sap, Lake Toba, Songkhla Lake, Laguna de Bay, Mekong River, Salween River, Irrawaddy River, Fly River.

Major Geographical Features: Volcanoes of Indonesia and the Philippine Islands, Malay Peninsula, Philippine Trench, Java Trench, New Guinea Island, Borneo Island, Sumatra Island.

SCANDINAVIA

Scandinavia is a group of countries in northern Europe that includes Norway and Sweden. The term is most often used linguistically, to mean places that speak Scandinavian languages (also called the North Germanic languages). Then it also includes Denmark.

The Scandinavian languages (Swedish, Norwegian, Danish, Icelandic and Faroese) are closely related, and many Scandinavians are able to understand some of the other languages, with some difficulty. Sometimes "Scandinavia" is a term of physical geography in which case it includes Finland instead.

The Scandinavian Peninsula is a large peninsula reaching west from northern Europe over the north side of the Baltic Sea. Norway, Sweden and some of Finland are on the peninsula, also known as Fennoscandia. Denmark, not Finland, however, is regarded as part of Scandinavia. This is because Danish is a Scandinavian language but Finnish is not.

Countries of Scandinavia

In general, Scandinavia denotes **Norway, Sweden, and Denmark**. The term Norden refers to Denmark, Finland, Iceland, Norway, and Sweden. These form a group of countries having affinities with each other and are distinct from the rest of continental Europe.

Some Facts about Finland and Scandinavia

Norway, Sweden and Finland seem wild. They are covered with forests and swift rivers.

- Norway and Sweden have many mountains while Finland and Denmark are low-lying. Denmark is known to have many farms.

- Most people in these countries live near the sea or near lakes.

- The people of Scandinavia have a high quality of life. They pay very high taxes, but this way the wealth is better shared; the Scandinavian people thus get good education, health and social benefits, great infrastructure and a safer, cleaner public transport system. Therefore, most of the population enjoy a good standard of living.

- The northern part of Scandinavia is called Lapland.

- The Lapland region is inhabited by Sami people. These people have their own language. The five Sami languages spoken in Lapland are North, South, Skolt, Inari and Lule.

- They herd reindeer for meat and milk in Lapland.

- The other languages spoken in Scandinavia include Danish, Swedish and Norwegian.

UNION OF SOVIET SOCIALIST REPUBLICS (USSR)

The Soviet Union (short for the Union of Soviet Socialist Republics or USSR) was a single-party Marxist–Leninist state. It existed for 69 years, from 1922 until 1991. It was the first country to declare itself socialist and build towards a communist society. It was a union of 14 Soviet socialist republics and one Soviet federative socialist republic (Russia).

The Soviet Union was created about five years after the Russian Revolution. It was announced after Vladimir Lenin overthrew Alexander Kerensky as Russian leader. The communist government developed industry and over time became a major, powerful union. The largest country in the Union was Russia, and Kazakhstan was the second. The capital city of the Soviet Union was Moscow.

The Soviet Union expanded its political control greatly after World War II. It took over the whole of Eastern Europe. Those countries were not made part of the Soviet Union, but they were controlled by the Soviet Union indirectly. These countries, like Poland, Czechoslovakia, and East Germany, were called satellite states.

Countries of USSR

The **15 countries** that were a part of the Soviet Union are:

Armenia, Azerbaijan, Belarus, Estonia, Georgia, Kazakhstan, Kyrgyzstan, Latvia, Lithuania, Moldova, Russia, Tajikistan, Turkmenistan, Ukraine, Uzbekistan

The UAE consists of a federation of seven emirates. Abu Dhabi is the largest emirate as it accounts for 84% of the total land area of the federation. Abu Dhabi is also home to the capital city also called Abu Dhabi.

Dubai is the second biggest emirate and the economic hub of the region. Dubai is also known for its three manmade archipelagos, two were designed to look like a palm tree, and one to resemble a world map.

The UAE's national airline is called 'Etihad' and based in Abu Dhabi, the capital city of the UAE. 'Emirates' which is the largest airline in the Middle East, and also one of the largest in the world, is also based in the UAE but in the emirate of Dubai, which is one of the seven emirates.

The United Arab Emirates are situated on the Arabian peninsula and border the Persian Gulf. In size, the UAE are slightly smaller than the US state of Maine or slightly bigger than South Carolina/USA.

The country has mountains in the eastern part and a dry desert with rolling sanddunes in the centre.

The landscape is generally barren and dry, even along the coastal plain bordering the Persian Gulf.

The UAE have a dry desert climate and temperatures can easily reach more than 40°C/104°F in summer. Natural hazards include sand storms, dust storms and haze.

7 Emirates of the UAE

Abu Dhabi, Dubai, Sharjah, Fujairah, Ajman, Ras Al Khaimah, Umm Al Quwain

Capital City: Abu Dhabi (The Arabic word abu means ‹father› and dhabi means ‹gazelle›). The name thus means ‹Father of the Gazelle› and according to a folk tale refers to the hunting of gazelles in the region.

Distinctions between United Kingdom, Great Britain and Britain

- **UK:** United Kingdom is a country belonging to the European continent that includes four separate countries on the British isles: England, Northern Ireland, Scotland and Wales.

◅ **Great Britain** is the name for three nations on the main isle: England, Scotland and Wales

◅ **Britain** is used only for including the mainland countries England and Wales.

The UK is short for The United Kingdom of Great Britain and Northern Ireland. It is a sovereign state (in the same way as France or the USA) but is made up of four countries; **England, Scotland, Wales** and **Northern Ireland.** The United Kingdom is a country in northwestern Europe. The UK consists of four countries: England, Scotland, Wales and Northern Ireland. The UK is located mainly on two large islands in the Atlantic Ocean: the islands of Great Britain and Ireland. No location in the UK is further away from the sea than 125 km/ 77 miles.

The only land border to a non-UK country is in Northern Ireland the border with Ireland. The United Kingdom is slightly smaller than the state of Oregon/USA and slightly bigger than Ghana. The UK lies on the prime meridian which marks the Greenwich meridian time zone (GMT).

The landscape is dominated by rolling plains and rugged hillsides. The UK has 13 British overseas territories; among them are Cayman Islands and British Virgin Islands in the Caribbean, Gibraltar on the Iberian Peninsula and Saint Helena in the South Atlantic Ocean.

The United Kingdom was part of the European Union from 1973 until 'Brexit' was finalised on 31 December 2020 when the transition period (from 31 January 2020) ended with new arrangements between the EU and the UK.

Important Facts

◅ The **largest country of the UK is England**. The smallest country is Northern Ireland.

◅ The UK has the **third longest coastline** in Europe with 12,430 km/ 7,723 miles - after Norway and Denmark (Greenland)

◅ The United Kingdom's **highest mountain** is Ben Nevis in Scotland with 1,345 m/4,412 ft.

◅ The **largest lake** in the UK is Lough Neagh in Northern Ireland.

◅ Loch Ness is the **largest fresh water lake** (by volume) in the UK.

◅ The **longest river** in the UK is the river Severn with 354 km/ 220 miles.

◅ London Heathrow is the **biggest airport** on the European continent.

◅ There is **only one land border** to Ireland.

◅ Bishop Rock off the Scilly Isles in southern England is the smallest of the UK islands.

International Organisations & Groups

Establishment – 24 October, 1945

Headquarter -- New York, USA

Objectives -- In accordance with the Charter, the organization's objectives include maintaining international peace and security, protecting human rights, delivering humanitarian aid, promoting sustainable development, and upholding international law.

Members – 193

Head -- António Guterres

United Nations Structure

The UN is structured around five principal organs:

1. General Assembly
2. United Nations Security Council (UNSC)
3. Economic and Social Council (ECOSOC)
4. International Court of Justice
5. UN Secretariat.

- A sixth principal organ, the Trusteeship Council, suspended operations on 1 November 1994, upon the independence of Palau, the last remaining UN trustee territory.
- **Five sovereign states** to whom the UN Charter of 1945 grants a permanent seat on the UN Security Council: China, France, Russia, the United Kingdom, and the United States.

Principal Organs of the United Nations

Name of the Organ	Primary Function	Primary Tasks of the Organ
UN General Assembly	Deliberative assembly of all the UN member states	• May resolve non-compulsory recommendations to states or suggestions to the Security Council (UNSC); • Decides on the admission of new members, following a proposal by the UNSC; • Adopts the budget; • Elects the non-permanent members of the UNSC; all members of ECOSOC; the UN Secretary-General (following his/her proposal by the UNSC); and the fifteen judges of the International Court of Justice (ICJ). Each country has one vote.

UN Secretariat	Administrative organ of the UN	• Supports the other UN bodies administratively (for example, in the organization of conferences, the writing of reports and studies the preparation of the budget); • Its chairperson – the **UN Secretary-General** – is elected by the General Assembly for a five-year mandate and is the UN's foremost representative.
International Court of Justice	Universal court of international law	• Decides disputes between states that recognize its jurisdiction; • Issues legal opinions; • Renders judgment by relative majority. Its fifteen judges are elected by the UN General Assembly for nine-year terms.
UN Security Council	Arbitrates international security issues	• Responsible for the maintenance of international peace and security; • May adopt compulsory resolutions; • Has fifteen members: five permanent members with veto power and ten elected non-permanent members (term – two years)
UN Economic and Social Council	For global economic and social affairs	• Responsible for cooperation between states concerning economic and social matters; • Coordinates cooperation between the numerous specialized agencies of UN; • Has 54 members, elected by the General Assembly to serve staggered three-year mandates.
UN Trusteeship Council	For administering trust territory (now disbanded)	• Was originally designed to manage former colonial possessions. • Has been inactive since 1994, when Palau, the last trust territory, attained independence.

Establishment – 11 December, 1946

Headquarter -- New York, USA

Objectives -- UNICEF works around the world to strengthen health systems; immunize and treat children for pneumonia, diarrhoea, malaria and other health conditions; help countries combat non-communicable diseases; and support children with mental health conditions, developmental delays and disabilities.

Members – 191

Head -- Henrietta H. Fore

INTERNATIONAL MONETARY FUND (IMF)

Establishment – 1944

Headquarter -- Washington DC, United States

Objectives -- The International Monetary Fund aims to reducing global poverty, encouraging international trade, and promoting financial stability and economic growth. The IMF has three main functions: overseeing economic development, lending, and capacity development.

Members – 190

Head -- Kristalina Georgieva

WORLD BANK GROUP (WBG)

Establishment – July 1944

Headquarter -- Washington DC, United States

Objectives -- i. To provide long term capital to members countries for economic reconstruction and development. ii. To induce long term capital investment for assuring BOP equilibrium and balanced development of international trade.

Members – 189

Head -- David Malpass

WORLD HEALTH ORGANISATION (WHO)

Establishment – 7 April, 1948

Headquarter -- Geneva, Switzerland

Objectives -- WHO's main functions can be summed up as follows: to act as a directing and coordinating authority on international health work, to ensure valid and productive technical cooperation, and to promote research. The objective of WHO is the attainment by all peoples of the highest possible level of health.

Members – 194

Head – Dr. Tedros Adhanom Ghebreyesus

INTERNATIONAL LABOUR ORGANISATION

Establishment – 1919

Headquarter -- Geneva, Switzerland

Objectives -- The organisation's main aims are to **promote rights at work**, encourage decent employment opportunities, enhance social protection and strengthen dialogue on work-related issues.

Members – 187

Head – Guy Ryder

INTERNATIONAL COMMITTEE OF THE RED CROSS

Establishment – 1863

Headquarter -- Geneva, Switzerland

Objectives -- The International Committee of the Red Cross is an impartial, neutral and independent organization whose exclusively humanitarian mission is to protect the lives and dignity of victims of armed conflict and other situations of violence and to provide them with assistance.

Head – Peter Maurer

Establishment – 1 January, 1995

Headquarter -- Geneva, Switzerland

Objectives -- The WTO has six key objectives: (1) to set and enforce rules for international trade, (2) to provide a forum for negotiating and monitoring further trade liberalization, (3) to resolve trade disputes, (4) to increase the transparency of decision-making processes, (5) to cooperate with other major international economic institutions involved in global economic management, and (6) to help developing countries benefit fully from the global trading system.

Members – 164

Head – Ngozi Okonjo-Iweala

WORLD METEOROLOGICAL ORGANISATION (WMO)

Establishment – 23 March, 1950

Headquarter -- Geneva, Switzerland

Objectives -- The vision of WMO is to provide world leadership in expertise and international cooperation in weather, climate, hydrology and water resources and related environmental issues and thereby contribute to the safety and well-being of people throughout the world and to the economic benefit of all nations.

Members – 187

Head – David Grimes

WORLD INTELLECTUAL PROPERTY ORGANIZATION (WIPO)

Establishment – 14 July, 1967

Headquarter -- Geneva, Switzerland

Objectives -- WIPO's two main objectives are (i) to promote the protection of intellectual property worldwide; and (ii) to ensure administrative cooperation among the intellectual property Unions established by the treaties that WIPO administers.

Members – 193

Head – Daren Tang

UNITED NATIONS EDUCATIONAL SCIENTIFIC AND CULTURAL ORGANISATION (UNESCO)

Establishment – 16 November, 1945

Headquarter -- Paris, France

Objectives -- The main objective of UNESCO is to contribute to peace and security in the world by promoting collaboration among nations through education, science, culture and communication in order to enhance universal respect for justice, for the rule of law and for the human rights and fundamental freedoms which are affirmed for the people of the world, without distinction of race, sex, language or religion, by the Charter of the UN.

Members – 193

Head – Audrey Azoulay

Establishment – 30 September, 1961

Headquarter -- Paris, France

Objectives -- The three main objectives as laid down in the OECD Convention were: 1. to achieve the highest sustainable economic growth and employment and a rising standard of living in Member Countries, while maintaining financial stability, and thus to contribute to the development of the world economy; 2. to contribute to sound economic expansion in Member as well as non-Member Countries in the process of economic development; 3. to contribute to the expansion of world trade on a multilateral, non-discriminatory basis in accordance with international objectives. The OECD therefore, represented a transformation and an extension of the OEEC.

Members – 38

Head – Mathias Cormann

INTERNATIONAL ATOMIC ENERGY AGENCY (IAEA)

Establishment – 29 July, 1957

Headquarter -- Vienna, Austria

Objectives -- Consistent with its statutory mandate "to accelerate and enlarge the contribution of atomic energy to peace, health and prosperity throughout the world", the IAEA's activities include: developing and transferring nuclear technologies for peaceful purposes to its Member States; contributing to the strengthening of the global nuclear safety framework and strengthening the security of nuclear material and facilities.

Members – 173

Head – Rafael Mariano Grossi

ORGANIZATION OF PETROLEUM EXPORTING COUNTRIES (OPEC)

Establishment – September 1960

Headquarter -- Vienna, Austria

Objectives -- OPEC's objective is to co-ordinate and unify petroleum policies among Member Countries, in order to secure fair and stable prices for petroleum producers; an efficient, economic and regular supply of petroleum to consuming nations and a fair return on capital to those investing in the industry.

Members – 15

Head – Mohammed Barkindo

INTERNATIONAL MARITIME ORGANISATION (IMO)

Establishment – 17 March, 1948

Headquarter -- London, United Kingdom

Objectives -- The International Maritime Organization's objectives can be best summed up by its slogan—"Safe, secure and efficient shipping on clean oceans." Basically, the IMO sets policy for international shipping, discouraging shippers from compromising on safety, security and environmental performance to address financial concerns, and encouraging innovation and efficiency.

Members – 174

Head – Kitack Lim

Establishment – 11 December, 1931

Headquarter -- London, United Kingdom

Objectives -- The instrument which sets out the Commonwealth's objectives is the 1971 Singapore Declaration, which committed the Commonwealth to the institution of world peace; promotion of representative democracy and individual liberty; the pursuit of equality and opposition to racism; the fight against poverty, ignorance, and disease; and free trade.

Members – 54

Head – Her Majesty Queen Elizabeth II

AMNESTY INTERNATIONAL

Establishment – July 1961

Headquarter -- London, United Kingdom

Objectives -- The main objective of Amnesty International is to conduct rigorous research and initiate measures to prevent and end grave abuses of human rights and to provide justice for the deprived section of the community.

Head – Swede Thomas Hammarberg

FOOD AND AGRICULTURAL ORGANISATION (FAO)

Establishment – 16 October, 1945

Headquarter -- Rome, Italy

Objectives -- Help eliminate hunger, food insecurity and malnutrition. Make agriculture, forestry and fisheries more productive and sustainable. Reduce rural poverty. Enable inclusive and efficient agricultural and food systems.

Members – 194

Head – Qu Dongyu

NORTH ATLANTIC TREATY ORGANISATION (NATO)

Establishment – 4 April, 1949

Headquarter -- Brussels, Belgium

Objectives -- The North Atlantic Treaty Organization or Atlantic Alliance (NATO) is an international political and military organization with the aim of guaranteeing the freedom and security of its members through political and military means.

Members – 30

Head – Jens Stoltenberg

ASSOCIATION OF SOUTHEAST ASIAN NATIONS (ASEAN)

Establishment – 8 August, 1967

Headquarter -- Jakarta, Indonesia

Objectives -- The ASEAN Declaration states that the aims and purposes of the Association are: (1) to accelerate economic growth, social progress and cultural development in the region and (2) to promote regional peace and stability through abiding respect for justice and the rule of law in the relationship among countries in the region and adherence to the principles of the United Nations Charter.

Members – 10

Head – Lim Jock Hoi

Establishment – November 1989

Headquarter -- Queenstown, Singapore

Objectives -- The objectives of APEC are summarized in the Seoul Declaration, adopted at the third APEC Ministerial Meeting in Seoul. They are: (1) to sustain the growth and development of the region for the common good of its peoples and, in this way, to contribute to the growth and development of the world economy; (2) to enhance the positive gains, both for the region and the world economy, resulting from increasing economic interdependence, including by encouraging the flow of goods, services, capital and technology; (3) to develop and strengthen the open multilateral trading system in the interest of Asia-Pacific and all other economies; and (4) to reduce barriers to trade in goods and services and investment among participants in a manner consistent with GATT principles, where applicable, and without detriment to other economics.

Members – 21

Head – Rebecca Sta Maria

Transparency International

Establishment – 4 May, 1993

Headquarter -- Berlin, Germany

Objectives -- Its nonprofit and non-governmental purpose is to take action to combat global corruption with civil societal anti-corruption measures and to prevent criminal activities arising from corruption.

Head – Delia Ferreira Rubio

INTERNATIONAL RENEWABLE ENERGY AGENCY

Establishment – 26 January, 2009

Headquarter -- Abu Dhabi (UAE)

Objectives -- IRENA promotes the widespread adoption and sustainable use of all forms of renewable energy, including bioenergy, geothermal, hydropower, ocean, solar and wind energy in the pursuit of sustainable development, energy access, energy security and low-carbon economic growth and prosperity.

Members – 166

Head – Francesco La Camera

SOUTH ASIAN ASSOCIATION FOR REGIONAL COOPERATION (SAARC)

Establishment – 8 December, 1985

Headquarter -- Kathmandu, Nepal

Objectives -- The objectives of the Association as outlined in the SAARC Charter are: to promote the welfare of the peoples of South Asia and to improve their quality of life; to accelerate economic growth, social progress and cultural development in the region and to provide all individuals the opportunity to live in dignity and to realize their full potentials; to promote and strengthen collective self-reliance among the countries of South Asia; to contribute to mutual trust, understanding and appreciation of one another's problems; to promote active collaboration and mutual assistance in the economic, social, cultural, technical and scientific fields; to strengthen cooperation with other developing countries; to strengthen cooperation among themselves in international forums on matters of common interests; and to cooperate with international and regional organizations with similar aims and purposes.

Members – 8

Head – Esala Weerakoon

ORGANIZATION OF ISLAMIC COOPERATION

Establishment – 25 September, 1969

Headquarter -- Jeddah, Saudi Arabia

Objectives -- According to its charter, the OIC aims to preserve Islamic social and economic values; promote solidarity amongst member states; increase cooperation in social, economic, cultural, scientific, and political areas; uphold international peace and security; and advance education, particularly in the fields of science and technology.

Members – 57

Head – Yousef bin Ahmad Al-Othaimeen

INDIAN OCEAN RIM ASSOCIATION FOR REGIONAL COOPERATION

Establishment – 7 March, 1997

Headquarter -- Ebene, Mauritius

Objectives -- To promote sustainable growth and balanced development of the region and member states. To focus on those areas of economic cooperation which provide maximum opportunities for development, shared interest and mutual benefits.

Members – 23

Head – Dr. Gatot Hari Gunawan

ORGANIZATION FOR THE PROHIBITION OF CHEMICAL WEAPONS

Establishment – 29 April, 1997

Headquarter -- The Hague, The Netherlands

Objectives -- The ultimate aim of the OPCW is to achieve a world permanently free of chemical weapons and to contribute to international security and stability, general and complete disarmament, and global economic development.

Members – 193

Head – Mr Fernando Arias

INTERNATIONAL OLYMPIC COMMITTEE

Establishment – 25 June, 1894

Headquarter -- Lausanne, Switzerland

Objectives -- The mission of the IOC is to lead the Olympic Movement for sound development throughout the world, promote ethics and act against discrimination and violence in sport, encourage fair play, promote sustainable development in sport, and use sport to improve well-being and promote peace.

Members – 102 active members, 44 honorary members, 1 honour member (United States), 206 NOCs officially recognised by the IOC

Head – Thomas Bach

Establishment – January 1971

Headquarter -- Cologny-Geneva, Switzerland

Objectives -- The World Economic Forum is the International Organization for Public-Private Cooperation. The Forum engages the foremost political, business, cultural and other leaders of society to shape global, regional and industry agendas.

Head – Professor Klaus Schwab

UNITED NATIONS ENVIRONMENT PROGRAMME (UNEP)

Establishment – 5 June, 1972

Headquarter -- Nairobi, Kenya

Objectives -- UNEP's mission is to provide leadership and encourage partnership in caring for the environment by inspiring, informing, and enabling nations and peoples to improve their quality of life without compromising that of future generations.

Members – 193

Head – Inger Andersen

UNITED NATIONS HIGH COMMISSIONER FOR REFUGEES (UNHCR)

Establishment – 14 December, 1950

Headquarter -- Geneva, Switzerland

Objectives -- UNHCR's goal is to guarantee the fundamental rules accepted by all States concerning the right of individuals to flee their country and seek asylum in another. To this end, it helps States face the administrative, legal, diplomatic, financial and human problems that are caused by the refugee phenomenon.

Head – Filippo Grandi

UNITED NATIONS OFFICE ON DRUGS AND CRIME (UNODC)

Establishment – 1997

Headquarter -- Vienna, Austria

Objectives -- The broad objective of GPML, as a unit within the United Nations Office on Drugs and Crime (UNODC), is to strengthen the ability of UN Member States to implement measures in anti-money laundering and countering the financing of terrorism (AML/CFT) and to assist them in detecting, seizing and confiscating illicit proceeds.

Head – Ghada Fathi Waly

UN OFFICE FOR DISASTER RISK REDUCTION (UNDRR)

Establishment – 22 December, 1999

Headquarter -- Geneva, Switzerland

Objectives -- The prevention of new and reduction of existing disaster risk and strengthening resilience through successful multi-hazard disaster risk management.

Members – 168

Head – Mami Mizutori

Establishment – 4 April, 1947

Headquarter -- Montreal, Canada

Objectives -- ICAO's aims and objectives, as stated in the Chicago Convention, are to foster the planning and development of international air transport so as to ensure the safe and orderly growth of international civil aviation throughout the world; encourage the arts of aircraft design and operation for peaceful purposes; encourage the development of airways, airports, and air navigation facilities for international civil aviation; meet the needs of the peoples of the world for safe, regular, efficient, and economical air transport; prevent economic waste caused by unreasonable competition; ensure that the rights of contracting states are fully respected and that every contracting state has a fair opportunity to operate international airlines; avoid discrimination between contracting states; promote safety of flight in international air navigation; and promote generally the development of all aspects of international civil aeronautics.

Members – 193

Head – Salvatore Sciacchitano

UNITED NATIONS DEVELOPMENT PROGRAMME (UNDP)

Establishment – 22 November, 1965

Headquarter -- New York, USA

Objectives -- UNDP's overall goal is to contribute to sustainable human development. UNDP has four focus areas in its mandate: poverty reduction, democratic governance, environment and energy, and crisis prevention and recovery.

Members – 170

Head – Achim Steiner

INTERNATIONAL FUND FOR AGRICULTURAL DEVELOPMENT (IFAD)

Establishment – December 1977

Headquarter -- Rome, Italy

Objectives -- IFAD's work aims to catalyse country and global progress for rural people to overcome poverty and achieve food security through remunerative, sustainable and resilient livelihoods.

Members – 177

Head – Kanayo F. Nwanze, Gilbert Houngbo

INTERNATIONAL TELECOMMUNICATION UNION (ITU)

Establishment – 17 May, 1865

Headquarter -- Geneva, Switzerland

Objectives -- The overall objectives of the International Telecommunication Union (ITU) are to promote the development of telecommunication networks and access to telecommunication services by fostering cooperation among governments and a range of non-governmental actors that includes network operators, service providers, equipment manufacturers, scientific and technical organisations, financial organisations and development organisations.

Members – 193

Head – Houlin Zhao

Establishment – 1 November, 1975

Headquarter -- Madrid, Spain

Objectives -- Through tourism, UNWTO aims at stimulating economic growth and job creation, providing incentives, protecting the environment, and cultural heritage, promoting peace, prosperity, and respect for rights.

Members – 159

Head – Zurab Pololikashvili

INTERNATIONAL COURT OF JUSTICE (ICJ)

Establishment – 26 June, 1945

Headquarter -- The Hague, Netherlands

Objectives -- The Court's role is to settle, in accordance with international law, legal disputes submitted to it by States and to give advisory opinions on legal questions referred to it by authorized United Nations organs and specialized agencies.

Members – 193

Head – Judge Joan E. Donoghue

UNITED NATIONS CONFERENCE ON TRADE AND DEVELOPMENT (UNCTAD)

Establishment – 30 December, 1964

Headquarter -- Geneva, Switzerland

Objectives -- The main goals of UNCTAD are to expand the capabilities of developing countries in the sphere of trade, investment and development, to assist them in overcoming the difficulties arisen as a result of globalization and to integrate on an equal footing into the world economy.

Members – 195

Head – Rebeca Grynspan

UN-HABITAT

Establishment – 1978

Headquarter -- Nairobi, Kenya

Objectives -- The United Nations Human Settlements Programme, UN-Habitat, is the United Nations agency for human settlements. It is mandated by the UN General Assembly to promote socially and environmentally sustainable towns and cities with the goal of providing adequate shelter for all.

Members – 58

Head – Maimunah Mohd Sharif

WORLD FOOD PROGRAMME (WFP)

Establishment – 1961

Headquarter -- Rome, Italy

Objectives -- WFP's mission is to provide access to food to hungry men, women and children in situations of acute and chronic food insecurity, thus contributing to the Millennium Development Goal of halving the number of people who suffer from hunger by the year 2015.

Head – David Beasley

Establishment – 20 December, 1993

Headquarter -- Geneva, Switzerland

Objectives -- The mandate of the Office of the High Commissioner for Human Rights (OHCHR) is to ensure universal enjoyment of all human rights, to remove obstacles to their effective implementation, and to enhance coordination and cooperation of human rights-related activities throughout the United Nations system.

Members – 47

Head – Michelle Bachelet

INTERNATIONAL CRIMINAL POLICE ORGANIZATION (INTERPOL)

Establishment – 7 September 1923

Headquarter – Lyon, France

Objectives -- INTERPOL's role is to enable police in our 194 member countries to work together to make the world a safer place. We provide secure access to global databases containing police information on criminals and crime, operational and forensic support, analytical services and training.

Members – 194

Head – Kim Jong Yang

Development of Technology

Invention/ Discovery	Inventor	Date
Centigrade scale	Anders Celsius	–
Watch	Peter Henlein	–
Amplitude Modulation	Reginald Fessiden	–
Barometer	Evangelista Torricelli	–
Railway Engine	George Stephenson	–
Rocket Engine	Robert Goddard	–
Taxol	Monroe Wall and Mansukh Wani	–
Anesthesia	William Morton	–
Pasteurization	Louis Pasteur	–
Polio Vaccine	Jonas Edward Stalk	–
Anthrax Vaccine	Louis Pasteur	–
Homeopathy & Allopathy	Samuel Hahnemann	–
Nucleus	Robert Brown	–
Printing Press	Johannes Gutenberg	1440
Anemometer(wind speed)	Leon Battista Alberti	1450
Telescope	Hans Lippershey and Zacharias Janssen; later Galileo	1608
Calculator	Blaise Pascal	1642
Cell	Robert Hooke	1665
Gravity	Sir Isaac Newton	1687
Steam engine	Thomas Newcomen	1698
Thermometer	Gabriel Farenheit	1714
Osmosis	Jean Antoine Nollet	1748
Electricity	Benjamin Franklin	1759

Hydrogen	Henry Cavendish	1766
Oxygen	Carl Wilhelm	1773
Battery	Alessandro Volta	1799
Atoms	John Dalton	1803
Calcium	Humphrey Davy	1808
Camera	Nicéphore Niépce	1816
Galvanometer	Johann Schweigger	1820
Electromagnetic induction	Michael Faraday	1830
Telegraph	Samuel Morse	1830
Electric Generator	Michael Faraday	1831
Seismograph	John Milne	1839
Lift	Elisha Otis	1853
Diesel Engine	Rudolf Diesel	1858
Dynamite	Alfred Nobel	1867
Periodic Table	Dmitri Mendeleev	1869
Air Brake	Westinghouse	1869
Telephone	Alexander Graham Bell	1876
Typewriter	Christopher Latham Sholes	1878
Electric Bulb	Thomas Edison	1879
Ionic Bonds	Svante August Arrhenius	1884
Automobile	Karl Benz	1885
Transformer	Michael Faraday	1885
Induction motor	Nikola Tesla	1885
Aluminium	Charles Martin Hall	1886
LCD	George H. Heilmeier	1888
Cholera Vaccine	Waldemar Haffkine	1892
Inert Gases	Sir William Ramsay	1894
Radio	Guglielmo Marconi	1895
X-Ray	William Rontgen	1895
Radioactivity	Henri Becquerel	1896
Cathode Ray Tube	Ferdinand Braun	1897

Electrons	JJ Thompson	1897
Radium	Marie slodo	1898
Aspirin	Felix Hofmann	1899
Blood Group	Karl Landsteiner	1900
Air conditioner	Willis Carrier	1902
Airplane	Wright Brothers	1903
Synthetic Rubber	Fritz Hofmann	1909
Protons	Ernest Rutherford	1911
Vitamin	Casimir Funk	1912
Quantum Mechanics	Werner Heisenberg, Max Born, and Pascual Jordan	1924
Television	John Logie Baird	1927
Refrigerator	William Cullen	1927
Penicillin	Alexander Fleming	1928
Polythene	Eric Fawcett	1933
PH Meter	Arnold O. Beckman	1934
Acid (LSD)	Albert hofmann	1938
Radar	Sir Robert Alexander Watson-Watt	1939
Titanium	William Kroll	1940
Nuclear Reactor	Enrico Fermi	1942
Transistor	John Bardeen, Walter brattain, and William Shockley	1947
Atomic bomb	Robert Oppenheimer, Edward Teller et al	1945
LED	Oleg Losev, Nick Holonyak	1962
Rubella Vaccine	Maurice Hilleman	1963
Laser	Theodore H. Maiman	1969
Mobile Phone	Martin Cooper	1973
DNA sequencer	Lloyd M. Smith	1987

Artificial Intelligence

◄ Artificial intelligence (AI) is the ability of a digital computer or computer-controlled robot to perform tasks commonly associated with intelligent beings.

◄ The term is frequently applied to the project of developing systems endowed with the intellectual processes characteristic of humans, such as the ability to reason, discover meaning, generalize, or learn from past experience.

◄ Since the development of the digital computer in the 1940s, it has been demonstrated that computers can be programmed to carry out very complex tasks—as, for example, discovering proofs for mathematical theorems or playing chess—with great proficiency.

◄ Despite continuing advances in computer processing speed and memory capacity, there are as yet no programs that can match human flexibility over wider domains or in tasks requiring much everyday knowledge.

◄ On the other hand, some programs have attained the performance levels of human experts and professionals in performing certain specific tasks, so that artificial intelligence in this limited sense is found in applications as diverse as medical diagnosis, computer search engines, and voice or handwriting recognition.

Machine Learning

◄ Machine learning (ML) is a type of artificial intelligence (AI) that allows software applications to become more accurate at predicting outcomes without being explicitly programmed to do so. Machine learning algorithms use historical data as input to predict new output values.

◄ Recommendation engines are a common use case for machine learning.

◄ Other popular uses include fraud detection, spam filtering, malware threat detection, business process automation (BPA) and predictive maintenance.

◄ Machine learning is important because it gives enterprises a view of trends in customer behaviour and business operational patterns, as well as supports the development of new products.

◄ Many of today's leading companies, such as Facebook, Google and Uber, make machine learning a central part of their operations. Machine learning has become a significant competitive differentiator for many companies.

Robotic Process Automation (RPA)

◄ With RPA, software users create software robots, or "bots", that can learn, mimic, and then execute rules-based business processes.

◄ RPA automation enables users to create bots by observing human digital actions. Show your bots what to do, then let them do the work.

◄ Robotic Process Automation software bots can interact with any application or system the same way people do—except that RPA bots can operate around the clock, nonstop, much faster and with 100% reliability and precision.

◄ Robotic Process Automation bots have the same digital skillset as people—and then some.

◄ For example, bots are able to copy-paste, scrape web data, make calculations, open and move files, parse emails, log into programs, connect to APIs, and extract unstructured data.

◄ Bots can adapt to any interface or workflow, there's no need to change business systems, applications, or existing processes in order to automate.

◄ RPA bots are easy to set up, use, and share. If you know how to record video on your phone, you'll be able to configure RPA bots. It's as intuitive as hitting record, play, and stop buttons and using drag-and-drop to move files around at work.

◁ RPA bots can be scheduled, cloned, customized, and shared to execute business processes throughout the organization.

Edge Computing

◁ Edge computing is a form of computing that is done on site or near a particular data source, minimizing the need for data to be processed in a remote data center.

◁ The origins of edge computing are in the 1990s with the creation of the first content delivery network (CDN), which put data collecting nodes closer to end users.

◁ But this technology was limited to images and videos, not massive workloads of data.

◁ In the 2000s, the increased shift to mobile and early smart devices increased the strain on existing IT infrastructure.

◁ Edge computing use case examples include Autonomous vehicles, Remote monitoring of assets in the oil and gas industry, Smart grid, Predictive maintenance, In-hospital patient monitoring, Virtualised radio networks and 5G (vRAN), Cloud gaming, Content delivery.

◁ Yet, with more end users demanding cloud-based applications and more businesses working from multiple locations, it became necessary to process more data outside of the data center right at the source and manage it from one central location. That's when mobile edge computing became a reality.

Cloud Computing

◁ Cloud computing is the delivery of computing services—including servers, storage, databases, networking, software, analytics, and intelligence—over the Internet ("the cloud") to offer faster innovation, flexible resources, and economies of scale.

◁ Cloud computing is a big shift from the traditional way businesses think about IT resources.

◁ Cloud computing eliminates the capital expense of buying hardware and software and setting up and running on-site datacenters—the racks of servers, the round-the-clock electricity for power and cooling, the IT experts for managing the infrastructure.

◁ Most cloud computing services are provided self service and on demand, so even vast amounts of computing resources can be provisioned in minutes, typically with just a few mouse clicks, giving businesses a lot of flexibility and taking the pressure off capacity planning.

◁ The benefits of cloud computing services include the ability to scale elastically.

◁ The biggest cloud computing services run on a worldwide network of secure datacenters, which are regularly upgraded to the latest generation of fast and efficient computing hardware.

◁ Cloud computing makes data backup, disaster recovery and business continuity easier and less expensive.

◁ Many cloud providers offer a broad set of policies, technologies and controls that strengthen your security posture.

Quantum Computing

- Quantum computing is an area of computing focused on developing computer technology based on the principles of quantum theory (which explains the behaviour of energy and material on the atomic and subatomic levels).

- Computers used today can only encode information in bits that take the value of 1 or 0—restricting their ability. Quantum computing, on the other hand, uses quantum bits or qubits.

- It harnesses the unique ability of subatomic particles that allows them to exist in more than one state (i.e., a 1 and a 0 at the same time).

- Quantum computing is the study of how to use phenomena in quantum physics to create new ways of computing.

- The power of quantum computers grows exponentially with more qubits.

- This is unlike classical computers, where adding more transistors only adds power linearly.

Virtual Reality and Augmented Reality

- Virtual reality (VR) is an artificial, computer-generated simulation or recreation of a real life environment or situation.

- It immerses the user by making them feel like they are experiencing the simulated reality firsthand, primarily by stimulating their vision and hearing.

- VR is typically achieved by wearing a headset like Facebook's Oculus equipped with the technology, and is used prominently in two different ways: to create and enhance an imaginary reality for gaming, entertainment, and play (Such as video and computer games, or 3D movies, head mounted display).

- Augmented reality (AR) is a technology that layers computer-generated enhancements atop an existing reality in order to make it more meaningful through the ability to interact with it.

- AR is developed into apps and used on mobile devices to blends digital components into the real world in such a way that they enhance one another, but can also be told apart easily.

Blockchain

- Blockchain is a specific type of database.

- It differs from a typical database in the way it stores information; blockchains store data in blocks that are then chained together.

- As new data comes in, it is entered into a fresh block.

- Once the block is filled with data it is chained onto the previous block, which makes the data chained together in chronological order.

- Different types of information can be stored on a blockchain but the most common use so far has been as a ledger for transactions.

- In Bitcoin's case, blockchain is used in a decentralized way so that no single person or group has control—rather, all users collectively retain control.

- Decentralized blockchains are immutable, which means that the data entered is irreversible. For Bitcoin, this means that transactions are permanently recorded and viewable to anyone.

Internet of Things (IoT)

- The Internet of Things is the concept of connecting any device (so long as it has an on/off switch) to the Internet and to other connected devices.
- The IoT is a giant network of connected things and people – all of which collect and share data about the way they are used and about the environment around them.
- That includes an extraordinary number of objects of all shapes and sizes – from smart microwaves, which automatically cook your food for the right length of time, to self-driving cars, whose complex sensors detect objects in their path, etc.
- There are even connected footballs that can track how far and fast they are thrown and record those statistics via an app for future training purposes.
- Devices and objects with built in sensors are connected to an Internet of Things platform, which integrates data from the different devices and applies analytics to share the most valuable information with applications built to address specific needs.

5G

- 5G is the 5th generation mobile network. It is a new global wireless standard after 1G, 2G, 3G, and 4G networks.
- 5G enables a new kind of network that is designed to connect virtually everyone and everything together including machines, objects, and devices.
- 5G wireless technology is meant to deliver higher multi-Gbps peak data speeds, ultra low latency, more reliability, massive network capacity, increased availability, and a more uniform user experience to more users.
- Higher performance and improved efficiency empower new user experiences and connects new industries.
- Like 4G LTE, 5G OFDM operates based on the same mobile networking principles. However, the new 5G NR air interface can further enhance OFDM to deliver a much higher degree of flexibility and scalability.
- This could provide more 5G access to more people and things for a variety of different use cases.

Cyber Security

- Cyber security is the practice of defending computers, servers, mobile devices, electronic systems, networks, and data from malicious attacks.
- It's also known as information technology security or electronic information security.
- The term applies in a variety of contexts, from business to mobile computing, and can be divided into a few common categories.
- Network security is the practice of securing a computer network from intruders, whether targeted attackers or opportunistic malware.
- Application security focuses on keeping software and devices free of threats.
- A compromised application could provide access to the data it's designed to protect.
- Successful security begins in the design stage, well before a program or device is deployed.
- One of the most common cyber threats, malware is software that a cybercriminal or hacker has created to disrupt or damage a legitimate user's computer.
- Those include Virus, Trojans, Spyware, Ransomware, Adware, Botnets, etc.

Other Inventions in the Field of IT

Invention	Inventor	Year
World Wide Web	Tim Berners and Robert Cailliau	1989
Search Engine	Alan Emtage	1990
Cable modem	Rouzbeh Yassini	–
Webcam	Quentin straford Fraser and Paul Jardetzky	1991
Smartphone	IBM	1992
JAVA	James Gosling	–
Surface Computing	Microsoft	2007
TCP/IP	Bob Kahn and Vint Cerf	–
Email	Ray Tomlinson	1971
Google	Larry Page and Sergey Brin	1998
Laptop	Adam Osborne	1981
C Language	Dennis Ritchie	1972
Python	Guido Van Rossum	1991
C++	Bjarne Stroustrup	1983
Facebook	Mark Zukerburg	2004
Yahoo	Jerry Yang and David Filo	1994
GPS	Ivan A. Getting Roger Bradford Parkinson	1995

SPACE

Major Milestones

◄ The first artificial Earth satellite, Sputnik 1, was launched by the Soviet Union on October 4, 1957.

◄ The first human to go into space, Yuri Gagarin, was launched, again by the Soviet Union, for a one-orbit journey around Earth on April 12, 1961.

◄ Within 10 years of that first human flight, American astronauts walked on the surface of the Moon.

◄ Apollo 11 crew members Neil Armstrong and Edwin ("Buzz") Aldrin made the first lunar landing on July 20, 1969.

◄ A total of 12 Americans on six separate Apollo missions set foot on the Moon between July 1969 and December 1972.

◄ Since then, no humans have left Earth orbit, but more than 500 men and women have spent as many as 438 consecutive days in space.

- Starting in the early 1970s, a series of Soviet (Russian from December 1991) space stations, the U.S. Skylab station, and numerous space shuttle flights provided Earth-orbiting bases for varying periods of human occupancy and activity.

- From November 2, 2000, when its first crew took up residence, to its completion in 2011, the International Space Station (ISS) served as a base for humans living and working in space on a permanent basis. It will continue to be used in this way until at least 2024.

Significant Milestones in Space Exploration

Date Accomplished	Event	Details	Country or Agency
Oct. 4, 1957	first artificial Earth satellite	Sputnik 1;	U.S.S.R.
Nov. 3, 1957;	first animal launched into space;	dog Laika aboard Sputnik 2;	U.S.S.R.
Sept. 14, 1959	first spacecraft to hard-land on another celestial object (the Moon)	Luna 2	U.S.S.R.
Oct. 7, 1959	first pictures of the far side of the Moon	Luna 3	U.S.S.R.
April 1, 1960	first applications satellite launched	TIROS 1 (weather observation)	U.S.
Aug. 11, 1960	first recovery of a payload from Earth orbit	Discoverer 13 (part of Corona reconnaissance satellite program)	U.S.
April 12, 1961	first human to orbit Earth	Yury Gagarin on Vostok 1	U.S.S.R.
Dec. 14, 1962	first data returned from another planet (Venus)	Mariner 2	U.S.
June 16, 1963	first woman in space	Valentina Tereshkova on Vostok 6	U.S.S.R.
July 26, 1963	first satellite to operate in geostationary orbit	Syncom 2 (telecommunications satellite)	U.S.
March 18, 1965	first space walk	Aleksey Leonov on Voskhod 2	U.S.S.R.
July 14, 1965	first spacecraft pictures of Mars	Mariner 4	U.S.

Date Accomplished	Event	Details	Country or Agency
Feb. 3, 1966	first spacecraft to soft-land on the Moon	Luna 9	U.S.S.R.
April 24, 1967	first death during a space mission	Vladimir Komarov on Soyuz 1	U.S.S.R.
Dec. 24, 1968	first humans to orbit the Moon	Frank Borman, James Lovell, and William Anders on Apollo 8	U.S.
July 20, 1969	first human to walk on the Moon	Neil Armstrong on Apollo 11	U.S.
Sept. 24, 1970	first return of lunar samples by an unmanned spacecraft	Luna 16	U.S.S.R.
Dec. 15, 1970	first soft landing on another planet (Venus)	Venera 7	U.S.S.R.
April 19, 1971	first space station launched	Salyut 1	U.S.S.R.
Nov. 13, 1971	first spacecraft to orbit another planet (Mars)	Mariner 9	U.S.
Dec. 2, 1971	first spacecraft to soft-land on Mars	Mars 3	U.S.S.R.
Dec. 3, 1973	first spacecraft to fly by Jupiter	Pioneer 10	U.S.
July 17, 1975	first international docking in space	Apollo and Soyuz spacecraft during Apollo-Soyuz Test Project	U.S., U.S.S.R.
July 20, 1976	first pictures transmitted from the surface of Mars	Viking 1	U.S.
Sept. 1, 1979	first spacecraft to fly by Saturn	Pioneer 11	U.S.
April 12–14, 1981	first reusable spacecraft launched and returned from space	Space shuttle Columbia	U.S.
Jan. 24, 1986	first spacecraft to fly by Uranus	Voyager 2	U.S.

Date Accomplished	Event	Details	Country or Agency
March 13, 1986	first spacecraft to make a close flyby of a comet nucleus	Giotto at Halley's Comet	European Space Agency
Aug. 24, 1989	first spacecraft to fly by Neptune	Voyager 2	U.S.
April 25, 1990	first large optical space telescope launched	Hubble Space Telescope	U.S., European Space Agency
Dec. 7, 1995	first spacecraft to orbit Jupiter	Galileo	U.S.
Nov. 2, 2000	first resident crew to occupy the International Space Station	William Shepherd, Yury Gidzenko, and Sergey Krikalyov	U.S., Russia
Feb. 14, 2000; Feb. 12, 2001	first spacecraft to orbit (2000) and land on (2001) an asteroid	NEAR at the asteroid Eros	U.S.
June 21, 2004	first privately funded manned spacecraft to achieve suborbital flight above 100 km (62 miles)	Mike Melvill on SpaceShipOne	Mojave Aerospace Ventures (commercial joint venture)
July 1, 2004	first spacecraft to orbit Saturn	Cassini-Huygens	U.S., European Space Agency, Italy
Jan. 14, 2005	first spacecraft to land on the moon of a planet other than Earth (Saturn's moon Titan)	Huygens probe of the Cassini-Huygens spacecraft	U.S., European Space Agency, Italy
June 13, 2010	first spacecraft to return to Earth with samples from an asteroid	Hayabusa	Japan
March 17, 2011	first spacecraft to orbit Mercury	Messenger	U.S.

Date Accomplished	Event	Details	Country or Agency
August 6, 2014	first spacecraft to orbit a comet	Rosetta	European Space Agency
November 12, 2014	first spacecraft to land on a comet	Philae	European Space Agency
March 6, 2015	first spacecraft to orbit a dwarf planet (Ceres)	Dawn	U.S.
July 14, 2015	first spacecraft to fly by Pluto	New Horizons	U.S.
December 21, 2015	first rocket stage to return to its launch site	Falcon 9	U.S.
January 1, 2019	farthest object (2014 MU69) explored by a spacecraft	New Horizons	U.S.
January 3, 2019	first landing on the Moon's far side	Chang'e 4	China

Major Military Inventions

Name	Date invented	Invented by	Original purpose
ASDIC	1910s	United Kingdom France	Submarine detection
Radar	mid-1930s	United Kingdom	Early warning radar, air defence systems
Walkie-talkie	1930s	Canada (Donald Hings) United States (Alfred J. Gross, Motorola SCR-300)	Portable two-way radio communications system for military
Night vision	1939 - 1940s	Nazi Germany United States	Visibility for military personnel in low light situations
Ballistic missiles	1940s	Nazi Germany Soviet Union	Long range attack

Name	Date invented	Invented by	Original purpose
Nuclear technology	1940s	United States United Kingdom Canada (Manhattan Project)	Nuclear weapons
Jet engine	1940s	Nazi Germany (Hans von Ohain) United Kingdom (Frank Whittle)	Jet fighters, jet bombers
Satellite navigation	1970s	United States Air Force Soviet Union	Nuclear weapons force multiplier, increased warhead accuracy through precise navigation

THE WORLD'S 20 STRONGEST MILITARIES

United States	**Budget**: $601 billion **Active frontline personnel**: 1,400,000 **Tanks**: 8,848 **Total aircraft**: 13,892 **Submarines**: 72

- Despite sequestration and other spending cuts, the United States spends more money — $601 billion — on defence than the next nine countries on Credit Suisse's index combined.

- America's biggest conventional military advantage is its fleet of 10 aircraft carriers.

- In comparison India, which is constructing its third carrier, has the second-most carriers in the world.

- The US also has by far the most aircraft of any country, cutting-edge technology like the Navy's new rail gun, a large and well-trained human force — and that's not even counting the world's largest nuclear arsenal.

Russia	**Budget**: $84.5 billion **Active frontline personnel**: 766,055 **Tanks**: 15,398 **Total aircraft**: 3,429 **Submarines**: 55

- The Russian armed forces are the unquestioned second strongest military power in the world.

- Russia has the world's largest tank fleet, the second largest aircraft fleet behind the US, and the third largest submarine fleet behind the US and China.

- The Kremlin's military spending has increased by almost a third since 2008 and is expected to grow 44% more in the next three years.

- Russia has also demonstrated its ability to project force abroad with its deployment of soldiers to Syria.

China	Budget: $216 billion Active frontline personnel: 2,333,000 Tanks: 9,150 Total aircraft: 2,860 Submarines: 67

◄ The Chinese military has grown rapidly in terms of both size and capability in the past few decades.

◄ In terms of raw manpower, it's the largest military in the world.

◄ It also has the second largest tank fleet behind Russia and the second largest submarine fleet behind the US.

◄ China has also made rapid strides in its military modernization program, now developing a range of potentially game-changing military technologies including ballistic missiles and fifth-generation aircraft.

Japan	Budget: $41.6 billion Active frontline personnel: 247,173 Tanks: 678 Total aircraft: 1,613 Submarines: 16

◄ In absolute terms, the Japanese military is relatively small. Nonetheless, the country is extremely well equipped.

◄ According to Credit Suisse, it has the fourth largest submarine fleet in the list.

◄ Japan also has four aircraft carriers, although these vessels are only equipped with helicopter fleets.

◄ Japan also has the fourth largest attack helicopter fleet behind China, Russia, and the US.

India	Budget: $50 billion Active frontline personnel: 1,325,000 Tanks: 6,464 Total aircraft: 1,905 Submarines: 15

◄ India is one of the largest military powers on the planet.

◄ It has the most active manpower of any country aside from China and the US, in addition to the most tanks and aircraft of any country besides the US, China, or Russia.

◄ India also has access to nuclear weapons.

France	Budget: $62.3 billion Active frontline personnel: 202,761 Tanks: 423 Total aircraft: 1,264 Submarines: 10

- ◄ The French military is relatively small but highly trained, professional, and capable of force projection.

- ◄ The country has the nearly new aircraft carrier the Charles de Gaulle, and France routinely engages in military deployments throughout Africa to help stabilize governments and fight against extremism.

South Korea	Budget: $62.3 billion
	Active frontline personnel: 624,465
	Tanks: 2,381
	Total aircraft: 1,412
	Submarines: 13

- ◄ South Korea has been left with little choice but to have a large and capable military in the face of potential North Korean aggression.

- ◄ With those realities in mind, South Korea has a number of submarines, attack helicopters, and active personnel.

- ◄ The country also has numerous tanks and the sixth largest air force in the world.

Italy	Budget: $34 billion
	Active frontline personnel: 320,000
	Tanks: 586
	Total aircraft: 760
	Submarines: 6

- ◄ The Italian military placed highly on Credit Suisse's report due to the country's possession of two active aircraft carriers.

- ◄ These carriers, in addition to the country's relatively large submarine and attack helicopter fleets, drastically boosted Italy's ranking.

United Kingdom	Budget: $60.5 billion
	Active frontline personnel: 146,980
	Tanks: 407
	Total aircraft: 936
	Submarines: 10

- ◄ Although the UK is planning to reduce the size of its armed forces by 20% between 2010 and 2018, it can count on being able to project its power around the world.

The Royal Navy is planning to put the HMS Queen Elizabeth, an aircraft carrier that has a flight deck measuring at 4.5 acres, into service in 2020, carrying 40 F-35B joint strike fighters across the globe.

Turkey	Budget: $18.2 billion
	Active frontline personnel: 410,500
	Tanks: 3,778
	Total aircraft: 1,020
	Submarines: 13

◄ Turkey's armed forces are one of the largest in the eastern Mediterranean.

◄ Although lacking an aircraft carrier, only five countries on Credit Suisse's list have more submarines than Turkey.

◄ In addition, the country can lay claim to an impressively large tank fleet as well as numerous aircraft and attack helicopters.

◄ Turkey is also a committed member of the F-35 program.

Pakistan	**Budget:** $7 billion **Active frontline personnel:** 617,000 **Tanks:** 2,924 **Total aircraft:** 914 **Submarines:** 8

◄ The Pakistani military is one of the largest forces in the world, in terms of active personnel.

◄ Credit Suisse also credits the country with having large tank, aircraft, and attack helicopter fleets.

◄ In addition, Pakistan is thought to be building nuclear weapons at a fast enough rate that it could have the world's third largest nuclear arsenal within the following decade.

Egypt	**Budget:** $4.4 billion **Active frontline personnel:** 468,500 **Tanks:** 4,624 **Total aircraft:** 1,107 **Submarines:** 4

◄ The Egyptian military is one of the oldest and largest armed forces in the Middle East.

◄ It receives substantial financial aid from the US and has the fifth largest tank fleet in the world.

◄ It has over 1,000 M1A1 Abrams tanks, many of which sit in storage and have never been used.

◄ Egypt also has a relatively large aircraft force.

Taiwan	**Budget:** $10.7 billion **Active frontline personnel:** 290,000 **Tanks:** 2,005 **Total aircraft:** 804 **Submarines:** 4

◄ Threatened by China, which continues to have plans for how to invade and retake the country, Tawain has focused its military development on defensive plans.

◄ The island has the fifth highest number of attack helicopters in the list. It also has a fairly large fleet of aircraft and a number of tanks.

Israel	Budget: $17 billion
	Active frontline personnel: 160,000
	Tanks: 4,170
	Total aircraft: 684
	Submarines: 5

- In absolute terms, Israel has a small military. But with mandatory military service a large percentage of the Israeli population is militarily ready.

- With a past history of being surrounded by aggressive neighbours, Israel also has a large tank, aircraft, and attack helicopter fleet.

- Israel also has qualitative military advantages. It has space assets, advanced fighter jets, high-tech armed drones, and nuclear weapons.

Australia	Budget: $26.1 billion
	Active frontline personnel: 58,000
	Tanks: 59
	Total aircraft: 408
	Submarines: 6

- Australia's military is comparatively small — it receives bottom scores on the report for the number of active personnel and the number of tanks.

- It also receives near bottom scores for the number of aircraft it has in its fleet.

- Credit Suisse boosts Australia's ranking due to its attack helicopters and submarines though.

Thailand	Budget: $5.39 billion
	Active frontline personnel: 306,000
	Tanks: 722
	Total aircraft: 573
	Submarines: 0

- Thailand's military is currently in control of the country following a coup in May 2014.

- The military is a major player in maintaining Thai unity, and Thailand receives strong scores from Credit Suisse for its number of active personnel, its number of tanks, and its possession of an aircraft carrier.

- Thailand also scores well as it has an aircraft carrier, although it does not have an aircraft fleet to complement the vessel.

Poland	Budget: $9.4 billion
	Active frontline personnel: 120,000
	Tanks: 1,009
	Total aircraft: 467
	Submarines: 5

- Poland edges out Germany in the list due to its larger number of tanks and a more fleshed out submarine fleet.

◅ Poland has also drastically increased its military spending in reaction to Russia's seizure of Crimea and the ongoing Ukraine crisis.

Germany	Budget: $40.2 billion
	Active frontline personnel: 179,046
	Tanks: 408
	Total aircraft: 663
	Submarines: 4

◅ The German military ended up low on the list due to their lack of power projection platforms.

◅ Germany does not have an aircraft carrier and has relatively few submarines which, according to the Credit Suisse methodology, drops its ranking.

◅ Germany does have a fair number of attack helicopters. Recently, the country has started considering offering military support to eastern European NATO members.

Indonesia	Budget: $6.9 billion
	Active frontline personnel: 476,000
	Tanks: 468
	Total aircraft: 405
	Submarines: 2

◅ The Indonesian military placed above Canada due its high numbers of active personnel and its relatively large number of tanks.

◅ The military, however, suffers from a lack of carriers and aircraft, as well as a minute number of submarines.

Canada	Budget: $15.7 billion
	Active frontline personnel: 92,000
	Tanks: 181
	Total aircraft: 420
	Submarines: 4

◅ Canada ended up at the bottom of the list due to the country's small number of active personnel, its lack of aircraft carriers and attack helicopters, and its small number of tanks and submarines.

◅ Canada has still taken part in US operations in Afghanistan and Iraq and it is a member of the NATO military alliance.

◅ Canada is also a partner in the US F-35 program, although it may decline the purchase of F-35s depending upon the outcome of elections in October.

Major Environmental Issues

Air Pollution

◄ Air pollution is a type of environmental pollution that affects the air and is usually caused by smoke or other harmful gases, mainly oxides of carbon, sulphur and nitrogen.

◄ In other words, air pollution is the contamination of air due to the presence or introduction of a substance which has a poisonous effect.

◄ There are many different types of air pollutants, such as gases (including ammonia, carbon monoxide, sulfur dioxide, nitrous oxides, methane, carbon dioxide and chlorofluorocarbons), particulates (both organic and inorganic), and biological molecules.

◄ Air pollution may cause diseases, allergies and even death to humans; it may also cause harm to other living organisms such as animals and food crops, and may damage the natural environment (for example, climate change, ozone depletion or habitat degradation) or built environment (for example, acid rain). Both human activity and natural processes can generate air pollution.

Human-made Sources

These are mostly related to the burning of fuel. Stationary sources include:

◄ Smoke stacks of fossil fuel power stations for example coal industry;

◄ manufacturing facilities (factories);

◄ waste incineration (incinerators as well as open and uncontrolled fires of mismanaged waste, making up a fourth of municipal solid terrestrial waste)

◄ furnaces and other types of fuel-burning heating devices;

◄ mobile sources include motor vehicles, trains (particularly diesel locomotives and DMUs),

◄ marine vessels and aircraft; controlled burn practices in agriculture and forest management.

Natural Sources

◄ Dust storm approaching Stratford, Texas; Dust from natural sources, usually large areas of land with little vegetation or no vegetation

◄ Methane, emitted by the digestion of food by animals, for example cattle

◄ Radon gas from radioactive decay within the Earth's crust

◄ Smoke and carbon monoxide from wildfires

◄ Vegetation, in some regions, emits environmentally significant amounts of volatile organic compounds (VOCs) on warmer days

◄ Volcanic activity, which produces sulfur, chlorine, and ash particulates

Major Air Pollutants

- Carbon Monoxide
- Lead
- Nitrogen Oxides
- Ozone
- Particulate Matter
- Sulfur Dioxide
- Other Air Pollutants: Acrolein; Acrolein; Asbestos; Benzene; Carbon Disulfide; Creosote; Fuel oils/Kerosene; Polycyclic Aromatic Hydrocarbons (PAHs); Synthetic Vitreous Fibers; Total Petroleum Hydrocarbons

Air Quality Index

- The air quality is measured by the Air Quality Index.
- Air quality indices have been created in different countries for the measurement of air quality.
- These indices measure the air quality in the country and indicate whether the amount of nitrogen dioxide, carbon monoxide and sulfur dioxide in the air exceeds the criteria set by the World Health Organization or not.
- India uses the National Air Quality Index (AQI), Canada uses the Air Quality Health Index, Singapore uses the Pollutant Standards Index and Malaysia uses the Air Pollution Index.
- There are many cities including Beijing, Paris where 'pollution emergency' is declared. However, India also declared the same in November 2019.
- The **AQI** is an index for reporting daily air quality.
- It focuses on health effects one might experience within a few hours or days after breathing polluted air.

AQI is calculated for eight major air pollutants:

- Ground-level ozone,
- PM10,
- PM2.5,
- Carbon monoxide,
- Sulfur dioxide,
- Nitrogen dioxide,
- Ammonia,
- Lead

How the Air Quality Index Works?

In more than 800 counties across the nation, air pollution levels are measured daily and ranked on a scale of 0 for perfect air all the way up to 500 for air pollution levels that pose an immediate danger to the public. The AQI further breaks air pollution levels into five categories, each of which has a name, an associated colour, and advice to go along with it.

World Capital City Ranking (World Air Quality Report 2020):

- Delhi ranked as the world's most polluted capital city followed by Dhaka (Bangladesh), Ulaanbaatar (Mongolia), Kabul (Afghanistan), Doha (Qatar).

- Bangladesh ranked as the most polluted country followed by Pakistan and India.
- The least polluted country Puerto Rico, followed by New Caledonia, US Virgin Islands respectively.

World City Ranking:

- Hotan in China is the most polluted city with an average concentration of 110.2 µg/m³ followed by Ghaziabad in Uttar Pradesh at 106.
- Delhi listed as the 10th most polluted city and the top polluted capital city in the world.

Air Quality and Pollution City Ranking

(02 November 2021)

	Major City	US AQI
1	Delhi, India	177
2	Mumbai, India	166
3	Karachi, Pakistan	162
4	Dhaka, Bangladesh	161
5	Wuhan, China	161
6	Beijing, China	161
7	Dubai, United Arab Emirates	160
8	Kyiv, Ukraine	153
9	Tehran, Iran	153
10	Kuwait City, Kuwait	152
11	Kolkata, India	140
12	Sofia, Bulgaria	124
13	Skopje, North Macedonia	121
14	Shenyang, China	117
15	Kathmandu, Nepal	114
16	Zagreb, Croatia	113
17	Moscow, Russia	113
18	Lima, Peru	107
19	Bishkek, Kyrgyzstan	107
20	Krakow, Poland	96
21	Warsaw, Poland	96
22	Hangzhou, China	94

	Major City	US AQI
23	Lahore, Pakistan	93
24	Kabul, Afghanistan	91
25	Belgrade, Serbia	88
26	Amsterdam, Netherlands	87
27	Guangzhou, China	84
28	Kaohsiung, Taiwan	83
29	Yangon, Myanmar	82
30	Hanoi, Vietnam	82
31	Tel Aviv-Yafo, Israel	81
32	Riyadh, Saudi Arabia	81
33	Chongqing, China	80
34	Shenzhen, China	78
35	Portland, USA	77
36	Jerusalem, Israel	76
37	Chengdu, China	76
38	Seoul, South Korea	76
39	Bogota, Colombia	74
40	Krasnoyarsk, Russia	72
41	Budapest, Hungary	70
42	Los Angeles, USA	69
43	Tashkent, Uzbekistan	68
44	Helsinki, Finland	68
45	Shanghai, China	65
46	Hong Kong, Hong Kong SAR	65
47	Busan, South Korea	65
48	Incheon, South Korea	65
49	Mexico City, Mexico	63
50	Pristina, Kosovo	62

Water Pollution

The water is life for human beings. About 70% of the earth is water, which has undeniably become one of our greatest resources. There are various ways to conserve water because water is used in almost every important human chores and processes. Water is an essential element in both domestic as well as industrial purposes.

However, a closer inspection of our water resources today gives us a terrible shock. Water is now infested with various wastes ranging from floating plastic bags to chemical waste, converting our water bodies into a pool of poison.

In simple words, the contamination of water bodies is water pollution. It is the abuse of lakes, ponds, oceans, rivers, reservoirs, etc. Pollution of water usually occurs when substances discharged in it negatively modify the water. This discharge of pollutants can be direct as well as indirect.

Water pollution is an appalling problem, powerful enough to lead the world on a path of destruction. Water is a natural solvent, enabling most pollutants to dissolve in it easily and contaminate it.

The effect of water pollution is directly suffered by the organisms and vegetation that survive in water, including amphibians. On a human level, several people die each day due to the consumption of polluted and infected water.

Water is polluted by both natural as well as human-made activities. Volcanic eruptions, earthquakes, tsunamis, etc. are known to alter water and contaminate it, also affecting the ecosystems that exist underwater.

Sources of Water Pollution

There are a number of classifications of water pollution, which are as follows:

Groundwater Pollution

Groundwater gets polluted when contaminants such as fertilizers, pesticides, and waste leaching from landfills and septic systems, making their way into an aquifer.

Once polluted, an aquifer becomes unsafe for humans and remains unusable for decades, or even thousands of years. Besides, groundwater can also spread contamination far from the original polluting source when it seeps into streams, lakes, and oceans.

Surface Water

As per the Environmental Protection Agency of the U.S., nearly 50% of our rivers and streams and over one-third of our lakes are polluted and unfit for swimming, fishing, and drinking.

Nutrient pollution that includes nitrates and phosphates, which plants and animals need to grow, causes major pollution in the freshwater sources due to farm waste and fertilizer runoff. Municipal and industrial waste discharges and also individuals' dumping directly into waterways contribute their fair share of toxins.

Ocean Water

Eighty percent of ocean pollution or marine pollution originates on land along the coast or far inland. Streams and rivers carry contaminants such as chemicals, nutrients, and heavy metals that are carried from farms, factories, and cities into our bays and estuaries, and from there, they reach the ocean.

Point Source

When contamination occurs from a single source, it's called point source pollution. Though this pollution originates from a specific place, it can affect miles of waterways and ocean.

Point sources include wastewater, which is known as effluent, legally or illegally discharged from a manufacturing unit, oil refinery, or wastewater treatment facility.

It can be from leaking septic systems, chemical and oil spills, and also illegal dumping. The EPA has set limits on what can be discharged by a facility directly into a body of water to regulate point source pollution.

Non-point Source

Non-point source pollution is contamination derived from multiple or diffused sources. These may include contaminated water travelled after rains, agricultural or stormwater runoff, or debris blown into waterways from the land.

Transboundary

A boundary line cannot contain water pollution on a map. Transboundary pollution happened when contaminated water from one country spilled into other countries' waters. It can result from a disaster like an oil spill or the slow, downriver creep of industrial, agricultural, or municipal discharge.

Causes of Water Pollution

1. Industrial Waste

Many industries, not having a proper waste management system, drain the waste in the freshwater, which goes into canals, rivers, and later into the sea.

The toxic chemicals may change the colour of water, increase the number of minerals, called eutrophication, change the temperature of the water, and pose a severe hazard to water organisms.

2. Sewage and Wastewater

The sewage and wastewater that is produced in each household are treated chemically and released into the sea along with fresh water. The sewage water carries pathogens, a typical water pollutant, other harmful bacterias, and chemicals that can cause serious health problems and thereby diseases.

3. Mining Activities

Mining is the process of crushing the rock and extracting coal and other minerals from the underground. These elements, when extracted in the raw form, contain harmful chemicals and can increase the number of toxic elements when mixed up with water, which may result in health problems.

Mining results in the extraction of minerals from the earth's core. These minerals also bring out harmful chemicals from deep inside the earth to the earth's surface. The toxic emissions from mining can cause air, water, and soil pollution.

Mining activities emit a large amount of metal waste and sulfides from the rocks, which is harmful to the water.

4. Marine Dumping

The garbage produced by households in the form of paper, plastic, food, aluminum, rubber, glass, is collected and dumped into the sea in some countries. These items take two weeks to 200 years to decompose.

5. Accidental Oil Leakage

Oil spill poses a huge threat to marine life when a large amount of oil spills into the sea and does not dissolve in water. It causes problems for local marine wildlife, including fish, birds, and sea otters.

6. The Burning of Fossil Fuels

Fossil fuels like coal and oil, when burnt, produce a substantial amount of ash in the atmosphere. The particles which contain toxic chemicals when mixed with water vapor result in acid rain. Also, carbon dioxide is released from the burning of fossil fuels, which results in global warming.

7. Chemical Fertilizers and Festicides

Chemical fertilizers and pesticides are used by farmers to protect crops from insects and bacterias. They are useful for the plant's growth. However, when these chemicals are mixed up with water, they produce harmful pollutants for plants and animals.

8. Global Warming

An increase in the earth's temperature results in global warming due to the greenhouse effect. It increases the water temperature and results in the death of aquatic animals and marine species, which later results in water pollution.

9. Radioactive Waste

The nuclear waste that is produced by radioactive material needs to be disposed of to prevent any nuclear accident. Nuclear waste can have serious environmental hazards if not disposed of properly. Few major accidents have already taken place in Russia and Japan.

10. Urban Development

As more cities and towns are developed, they have resulted in increasing use of fertilizers to produce more food, soil erosion due to deforestation, rise in construction activities, inadequate sewer collection and treatment, landfills as more garbage is produced, increase in chemicals from industries to produce more materials.

11. Leakage from the Landfills

Landfills are nothing but a massive pile of garbage that produces the awful smell and can be seen across the city. When it rains, the landfills may leak, and the leaking landfills can pollute the underground water with a large variety of contaminants.

12. Acid Rain

Acid rain is essentially water pollution caused by air pollution. When the acidic particles released in the atmosphere by air pollution mix with water vapor, it results in acid rain.

Global Warming

- Global warming is the gradual heating of Earth's surface, oceans and atmosphere. As greenhouse gas emissions blanket the Earth, they trap the sun's heat. This leads to global warming and climate change. The world is now warming faster than at any point in recorded history.

◁ Global warming is due to human activities, primarily fossil fuel burning, which increases heat-trapping greenhouse gas levels in Earth's atmosphere.

◁ The term is frequently used interchangeably with the term climate change, though the latter refers to both human- and naturally produced warming and the effects it has on our planet.

◁ It is most commonly measured as the average increase in Earth's global surface temperature.

◁ Since the pre-industrial period, human activities are estimated to have increased Earth's global average temperature by about 1 degree Celsius (1.8 degrees Fahrenheit), a number that is currently increasing by 0.2 degrees Celsius (0.36 degrees Fahrenheit) per decade.

◁ It is unequivocal that human influence has warmed the atmosphere, ocean and land.

The Greenhouse Effect

Fossil fuel related CO_2 emissions compared to five IPCC scenarios. The dips are related to global recessions. Coal-burning power plants, car exhausts, factory smokestacks, and other man-made waste gas vents give off about 23 billion tons of carbon dioxide and other greenhouse gases into the Earth's atmosphere each year.

Climate Change

◁ Climate is the average weather in a place over many years.

◁ Climate change is a shift in those average conditions.

◁ The rapid climate change we are now seeing is caused by humans using oil, gas and coal for their homes, factories and transport.

◁ When these fossil fuels burn, they release greenhouse gases - mostly carbon dioxide (CO_2). These gases trap the Sun's heat and cause the planet's temperature to rise.

Ozone Holes

◁ The term 'ozone hole' refers to the depletion of the protective ozone layer in the upper atmosphere (stratosphere) over Earth's polar regions.

◁ People, plants, and animals living under the ozone hole are harmed by the solar radiation now reaching the Earth's surface—where it causes health problems, from eye damage to skin cancer.

◁ Stratospheric ozone is constantly produced by the action of the sun's ultraviolet radiation on oxygen molecules (known as photochemical reactions).

◁ Although ozone is created primarily at tropical latitudes, large-scale air circulation patterns in the lower stratosphere move ozone toward the poles, where its concentration builds up.

◁ In addition to this global motion, strong winter polar vortices are also important to concentrating ozone at the poles.

◁ During the continuously dark polar winter, the air inside the polar vortices becomes extremely cold, a necessary condition for polar stratospheric cloud formation.

Causes

◁ The main causes of ozone depletion and the ozone hole are manufactured chemicals, especially manufactured halocarbon refrigerants, solvents, propellants, and foam-blowing agents (chlorofluorocarbons (CFCs), HCFCs, halons), referred to as ozone-depleting substances (ODS).

- ◄ These compounds are transported into the stratosphere by turbulent mixing after being emitted from the surface, mixing much faster than the molecules can settle.
- ◄ Once in the stratosphere, they release atoms from the halogen group through photodissociation, which catalyze the breakdown of ozone (O_3) into oxygen (O_2).
- ◄ Both types of ozone depletion were observed to increase as emissions of halocarbons increased.

Ozone Layer Depletion

The ozone layer is an undetectable layer of protection around the planet that secures us from the sun's unsafe beams. The depletion of the critical Ozone layer of the air is credited to contamination brought about by Bromide and Chlorine found in Chlorofloro carbons (CFCs). When these poisonous gasses reach the upper parts of the atmosphere, they cause a gap in the ozone layer, the greatest of which is over the Antarctic.

Acid Rain

Acid rain, or acid deposition, is a broad term that includes any form of precipitation with acidic components, such as sulfuric or nitric acid that fall to the ground from the atmosphere in wet or dry forms. This can include rain, snow, fog, hail or even dust that is acidic.

Causes of Acid Rain

Acid rain results when sulfur dioxide (SO_2) and nitrogen oxides (NOX) are emitted into the atmosphere and transported by wind and air currents. The SO_2 and NOX react with water, oxygen and other chemicals to form sulfuric and nitric acids. These then mix with water and other materials before falling to the ground.

While a small portion of the SO_2 and NOX that cause acid rain is from natural sources such as volcanoes, most of it comes from the burning of fossil fuels. The major sources of SO_2 and NOX in the atmosphere are:

- ◄ Burning of fossil fuels to generate electricity. Two thirds of SO_2 and one fourth of NOX in the atmosphere come from electric power generators.
- ◄ Vehicles and heavy equipment
- ◄ Manufacturing, oil refineries and other industries
- ◄ Winds can blow SO_2 and NOX over long distances and across borders making acid rain a problem for everyone and not just those who live close to these sources.

Nuclear Issues

Radioactive waste is a nuclear fuel that contains radioactive substances and is a by-product of nuclear power generation. The radioactive waste is an environmental concern that is extremely toxic and can have a devastating effect on the lives of the people living nearby, if not disposed of properly. Radioactive waste is considered to be harmful to humans, plants, animals, and the surrounding environment.

Ice Ages

- ◄ An ice age is a long period of reduction in the temperature of Earth's surface and atmosphere, resulting in the presence or expansion of continental and polar ice sheets and alpine glaciers.
- ◄ Earth's climate alternates between ice ages and greenhouse periods, during which there are no glaciers on the planet.

- ◁ In glaciology, ice age implies the presence of extensive ice sheets in both northern and southern hemispheres. By this definition, Earth is currently in an interglacial period—the Holocene.
- ◁ The amount of anthropogenic greenhouse gases emitted into Earth's oceans and atmosphere is predicted to prevent the next glacial period for the next 500,000 years, which otherwise would begin in around 50,000 years, and likely more glacial cycles after.

Scientists have recorded five significant ice ages throughout the Earth's history:

- ◁ The Huronian (2.4-2.1 billion years ago),
- ◁ Cryogenian (850-635 million years ago),
- ◁ Andean-Saharan (460-430 mya),
- ◁ Karoo (360-260 mya),
- ◁ Quaternary (2.6 mya-present).

Approximately a dozen major glaciations have occurred over the past 1 million years, the largest of which peaked 650,000 years ago and lasted for 50,000 years. The most recent glaciation period, often known simply as the "Ice Age," reached peak conditions some 18,000 years ago before giving way to the interglacial Holocene epoch 11,700 years ago.

Oil Spills

- ◁ An oil spill is the release of a liquid petroleum hydrocarbon into the environment, especially the marine ecosystem, due to human activity, and is a form of pollution.
- ◁ The term is usually given to marine oil spills, where oil is released into the ocean or coastal waters, but spills may also occur on land.
- ◁ Oil spills may be due to releases of crude oil from tankers, offshore platforms, drilling rigs and wells, as well as spills of refined petroleum products (such as gasoline, diesel) and their by-products, heavier fuels used by large ships such as bunker fuel, or the spill of any oily refuse or waste oil.
- ◁ Oil spills penetrate into the structure of the plumage of birds and the fur of mammals, reducing its insulating ability, and making them more vulnerable to temperature fluctuations and much less buoyant in the water.
- ◁ Cleanup and recovery from an oil spill is difficult and depends upon many factors, including the type of oil spilled, the temperature of the water (affecting evaporation and biodegradation), and the types of shorelines and beaches involved.
- ◁ Spills may take weeks, months or even years to clean up.
- ◁ Oil spills can have disastrous consequences for society; economically, environmentally, and socially.
- ◁ Oil spill accidents have initiated intense media attention and political uproar, bringing many together in a political struggle concerning government response to oil spills and what actions can best prevent them from happening.

Deforestation & Logging

With a desperate need for land for agricultural, industrial and most importantly, urban requirements to contain cities and their growing population, a direct action that we have come to recognize as "Deforestation" occurs. Deforestation in simple terms means the felling and clearing of forest cover or tree plantations to accommodate agricultural, industrial or urban use. It involves the permanent end of forest cover to make that land available for residential, commercial or industrial purposes.

Over the last century, the forest cover around the globe has been significantly compromised, leaving the green cover down to an all-time low of about 30 percent. According to the United Nations Food and Agriculture Organization (FAO), an estimated 18 million acres (7.3 million hectares) of forest are lost each year.

Deforestation can also be seen as removal of forests leading to several imbalances, both ecologically and environmentally. What makes deforestation alarming is the immediate and long term effects it is bound to inflict if continued at the current pace. Some predictions state that the rainforests of the world will be eradicated if deforestation continues at its current pace.

Logging is the process of cutting, processing, and moving trees to a location for transport. It may include skidding, on-site processing, and loading of trees or logs onto trucks or skeleton cars.

Logging is the beginning of a supply chain that provides raw material for many products societies worldwide use for housing, construction, energy, and consumer paper products. Logging systems are also used to manage forests, reduce the risk of wildfires, and restore ecosystem functions.

Primary Causes of Deforestation

- Agricultural Activities
- Livestock Ranching
- Illegal Logging
- Urbanization
- Desertification of Land
- Mining
- Forest Fires
- Paper
- Overpopulation

Effects of Deforestation

- Climate Imbalance and Climate Change
- Increase in Global Warming
- Increase in Greenhouse Gas Emissions
- Soil Erosion
- Floods
- Wildlife Extinction & Habitat Loss
- Acidic Oceans
- The Decline in Life Quality of People
- Food Insecurity in the Future
- Loss of Biodiversity

Biodiversity

- Biodiversity is all the different kinds of life you'll find in one area—the variety of animals, plants, fungi, and even microorganisms like bacteria that make up our natural world.

- Each of these species and organisms work together in ecosystems, like an intricate web, to maintain balance and support life.

- Biodiversity supports everything in nature that we need to survive: food, clean water, medicine, and shelter.

- But as humans put increasing pressure on the planet, using and consuming more resources than ever before, we risk upsetting the balance of ecosystems and losing biodiversity.

- WWF's 2018 Living Planet Report found an average 60% decline in global populations of mammals, fish, birds, reptiles, and amphibians since 1970.

◁ The 2019 landmark Global Assessment Report by the Intergovernmental Platform on Biodiversity and Ecosystem Services reported one million animal and plant species are now threatened with extinction – the highest number in human history.

Biodiversity is usually explored at three levels - genetic diversity, species diversity and ecosystem diversity. These three levels work together to create the complexity of life on Earth.

Coral Reefs

◁ A coral reef is an underwater ecosystem characterized by reef-building corals.

◁ Reefs are formed of colonies of coral polyps held together by calcium carbonate. Most coral reefs are built from stony corals, whose polyps cluster in groups.

◁ Coral belongs to the class Anthozoa in the animal phylum Cnidaria, which includes sea anemones and jellyfish.

◁ Unlike sea anemones, corals secrete hard carbonate exoskeletons that support and protect the coral.

◁ Most reefs grow best in warm, shallow, clear, sunny and agitated water.

◁ Coral reefs first appeared 485 million years ago, at the dawn of the Early Ordovician, displacing the microbial and sponge reefs of the Cambrian.

◁ Sometimes called rainforests of the sea, shallow coral reefs form some of Earth's most diverse ecosystems.

◁ They occupy less than 0.1% of the world's ocean area, about half the area of France, yet they provide a home for at least 25% of all marine species, including fish, mollusks, worms, crustaceans, echinoderms, sponges, tunicates and other cnidarians.

◁ Coral reefs flourish in ocean waters that provide few nutrients. They are most commonly found at shallow depths in tropical waters, but deep water and cold water coral reefs exist on smaller scales in other areas.

◁ Coral reefs have declined by 50% since 1950, partly because they are sensitive to water conditions.

◁ Coral reefs deliver ecosystem services for tourism, fisheries and shoreline protection.

◁ The annual global economic value of coral reefs has been estimated at anywhere from US$30–375 billion (1997 and 2003 estimates) to US$2.7 trillion (a 2020 estimate) to US$9.9 trillion (a 2014 estimate).

Types

While some sources find only three, Thomas and Goudie list four "principal large-scale coral reef types" – the fringing reef, barrier reef, atoll and table reef – while Spalding *et al.* list five «main types» – the fringing reef, barrier reef, atoll, «bank or platform reef» and patch reef.

Algae

Reefs are chronically at risk of algal encroachment. Overfishing and excess nutrient supply from onshore can enable algae to outcompete and kill the coral. Increased nutrient levels can be a result of sewage or chemical fertilizer runoff. Runoff can carry nitrogen and phosphorus which promote excess algae growth.

Ecology

◁ Ecology is the study of the relationships between living organisms, including humans, and their physical environment.

◄ Ecology considers organisms at the individual, population, community, ecosystems, and biosphere level.

◄ Ecology is a branch of biology, and it is not synonymous with environmentalism. Among other things, ecology is the study of:

◄ Life processes, interactions, and adaptations

◄ The movement of materials and energy through living communities

◄ The successional development of ecosystems

◄ Cooperation, competition and predation within and between species.

◄ The abundance, biomass, and distribution of organisms in the context of the environment.

◄ Patterns of biodiversity and its effect on ecosystem processes.

Ecosystems

◄ An ecosystem is a geographic area where plants, animals, and other organisms, as well as weather and landscape, work together to form a bubble of life.

◄ Ecosystems contain biotic or living, parts, as well as abiotic factors, or nonliving parts.

◄ Biotic factors include plants, animals, and other organisms.

◄ Abiotic factors include rocks, temperature, and humidity.

◄ Every factor in an ecosystem depends on every other factor, either directly or indirectly.

◄ A change in the temperature of an ecosystem will often affect what plants will grow there, for instance.

◄ Animals that depend on plants for food and shelter will have to adapt to the changes, move to another ecosystem, or perish.

Ecosystems can be very large or very small. Tide pools, the ponds left by the ocean as the tide goes out, are complete, tiny ecosystems. Tide pools contain seaweed, a kind of algae, which uses photosynthesis to create food. Herbivores such as abalone eat the seaweed. Carnivores such as sea stars eat other animals in the tide pool, such as clams or mussels. Tide pools depend on the changing level of ocean water.

Threats to Ecosystems

As human populations have grown, however, people have overtaken many ecosystems. The tallgrass prairie of the Great Plains, for instance, became farmland.

As the ecosystem shrunk, fewer bison could survive. Today, a few herds survive in protected ecosystems such as Yellowstone National Park.

In the tropical rain forest ecosystems surrounding the Amazon River in South America, a similar situation is taking place. The Amazon rain forest includes hundreds of ecosystems, including canopies, understories, and forest floors. These ecosystems support vast food webs.

Exotic Species

An introduced species, alien species, exotic species, adventive species, immigrant species, foreign species, non-indigenous species, or non-native species is a species living outside its native distributional range, but which has arrived there by human activity, directly or indirectly, and either deliberately or accidentally.

The presence of an exotic species may have a significant effect on the local ecosystem. The ecological impact varies; it may generally bring adverse effects to the ecological balance in an ecosystem or it may be beneficial. At other times, the effect is not too significant to cause major changes in the ecosystem.

Introduced Animals

Most introduced species do not become invasive. Examples of introduced animals that have become invasive include the gypsy moth in eastern North America, the zebra mussel and alewife in the Great Lakes, the Canada goose and gray squirrel in Europe, the beaver in Tierra del Fuego, the muskrat in Europe and Asia, the cane toad and red fox in Australia, nutria in North America, Eurasia, and Africa, and the common brushtail possum in New Zealand.

Some species, such as the Western honey bee, brown rat, house sparrow, ring-necked pheasant, and European starling, have been introduced very widely. In addition there are some agricultural and pet species that frequently become feral; these include rabbits, dogs, ducks, snakes, goats, fish, pigs, and cats.

Wildfires

- A wildfire is an unplanned fire that burns in a natural area such as a forest, grassland, or prairie.
- Wildfires are often caused by human activity or a natural phenomenon such as lightning, and they can happen at any time or anywhere.
- In 50% of wildfires recorded, it is not known how they started.
- The risk of wildfires increases in extremely dry conditions, such as drought, and during high winds.
- Wildfires can disrupt transportation, communications, power and gas services, and water supply.
- They also lead to a deterioration of the air quality, and loss of property, crops, resources, animals and people.
- Wildfires and volcanic activities affected 6.2 million people between 1998-2017 with 2400 attributable deaths worldwide from suffocation, injuries, and burns, but the size and frequency of wildfires are growing due to climate change.
- Hotter and drier conditions are drying out ecosystems and increasing the risk of wildfires.
- Wildfires also simultaneously impact weather and the climate by releasing large quantities of carbon dioxide, carbon monoxide and fine particulate matter into the atmosphere.
- Resulting air pollution can cause a range of health issues, including respiratory and cardiovascular problems. Another significant health effect of wildfires is on mental health and psychosocial well-being.
- Wildfires are among the most common forms of natural disaster in some regions, including Siberia, California, and Australia. Areas with Mediterranean climates or in the taiga biome are particularly susceptible.

Natural Disasters

A natural disaster is a major adverse event resulting from natural processes of the Earth; examples include firestorms, duststorms, floods, hurricanes, tornadoes, volcanic eruptions, earthquakes, tsunamis, storms, and other geologic processes.

A natural disaster can cause loss of life or damage property, and typically leaves some economic damage in its wake, the severity of which depends on the affected population's resilience and on the infrastructure available.

Avalanches and Landslides

An avalanche is a rapid flow of snow down a hill or mountainside. Although avalanches can occur on any slope given the right conditions, certain times of the year and certain locations are naturally more dangerous than others. Wintertime, particularly from December to April, is when most avalanches tend to happen.

A landslide is described as an outward and downward slope movement of an abundance of slope-forming materials including rock, soil, artificial materials, or a combination of these.

Earthquakes

An earthquake is the result of a sudden release of energy in the Earth's crust that creates seismic waves. At the Earth's surface, earthquakes manifest themselves by vibration, shaking, and sometimes displacement of the ground. Earthquakes are caused by slippage within geological faults.

Earthquakes by themselves rarely kill people or wildlife — it is usually the secondary events that they trigger, such as building collapse, fires, tsunamis and volcanic eruptions that cause death.

Volcanic Eruptions

When a part of the earth's upper mantle or lower crust melts, magma forms. A volcano is essentially an opening or a vent through which this magma and the dissolved gases it contains are discharged.

Although there are several factors triggering a volcanic eruption, three predominate: the buoyancy of the magma, the pressure from the exsolved gases in the magma and the injection of a new batch of magma into an already filled magma chamber.

Storms

A storm is a violent meteorological phenomena in which there is heavy rain, and wind due to moisture in the air. Hail and Lightning are also common in storms. More rarely, Tornadoes can occur in storms. Hurricanes, typhoons, and tornadoes are, often, called storms too but they have special names because they are very, very strong.

There are many varieties and names for storms: icestorm, blizzard, snowstorm, ocean-storm, firestorm, etc.

Floods

A flood is an overflow of water that 'submerges' land. The EU Floods Directive defines a flood as a temporary covering of land that is usually dry with water. In the sense of 'flowing water', the word may also be applied to the inflow of the tides.

Flooding may result from the volume of a body of water, such as a river or lake, becoming higher than usual, causing some of the water to escape its usual boundaries.

Tsunami

A tsunami is a series of waves in a water body caused by the displacement of a large volume of water, generally in an ocean or a large lake. Tsunamis can be caused by undersea earthquakes such as the 2004 Boxing Day tsunami, or by landslides such as the one in 1958 at Lituya Bay, Alaska, or by volcanic eruptions such as the ancient eruption of Santorini.

Tropical Cyclone

Typhoon, cyclone, cyclonic storm and hurricane are different names for the same phenomenon: a tropical storm that forms over an ocean. It is characterized by strong winds, heavy rainfall and thunderstorms.

Tornadoes

A tornado is a violently rotating column of air that is in contact with both the surface of the Earth and a cumulonimbus cloud or, in rare cases, the base of a cumulus cloud. It is often referred to as a twister, whirlwind or cyclone.

Tornadoes come in many shapes and sizes, and they are often visible in the form of a condensation funnel originating from the base of a cumulonimbus cloud, with a cloud of rotating debris and dust beneath it. Most tornadoes have wind speeds less than 110 miles per hour (180 km/h), are about 250 feet (80 m) across, and travel a few miles (several kilometers) before dissipating.

El Nino and La Nina

El Niño and La Niña are climate patterns in the Pacific Ocean that can affect weather worldwide. During El Niño, trade winds weaken. Warm water is pushed back east, toward the west coast of the Americas.

During La Niña events, trade winds are even stronger than usual, pushing more warm water toward Asia. Off the west coast of the Americas, upwelling increases, bringing cold, nutrient-rich water to the surface.

Hazardous Waste

Hazardous wastes are wastes with properties that make them dangerous or potentially harmful to human health or the environment. Hazardous wastes can be liquids, solids, contained gases, or sludges. They can be by-products of manufacturing processes or simply discarded commercial products, like cleaning fluids or pesticides.

Household Hazardous Waste

Household Hazardous Waste (HHW), also referred to as domestic hazardous waste or home generated special materials, is a waste that is generated from residential households. HHW only applies to waste coming from the use of materials that are labelled for and sold for "home use".

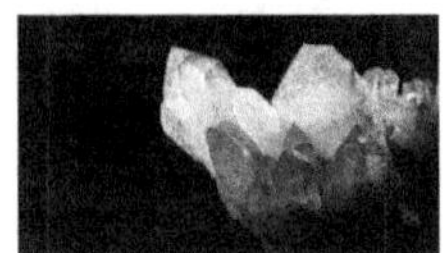

Major Minerals of the World

- Production of bauxite, a key component in the production of aluminium, has fluctuated over the last five years, peaking in 2013 at 299 million tonnes.
- The world's five largest producers – India, Guinea, Brazil, China and Australia, who between them produced 246.1 million tonnes in 2016 – have all seen increases in bauxite production since 2012.
- Guinea, which was the fourth-highest producer in 2016, has seen the most dramatic rate of change.
- The West African country has seen bauxite production almost double from 17.8 million tonnes in 2012 to 30.8 million tonnes in 2016.
- Despite having the world's largest bauxite reserves, Guinea has historically processed very little of the mineral, instead exporting it to foreign countries in deals that favour overseas companies.
- Guinea has reached an agreement with Russian company Rusal where the latter only has to return 0.01% of its bauxite profits to Guinea, equivalent to around $1 per tonne.
- Many in Guinea hope that the new MetalCorp plant will enable Guineans to better profit from the country's bauxite reserves.

Top 10 Countries by Bauxite Production (2020)

Country	Production in thousand tonnes	Country	Production in thousand tonnes
World	**327,000**	**World**	**327,000**
Australia	110,000	India	22,000
Guinea	82,000	Jamaica	7,700
China	60,000	Russia	6,100
Brazil	35,000	Kazakhstan	5,800
Indonesia	23,000	Vietnam	4,000

- In 2010, China's zinc mines produced approximately 3.7 million metric tons of zinc.
- By 2020, this amount increased to 4.2 million metric tons.
- Accordingly, China is the world's largest producer of the base metal zinc.
- Australia and Peru are the second and third-largest zinc mining countries in the world, respectively.
- In the United States, zinc production has remained fairly stable, reaching approximately 780,000 metric tons in 2019.

Top 10 Countries by Zinc Production (2019)

Rank	Country/Region	Zinc production (tonnes)	Rank	Country/Region	Zinc production (tonnes)
—	World total	13,000,000	—	World total	13,000,000
—	Other countries	1,900,000	—	Other countries	1,900,000
1	China	4,300,000	6	Mexico	690,000
2	Peru	1,400,000	7	Bolivia	460,000
3	Australia	1,300,000	8	Russia	300,000
4	India	800,000	8	Canada	300,000
5	United States	780,000	10	Kazakhstan	290,000

URANIUM

- Global uranium production stood at some 54,752 metric tons in 2019.
- With a production of approximately 22,808 metric tons, Kazakhstan is the largest single producer of uranium in the world.
- Other top uranium producers include Canada, Australia, and Namibia.
- The world's largest uranium producing mine is Cigar Lake in Canada. Some 6,924 metric tons of uranium were generated there in 2019.
- The second-largest mine is Husab in Namibia with 3,400 metric tons of uranium produced in 2019.
- Approximately 57 percent of the uranium worldwide is produced by the mining method of in-situ leaching.
- Kazakh state-owned KazAtomProm is the world's leading uranium company, having produced about 12,229 metric tons in 2019 (or 13,291 metric tons when the company's fifty percent stake of Energy Asia's production is included).
- French Orano and Canadian Cameco follow in second and third place, respectively.
- In the same year, only 14 companies accounted for 94 percent of the total global mine production of uranium.
- The leading consumers of uranium worldwide are the countries with the highest share of nuclear energy: the United States, France, and China.

Top 10 Countries by Uranium Production

(Source: World Nuclear Association 2018)

Rank	Country/Region	Uranium production (2018) (tonnes U)	Percentage of World Production (2018)
	World	53,498	100.00%
1	Kazakhstan	21,705	40.57%
2	Canada	7,001	13.09%
3	Australia	6,517	12.18%
4	Namibia	5,525	10.33%
5	Niger	2,911	5.44%
6	Russia	2,904	5.43%
7	Uzbekistan	2,404	4.49%
8	China	1,885	3.52%
9	Ukraine	1,180	2.21%
10	United States	582	1.09%

◁ The mine production of iron ore in the United States reached approximately 56 million metric tons in 2014.

◁ By 2020, the annual production decreased to an estimated 37 million metric tons.

◁ Australia and Brazil are among the world's largest iron ore mine producers, producing 900 million metric tons and 400 million metric tons, respectively, in 2020.

◁ Subsequently, iron ore reserves are among the highest in Australia with 24 billion metric tons of iron content and 50 billion metric tons of crude ore, as of 2020.

◁ Over 90 percent of Australia's identified resource resides in Western Australia.

◁ Hamersley Province contains a large portion of this resource and is considered one of the world's largest iron ore reserves.

◁ The Pilbara region in Western Australia has two major producers, including BHP Billiton and Rio Tinto Ltd. Pilbara Iron is a subsidiary of the Rio Tinto group and has about 15 sites in the region.

◁ As of 2011, Australia exported about 40 percent of the world's iron ore resources. Along with Brazil, the two countries account of over half of the world's exports.

◁ Iron ore are rocks and minerals that can be heated in the presence of a reductant to extract metallic iron.

Top 10 Countries by Iron Ore Production (2019)

Rank	Country	Usable iron ore production (1000 tonnes)
	World	**2,500,000**
1	Australia	930,000
2	Brazil	480,000
3	China	350,000
4	India	210,000
5	Russia	99,000
6	South Africa	77,000
7	Ukraine	62,000
8	Canada	54,000
9	United States	48,000
10	Kazakhstan	43,000

◁ Primary aluminium is aluminium tapped from electrolytic cells or pots during the electrolytic reduction of metallurgical alumina (aluminium oxide).

◁ In 2020, China had a total smelter production of some 37 million metric tons of aluminum.

◁ In 2019, the leading producer of primary aluminum worldwide was Chalco from China. That year, they produced 6.1 million metric tons of aluminum.

◁ Rio Tinto Alcan from Canada was the fifth leading producer of aluminum that year. In 2019, they produced about 3.17 million metric tons of aluminum.

◁ Alcoa, from the United States, brought in about 5.4 billion U.S. dollars in sales from its aluminum segment in the 2019 fiscal year. Following aluminum was alumina, which generated 1.4 billion U.S. dollars in sales that year.

◁ U.S. primary aluminum production has slowly decreased since 2009. In 2009, the U.S. produced about 1.7 million metric tons of primary aluminum.

◁ In 2020, they produced one million metric tons of aluminum.

Top 10 Countries by Primary Aluminium Production

(Countries with a minimum production of 100,000 tonnes)

Country	Production in thousand tonnes	Year
World	**64,000**	**2019**
China	36,000	2019
India	3,700	2019
Russia	3,600	2019
Canada	2,900	2019
United Arab Emirates	2,700	2019
Australia	1,580	2018
Bahrain	1,400	2019
Norway	1,300	2019
United States	1,100	2019
Saudi Arabia	932	2018

COPPER

- In 2020, Peru produced 2.2 million metric tons of copper.
- The ten leading countries in world copper production as of 2019 were Chile, Peru, China, the United States, Australia, the Democratic Republic of the Congo, Zambia, Mexico, Russia, and Kazakhstan.
- Chile, the world's leading copper producer by far, produced an estimated 5.7 million metric tons of copper in 2020.
- In second place is Peru, with an estimated copper mine production of 2.2 million metric tons in the same year.
- The world's third-largest copper producer from mines is China. In 2020, China produced an estimated 1.7 million metric tons of copper from mines, which is over three times less than Chile's production.
- Chile is the world's largest producer of copper, so 3 of the world's ten largest copper mines based on capacity are located there.
- At the top of the list is the Escondida mine, located in the Atacama Desert in Chile's Antofagasta Region.
- It had a capacity of some 1.4 million metric tons of copper in 2020, which is nearly twice the capacity of the world's second-largest copper mine, located in Indonesia.

Top 10 Countries by Copper Production (2020)

Rank	Country/ region	Production (thousand tons of)
	World	**16,890**
1	Chile	5,700
2	Peru	2,200
3	China	1,700
4	Congo, Democratic Republic of the	1,300
5	United States	1,200
6	Australia	870
7	Russia	850

Rank	Country/ region	Production (thousand tons of)
8	Zambia	830
9	Mexico	690
10	Kazakhstan	580

- In 2020, China's mines produced an estimated 380 metric tons of gold.
- China is the largest gold producer in the world.
- China, Australia, Russia, and the United States are respectively the largest producers of gold in the world.
- Global production of gold reached approximately 3,200 metric tons in 2020.
- Production in China has increased from 320 metric tons in 2009 to an estimated 380 metric tons in 2020. However, large-scale gold production is minimal with only one mine exceeding 300,000 ounces of gold, the Zijinshan gold-copper mine in the Fujan Province.
- The production value of gold in the United States has increased from 4.9 billion U.S. dollars in 2006 to 9.6 billion U.S. dollars in 2017.
- One of the largest gold companies in the world, AngloGold Ashanti, is headquartered in Johannesburg, South Africa and was founded in 2004.
- AngloGold Ashanti generated revenues of 4.43 billion U.S. dollars in 2020. It produced over three million ounces of gold in 2020, with over half of it being produced in Africa.
- Most gold mining is performed by large corporations around the world. However, there are smaller independent operations and in some cases, illegal mines have also been formed.

Top 10 Countries by Gold Production (2018)

2018 Rank	Country	Gold production (tonnes)	Reserves (tonnes)
1	China	404	2,000
2	Australia	319	9,800
3	Russia	297	5,300
4	United States	222	3,000
5	Canada	189	2,200
6	Peru	158	2,600
7	Indonesia	137	2,500
8	Ghana	130	1,000
9	South Africa	130	6,000
10	Mexico	115	1,400

- The estimated global production of silver in 2020 amounted to 25,000 metric tons.
- Production of this precious metal has thus increased considerably from the production volume of 20,800 in 2005.
- The three leading silver producing countries worldwide in 2019 were Mexico, Peru, and China.
- In that year Mexico produced 190.3 million ounces, Peru produced 135.4 million ounces, and China produced 110.7 million ounces.

◅ Fresnillo plc was the leading global silver mining company in 2019.

◅ The Mexico-based company produced 61.8 million ounces of silver in 2018, and 51.8 million ounces of silver in 2019.

◅ In 2018 they generated a revenue of about 2.2 billion U.S. dollars.

◅ The second largest silver mining company in the world in 2019 was KGHM Polska Miedz S.A.; a Polish based mining company.

Top 10 Countries by Silver Production (2018)

Rank	Country/Region	Silver production (tonnes)
—	**World**	**26,900**
1	Mexico	6,120
2	Peru	4,160
3	China	3,570
4	Russia	2,100
5	Poland	1,470
6	Chile	1,370
7	Bolivia	1,190
8	Australia	1,220
9	Argentina	1,020
10	United States	930

DIAMOND

◅ In 2020, Russia produced approximately 19 million carats of diamonds, making it the world's largest natural industrial diamond producer that year.

◅ In 2016, the global production of industrial diamonds was about 4.41 billion carats.

◅ The production of natural diamonds is expected to remain the same from 2015 to 2025, at around 100 million carats.

◅ For synthetic industrial diamond production, a forecasted five billion carats is expected in 2025.

◅ The largest diamond producing country in 2020 was Russia, and secondly Australia.

◅ In that year Australia produced about 12 million carats of diamonds.

◅ The total global production of rough diamonds amounted to 142 million carats in 2019.

Top 10 Countries by Diamond Production

(Source: the British Geological Survey Mineral Statistics Summary for 2016)

2016 Diamond Production (million carats)			
Country	Production	Country	Production
World	**121.7**	**World**	**121.7**
Russia	40	Angola	9
Botswana	20.9	South Africa	8.4
Australia	13.9	Zimbabwe	2.1
DR Congo	12.3	Namibia	1.5
Canada	11.1		

Major Crops of the World

- Rice is among the three leading food crops of the world, with maize (corn) and wheat being the other two.
- All three directly provide no less than 42% of the world's required caloric intake and, in 2009, human consumption was responsible for 78% of the total usage of produced rice.
- More than 3.5 billion of the world's population think of rice as their staple food, which translates to at least half of the people living in the world.
- Because of this, experts do not see a future decline of rice consumption, especially among African and Asian countries food source.

The Geographical Conditions

- It is a kharif crop which requires hot and humid climate for cultivation. Temperature (above 25°C) and high humidity with annual rainfall above 100 cm-150 cm are favourable for the growth of rice.
- Rich alluvial soils of the floodplains and deltaic areas which are renewed every year are ideal for rice cultivation.
- Rice requires abundant rainfall or good water supply through irrigation and flooded fields during the earlier part of its growing season in June-July.

Top Rice Producing Countries of World

Rank	Country	Rice Production (millions of hectares)	Rank	Country	Rice Production (millions of hectares)
1	India	143.20	6	Vietnam	7.66
2	China	30.35	7	Burma	6.80
3	Indonesia	12.16	8.	Philippines	4.50
4	Bangladesh	12.00	9.	Cambodia	2.90
5	Thailand	9.65	10.	Pakistan	2.85

- Conditions of growth for the wheat are more flexible than rice, Wheat is a Rabi crops which is shown in the beginning of winter and is harvested in the beginning of summer.
- India is second largest producer of wheat. According to FAOSTAT, China produces more wheat than any other country, followed by India, Russia, and the United States.

The Geographical Conditions

- Wheat is predominantly a crop of mid-latitude grasslands and requires a cool climate with moderate rainfall.

◅ The ideal wheat climate has winter temperature 10°- 15° C and summer temperature varying from 21° to 26° C.

◅ The temperature should be low at the time of sowing but harvesting time approaches higher temperature.

◅ Annual rainfall about 75cm to 100 cm.

Top Wheat Producing Countries of World

Rank	Country	Wheat Production (Tonnes)	Rank	Country	Wheat Production (Tonnes)
1	China	1 134,340,630	6	Australia	31,818,744
2	India	98,510,000	7	Canada	29,984,200
3	Russian Federation	85,863,132	8	Pakistan	26,674,000
4	USA	47,370,880	9	Ukraine	26,208,980
5	France	36,924,938	10	Germany	24,481,600

MAIZE

◅ Maize is widely cultivated throughout the world, and a greater weight of maize is produced than any other grain.

◅ The United States produces 40% of the world's harvest; other top producing countries include China, Brazil, Mexico, Indonesia, India, France and Argentina.

The Geographical Conditions

◅ It requires 50-100 cm of rainfall and it cannot be grown in lesser rainfall, the crop is irrigated.

◅ Temperature varying from 21°C to 27 Frost is injurious to maize and this crop is grown only in those areas where there are about four and a half frost free months in a year.

◅ Fertile well-drained alluvial or red loams free from coarse materials and rich in nitrogen are the best soil for its growth.

Top Maize Producing Countries of World

Rank	Country	Production (Tonnes)	Rank	Country	Production (Tonnes)
1	United States	333,010,910	6	India	17,300,000
2	China	163,118,097	7	France	15,299,900
3	Brazil	51,232,447	8	Argentina	13,121,380
4	Mexico	17,629,740	9	South Africa	12,050,000
5	Indonesia	20,202,600	10	Ukraine	10,486,300

RYE

◅ Rye is a type of cereal grain that belongs to the wheat family. This plant is native to the central and eastern regions of present-day Turkey.

◅ Archaeological evidence suggests that it may have been cultivated in small amounts during the Neolithic era. Rye made its way to central Europe and by the Bronze era, it was grown in large amounts.

➤   Today, rye is used to make flour, bread, beer, whiskey, and animal feed. It can also be consumed whole as a cereal.

The Geographical Conditions

➤   Rye prefers **light loams or sandy soils** and will germinate even in fairly dry soil. It also will grow in heavy clays and poorly drained soils, and many cultivars tolerate waterlogging.

➤   Rye can establish in very cool weather. It will germinate at temperatures as low as 34° F.

➤   Most farmers grow winter ryes, which are planted and begin to grow in autumn. In spring, the plants develop and produce their crop.

➤   By the summer solstice, plants reach their maximum height of about a 120 cm (4 ft) while spring-planted wheat has only recently germinated.

Top Rye Producing Countries of World

Rank	Country	Rey Production (in metric ton)	Rank	Country	Rey Production (in metric ton)
1.	Germany	3893000	6	Ukraine	676800
2.	Poland	2888137	7	Denmark	384400
3.	Russia	2131519	8	Turkey	370000
4.	Belarus	1082405	9	Canada	336600
5.	China	678000	10	Spain	296700

JOWAR (SORGHUM)

➤   Sorghum is a cereal plant drawn from the grass family and has been ranked among the top leading cereals grown around the world.

➤   Sorghum grows well in areas with warm climates. The crop is grown for both domestic consumption and as a cash crop.

➤   Sorghum has a wide range of uses, which include human food, animal feed, and the production of alcoholic beverages, and biofuels.

➤   Nutritionists categorize sorghum as very healthy, as it is rich with essential nutrients that are significant in the body.

The Geographical Conditions

➤   It grows well in areas having mean monthly temperature of 26 to 33C. Requires more than 30 cm rainfall during the growing period and does not grow where the rainfall exceeds 100cm.

➤   Jowar is per excellence a rain fed crop of dry farming areas where irrigation is not used. Excessive drought moisture and prolonged droughts are harmful for its proper growth. Soil including loamy and sandy soils, clay deep regur and alluvium are the best suited soil for jowar. It grown in plain areas but it can also be raised on gentle slopes up to 1200 metres height.

Top Jowar Producing Countries of World

Rank	Country	Sorghum Production (Million Metric Tons)
1	United States	11.5
2	India	7.5
3	Nigeria	7.4
4	Mexico	6.1
5	Sudan	4.4
6	Sudan (former)	3.7
7	China	3.1
8	Argentina	2.9
9	Ethiopia	2.2
10	Australia	1.9

MILLET

- Millet constitutes a variety of small-grained, warm-weather, annual cereals that are part of the grass family. These crops are highly drought tolerant in nature.
- Millet is grown widely around the world for use as food and fodder. Millets are important crops in the semiarid tropical regions and are indigenous to many parts of the world.
- For centuries, millets have served as an important staple in parts of Asia and Africa. The crop has been cultivated for at least 10,000 years in East Asia.

The Geographical Conditions

- Generally the Millets are grown in tropical as well as sub-tropical up to an altitude of 2,100m.
- It is a heat loving plant and for its germination the minimum temperature required is 8- 10°C. A mean temperature range of 26-29°C during the growth is best for proper development and good crop yield.
- It is grown where rainfall ranges from 500-900mm.
- The best soils are alluvial, loamy and sandy soil with good drainage. Kodo millet can be grown in gravelly and stony soil such as in the hilly region.

Top Millet Producing Countries of World

Rank	Country	Production (Tonnes)	Rank	Country	Production (Tonnes)
1	India	10,910,000	6	Burkina Faso	1,109,000
2	Nigeria	5,000,000	7	Sudan	1,090,000
3	Niger	2,955,000	8	Ethiopia	807,056
4	China	1,620,000	9	Chad	582,000
5	Mali	1,152,331	10	Senegal	572,155

- Jute is a long natural fiber that is produced from plants of the Corchorus genus and is made of the plant's cellulose and lignin.
- The fiber has numerous uses including the manufacturing of biodegradable packing material, such as gunny bags.
- Jute is recognized as the second most important vegetable fiber in the world, behind only cotton, in terms of global consumption and production.
- India and Bangladesh produce the greatest amounts of jute in the world, and global production is estimated at more than 3.3 million tonnes each year.

The Geographical Conditions

- Jute is the crop of hot and humid climate. It requires temperature varying from 24°C to 35°C and heavy rainfall of 120 to 150 cm with 80 to 90 percent relative humidity during the period of its growth.
- Rainfall between 2.5 to 7.5 cm in a month, during the sowing period, is considered to be sufficient. Occasional showers varying from 2 to 3 cm at intervals of a week's time during the growing period are very useful.
- Large quantity of water is required not only for growing the jute crop but also for processing the fibre after the crop is harvested.
- Light sandy or clayey loams are considered to be best suited soils for jute. Jute rapidly exhausts the fierily of soil, it is necessary that the soil is replenished annually by the silt-laden food water of the rivers.
- Large number of cheap labour is also necessary for growing and processing the jute fibre.

Top Jute Producing Countries of the World

Rank	Country	Annual Jute Production (Tonnes)
1	India	1,968,000
2	Bangladesh	1,349,000
3	China	29,628
4	Uzbekistan	20,000
5	Nepal	14,890
6	South Sudan	3,300
7	Zimbabwe	2,519
8	Egypt	2,508
9	Brazil	1,172
10	Vietnam	970

COTTON

- Cotton is the most important fibre that used to make clothes and number of textile products. Cotton has history about 7000 years.
- It cultivated by the many civilization around the globe, there are four types of cotton growing commonly that is Gossypium hirsutum, Gossypium barbadense, Gossypium arboretum, Gossypium herbaceum.
- Cotton measured in 'Bales' that about 480 pound for A Bale.

The Geographical Conditions

⊰ Cotton is the crop of tropical and sub-tropical areas and requires uniformly high temperature varying between 21° C and 30° C.

⊰ The growth of cotton is retreated when the temperature falls below 20° C. Frost is the enemy of the cotton and plant and it is grown in areas having atleast 210 frost free days in a year.

⊰ The modest requirement of water can be made by an average annual rainfall of 50-100cm.

⊰ High amount of rainfall in beginning and Sunny and dry weather at ripening time are very usefull. Cotton cultivation is closely related to deep black soils (regur).

Top Cotton Producing Countries in the World

Rank	Countries	Production (Million Bales/Year)
1	China	33
2	India	27
3	USA	18
4	Pakistan	10.3
5	Brazil	9.3
6	Uzbekistan	4.6
7	Australia	4.2
8	Turkey	2.8
9	Turkmenstan	1.6
10	Greece	1.4

SUGARCANE

⊰ Sugarcane is several species of tall perennial true grasses of the genus Saccharum, tribe Andropogoneae, used for sugar production.

⊰ The plant is two to six metres (six to twenty feet) tall.

⊰ It has stout, jointed, fibrous stalks that are rich in sucrose, which accumulates in the stalk internodes.

⊰ It is native to the warm temperate to tropical regions of Southeast Asia and New Guinea.

The Geographical Conditions

⊰ Sugarcane cultivation requires a tropical or subtropical climate, with a minimum of 60 cm (24 in) of annual moisture.

⊰ It is one of the most efficient photosynthesizers in the plant kingdom. It is a C4 plant, able to convert up to 1% of incident solar energy into biomass.

Top Sugarcane Producing Countries in the World

Countries	Millions of tonnes
Brazil	746.8
India	376.9
China	108.1
Thailand	104.4
Pakistan	67.2
Mexico	56.8
World	1,907

MUSTARD SEED

- Mustard seed are the small seeds of the mustard plant. These 1 to 2-millimeter seeds can be found in several colours, depending on the plant.
- These plants include black mustard, brown Indian mustard, and white mustard.

The Geographical Conditions

- Mustard seeds require a cold climate and moist soil to germinate, which takes between 3 and 10 days. When allowed to mature, the mustard plant grows into a shrub-like plant.
- Around 1 month to 1.5 months after germination, the mustard plant flowers. These flowers can be seen for around 2 weeks before they become pods over a 35 to 45-day period. Once the pods turn brown, the seeds are ready.
- In total, mustard plants take approximately 3 months to produce seeds. The black and brown varieties produce a higher quantity of seeds than the yellow mustard plant.
- Depending on the water content of harvested seeds, cultivators may place them on mesh screens to dry out slightly.

Top Mustard Producing Countries in the World

Rank	Country	Production (Tonnes)
1	Nepal	159,710
2	Canada	121,600
3	Russia	98,319
4	Myanmar	42,760
5	Ukraine	31,000
6	United States of America	27,330
7	China	18,415
8	Kazakhstan	15,121
9	France	14,160
10	Czechia	9,542

- Tea is a typical preferable beverage as well as coffee. Therefore, tea is produced in a lot of countries. China is the one of the largest tea producing country that produces non-fermented tea (Green tea), semi-fermented tea (Oolong tea) and various kind of fermented tea (Black tea).
- Other than in China, Oolong tea is produced mainly in Taiwan. Black tea is produced in India, Sri Lanka, Indonesia, Kenya, etc. Green tea is produced also in the old Soviet Union, Japan, and some other places.

The Geographical Conditions

- A suitable climate has a minimum annual rainfall of 1,140 to 1,270 mm, with proper distribution.
- If there is a cool season, with average temperatures 20 °F (11 °C) or more below those of the warm season, the growth rate will decrease and a dormant period will follow, even when the cool season is the wetter one.
- Tea soils must be acid; tea cannot be grown in alkaline soils. A desirable pH value is 5.8 to 5.4 or less.

Top Tea Producing Countries in the World

Rank	Country	Tea Production (Tonnes)
1	China	2,473,443
2	India	1,325,050
3	Kenya	439,857
4	Sri Lanka	349,699
5	Vietnam	260,000
6	Turkey	234,000
7	Indonesia	139,362
8	Myanmar	104,743
9	Iran	100,580
10	Bangladesh	81,850

- Coffee is world's most favourite beverage with 2.5 billion cups consumed every day.
- Coffee is produced in about 70 countries most of them belonging to the developing world from Africa, Latin America and Asia.
- It is the world's highest traded commodity after petroleum. Coffee is categorized into two varieties namely Robusta and Arabica.

The Geographical Conditions

- Coffee is a tropical plant which is also grown in semi-tropical climate. It needs abundant rainfall, i.e., 100 to 200 cm annually.
- It requires an average temperature between 20°-27°C. Although it grows in day temperature over 32°C in the Arabian Peninsula.
- Growth is most rapid during hot rainy season and during cool dry season berries ripen and ready for picking.
- Bright sunshine and warm weather are necessary for the harvesting.

◅ The ideal soil is one with a good sub-surface drainage, and one that is easily workable. The presence of humus and other nitrogenous matter in the soil is an advantage.

Top Coffee Producing Countries in the World

Rank	Countries	Coffee Production(Tons)
1	Brazil	2,592,000
2	Vietnam	1,650,000
3	Colombia	810,000
4	Indonesia	660,000
5	Ethiopia	384,000
6	Honduras	348,000
7	India	348,000
8	Uganda	288,000
9	Mexico	234,000
10	Guatemala	204,000

CHILLI

◅ Chilli is a fruit of plants which are members of the Nightshade family. To narrow it down, its genus is that of the more popular capsicum.

◅ Capsaicin and similar compounds mainly cause the "hotness" that comes after eating it. Astonishingly, humans have been eating them since 7500 BCE.

◅ Recent studies show that they were first domesticated in the Americas, particularly in Mexico. That today Asia is a significant player in the chilli sector can be attributed to trade in the past primarily by the Portuguese and Arabs.

The Geographical Conditions

◅ Chilli is a tropical and sub-tropical plant requiring a combination of warm, humid yet dry weather. During the growth stage it needs a warm and humid weather.

◅ 20°-25°C is ideal temperature range for chilli growth. At 37°C or higher the crop development is affected.

◅ Chillies need moisture for growth. It has been found that black soil which retains moisture is ideal in case they are grown as rainfed crops.

◅ PH of soil should be between 6.5 and 7.5 (neutral soil). It cannot tolerate neither acidic nor alkaline soil.

Top Chilli Producing Countries in the World

Rank	Country	Production (Millions of Tonnes)
1	China	16.1
2	Mexico	2.7
3	Turkey	2.4
4	Indonesia	1.9
5	India	1.5
6	Spain	1.1
7	United States	0.9

Apple

- Apples are a deciduous variety of fruits which grow on trees in mostly temperate regions around the world.
- The apple fruit was originated from Central Asia and with time it was spread all over the contains vitamins and minerals in it.

Which Country Grows the Most Apples?

China, the USA, and Poland are the world's top producers of apples. In the United States alone, there an average of 4.6 million tonnes of apples produced every year.

Mango

- India, China, Thailand, Indonesia and Mexico are the world leaders in mango production.
- Mango is a tropical fruit that grows on extremely large trees that reach over 100 feet in height and 12 feet in diameter.
- The fruit itself is considered a stone fruit due to its single pit. Mangoes can come in a variety of colours, including orange, red, green and yellow. This fruit is native to India, Bangladesh and Pakistan.
- Its importance to humans dates back to around 2000 BC when it was domesticated in India. After domestication, the mango was introduced to East Asia between 500 and 400 BC. By the 15th century, it had made its way to the Philippines, followed by Africa and Brazil in the 16th century.
- Akbar, a Mughal emperor, planted over 100,000 mango trees in a place now known as Lakhi Bagh in India.
- Today, it is an important crop in tropical regions throughout South America, Hawaii, Central America, Asia, the Caribbean and Africa. Mango farmers often practice grafting in order to ensure fruit production.

Banana

- Banana is the fruit cultivated around the world, the fruit famous and used widely as part of the food.
- India is the largest producer of Bananas with around 30 million tonnes of production annually, most bananas cultivated in south Indian states and exports to other states of the country. China, Philippines and Ecuador are the next largest Bananas producers.
- Banana is the largest cultivated fruits and fourth-largest cultivated food after Rice, Wheat and Maize.
- Ecuador, Costa Rica and Colombia are the largest exporters of bananas, it exports annually.

World Transport

According to the World Bank, the world transport market is estimated at 4.2 trillion (6.8% of world GDP). Like the global economy itself, transport has turned into a very complex, interdependent, advanced technology-oriented industry that consumes a significant part of the world's energy and natural resources.

The quantitative indicators of the transport system are: the length of communications, the number of employees, freight and passenger turnover.

- The global transport network, the total length of which exceeds 50 million km

- More than 210,000 locomotives and millions of railroad cars carry cargoes by railways, over a trillion cars by road, over 90,000 ships along the sea routes, and over 30,000 flights on airways.

- The total carrying capacity of all vehicles of world transport has already exceeded 2.0 billion tons.

- The work of transport annually transports more than 110 billion tons of cargo and more than a trillion passengers.

- The number of employees in transport exceeds 100 million people (which can be compared with the entire population of the Philippines).

Transport is divided into land (rail and road), water (sea and river), air and pipeline. Here are the main parameters of the global transport system:

No.	Parameter	Mode of transport					
		Land		Water		Air	Pipeline
		Rail	Road	Sea	River		
1	Length, mm km	13,2	12,8	–	0,9	–	2,0
2.	Cargo turnover, % of world volume	9,0	13,0	62,0	4,0	1,0	11,0
3	Passenger transportations, % of world volume	11,0	82	1,0	3,0	3,0	–
4	Number of employed	Over 100 mm people (more than population of Philippines)					

ROAD TRANSPORT

Road transport from the middle of the 20th century became the leading among the types of land transport. The length of its network is growing and has reached 27.8 million km, with about 1/2 of that in the USA, India, Russia, Japan, and China. The level of motorization in the world is dominated by the US and Western European countries. Road transport also belongs to the priority in the volume of passenger transportation - 82% of the world volume.

Top 10 Biggest Road Networks (as of 2018)

1. US 6.59 million kilometres
2. China 4.77 million kilometres
3. India 4.7 million kilometres   (5897671 km as of the year 2020)
4. Brazil 2.0 million kilometres
5. Russia 1.28 million kilometres
6. Japan 1.22 million kilometres
7. France's 1.05 million kilometre
8. Canada 1.04 million kilometres
9. Australia 0.87 km
10. Spain 0.68 km

Top 10 Longest Highways in the World

Name	Approximate Length	Route
1. Pan American	48,000 km	Connects 14 countries including the United States of America, Canada (British Columbia, Yukon, Alberta), Mexico, El Salvador, Nicaragua, Honduras, Panama, Costa Rica, Chile, Peru, Ecuador, Argentina, Columbia, and Guatemala.
2. Highway 1, Australia	14,500 km	All Australian states and territories (but the Australian Capital Territory)
3. Trans-Siberian	11,000 km	St. Petersburg (Baltic Sea) to Vladivostok (Sea of Japan)
4. Trans-Canada	7,821 km	All ten Canadian provinces (covering the Pacific-Atlantic ocean from west to east)
5. Golden Quadrilateral Highway Network, India	5,846 km	The four major metropolitan cities (Delhi to the north, Kolkata to the east, Mumbai to the west, Chennai to the south) apart from other cities (Ahmedabad, Bhubaneswar, Bengaluru, Kanpur, Cuttack, Surat, Jaipur, Vizag, Pune, Varanasi, Vadodara, Gandhinagar, Agar, Mathura, Dhanbad) that are also a part of this network.
6. China National Highway 010	5700 km	Provinces of Jilin, Heilongjiang, Shandong, Liaoning, Jiangsu, Fujian, Shanghai, Guangdong, Zhejiang
7. US Route 20	5415 km	Newport to Boston in Oregon and Massachusetts respectively
8. US Route 6	5148 km	California's Bishop to Massachusetts' Provincetown

| 9. I-90 | 4,861 km | Western terminus: Seattle (in Washington at State Route 519 adjacent to Century Link Field and T Mobile Park); Eastern terminus: Boston (in Massachusetts, at Route 1A, adjacent to Logan International Airport) |
| 10. I-80 | 4,666 km | San Francisco (California) to Teaneck (New Jersey), also running through cities like Sacramento, Oakland, Reno, Omaha, Salt Lake City, Toledo, and Des Moines |

RAILWAY TRANSPORT

Railway transport is inferior to road transport by volume of transported cargo (9% of world volume), but it remains an important type of land transport. The world railway network as a whole developed back in the beginning of the 20th century, its length now amounts to 13.2 million km with considerable unevenness of location.

Although there are railways in 140 countries, more than 1/2 of their total length falls on the "top ten countries": the USA, Russia, Canada, India, China, Australia, Argentina, France, Germany and Brazil. Especially in the density of the network, the countries of Europe are allocated. But along with this there are huge spaces where the railway network is very rare or absent.

Top 10 Longest Railway Networks

1. United States: 250,000 km
2. China: 100,000 km
3. Russia: 85,500 km
4. India: 65,000 km
5. Canada: 48,000 km
6. Germany: 41,000 km
7. Australia: 40,000 km
8. Argentina: 36,000 km
9. France: 29,000 km
10. Brazil: 28,000 km

Top 10 Longest Train Journeys

1. Trans-Siberian: Moscow to Vladivostok (Russia)   Length: 9,289 km
2. The Canadian: Toronto to Vancouver (Canada)   Length: 3359 km
3. Shanghai to Lhasa (China)   Length: 4,373 km
4. Indian Pacific: Sydney to Perth (Australia)   Length: 4,352 km
5. Vivek Express: Dibrugarh to Kanyakumari (India)   Length: 4,286 km
6. California Zephyr: Emeryville (San Francisco) to Chicago Length: 3,924 km
7. Paris-Moscow Express: Paris (France) to Moscow (Russia) Length: 3,483 km

8.   The Ghan: Darwin to Adelaide (Australia)   Length: 2,979 km
9.   Eastern and Oriental Express: Bangkok (Thailand) to Singapore Length: 2,000 km
10. Blue Train: Pretoria to Cape Town (South Africa)   Length: 1,600 km

AIR TRANSPORT

Air Transport is the most high-speed, but quite expensive transport plays an important role in international passenger transportation. Its advantages apart from speed are the quality of supplies, geographic mobility, which makes it easy to expand and change routes. The network of regular airlines now encircles the entire globe, stretching for millions of kilometers. Its control points are more than 5 thousand airports. The main air powers of the world are the USA, Russia, Japan, Great Britain, France, Canada and Germany.

Top 10 Airlines of 2021

Here are Skytrax's top 10 airlines of 2021, by overall rating:

1.   Qatar Airways
2.   Singapore Airlines
3.   ANA All Nippon Airways
4.   Emirates
5.   Japan Airlines
6.   Cathay Pacific Airways
7.   EVA Air
8.   Qantas Airways
9.   Hainan Airlines
10. Air France

Forbes' World's Biggest Public Airline Companies by Revenue (as of January 2020)

Rank	Airline	Country	Revenue (US$ billions)
1	Delta Air Lines	United States	44.9
2	American Airlines Group	United States	44.5
3	Lufthansa Group	Germany	42.3
4	United Airlines	United States	41.9
5	Air France–KLM	France/ Netherlands	31.3
6	IAG	Spain/ UK	28.8
7	Southwest Airlines	United States	22.0
8	China Southern Airlines	China	21.7
9	All Nippon Airways	Japan	18.6
10	China Eastern Airlines	China	17.3

Note: Emirates is a state-owned company.

Top 10 Busiest Airports by Passenger Traffic

Source: 2020 reports from the Port Authority of New York and New Jersey and the Ministry of Transport of the People's Republic of China

Rank	Airport	Location	Country	Total passengers
1.	Guangzhou Baiyun International Airport	Baiyun-Huadu, Guangzhou, Guangdong	China	43,760,427
2.	Hartsfield–Jackson Atlanta International Airport	Atlanta, Georgia	United States	42,918,685
3.	Chengdu Shuangliu International Airport	Shuangliu-Wuhou, Chengdu, Sichuan	China	40,741,509
4.	Dallas/Fort Worth International Airport	Dallas-Fort Worth, Texas	United States	39,364,990
5.	Shenzhen Bao'an International Airport	Bao'an, Shenzhen, Guangdong	China	37,916,059
6.	Chongqing Jiangbei International Airport	Yubei, Chongqing	China	34,937,789
7.	Beijing Capital International Airport	Chaoyang-Shunyi, Beijing	China	34,513,827
8.	Denver International Airport	Denver, Colorado	United States	33,741,129
9.	Kunming Changshui International Airport	Guandu, Kunming, Yunnan	China	32,989,127
10.	Shanghai Hongqiao International Airport	Changning-Minhang, Shanghai	China	31,165,641

WATER TRANSPORT

Water transport is primarily characterized by the outstanding role of maritime transport. It accounts for 62% of world freight turnover, it also serves about 4/5 of all international trade. It is thanks to the development of sea transport that the ocean no longer divides, but connects countries and continents.

Naval vessels transport mainly bulk cargo: oil, oil products, coal, ore, grain and others, usually at a distance of 8-10 thousand km. "Container revolution" in maritime transport led to a rapid growth in transportation and the so-called general cargo - finished goods and semi-finished products.

Sea shipping is provided by the merchant marine fleet, the total tonnage of which exceeds 456 million tons. World shipping belongs to the Atlantic Ocean, the Pacific Ocean takes the second place in terms of shipping and the Indian Ocean takes the third place. The international sea channels (especially Suez and Panama) and the sea straits (La Manche, Gibraltar, etc.) have a very great influence on the geography of sea transport.

Inland Waterway

Inland waterway occupies the last place in the world transport system along the length of the network. The development and placement of inland waterway transport is primarily due to the natural prerequisites - the availability of rivers and lakes suitable for navigation, the Amazon, Mississippi, Volga, Ob, Yenisei, Yangtze, Congo have greater capacity than the most powerful railroads. Therefore, the United States, Russia, Canada, Germany, the Netherlands, Belgium, as well as China, are allocated for the freight turnover of inland waterways in the world.

Top 10 Shipping Companies (by TEU capacity)

1. P. Moller–Maersk – 4.1m TEU
2. Mediterranean Shipping Company – 3.8m TEU
3. COSCO Shipping Lines – 3.1m TEU
4. CMA CGM Group – 2.7m TEU
5. Hapag-Lloyd – 1.7m TEU
6. Ocean Network Express – 1.5m TEU
7. Evergreen Line – 1.2m TEU
8. Orient Overseas Container Line – 733,580 TEU
9. HMM – 728,416 TEU
10. Yang Ming – 616,000 TEU

PIPELINE TRANSPORTATION

Pipeline transport is the long-distance transportation of a liquid or gas through a system of pipes—a pipeline—typically to a market area for consumption. Pipeline transportation is actively developing due to the rapid growth of oil and natural gas production and the territorial gap that exists between the main areas of their production and consumption. Pipeline transportation accounts for 11% of the world cargo turnover with the length of the networks - more than 2.0 million km.

The latest data from 2014 gives a total of slightly less than 3,500,000 km of pipeline in 120 countries of the world. The United States had 65%, Russia had 8%, and Canada had 3%, thus 75% of all pipeline were in these three countries.

Pipeline and Gas Journal's worldwide survey figures indicate that 190,905 km of pipelines are planned and under construction. Liquids and gases are transported in pipelines, and any chemically stable substance can be sent through a pipeline. Pipelines exist for the transport of crude and refined petroleum, fuels – such as oil, natural gas and biofuels – and other fluids including sewage, slurry, water, beer, hot water or steam for shorter distances.

Oil pipelines are made from steel or plastic tubes which are usually buried. The oil is moved through the pipelines by pump stations along the pipeline. Natural gas (and similar gaseous fuels) are pressurized into liquids known as Natural Gas Liquids (NGLs).

Religions of the World

- Today the largest religion in the world, Christianity began 2,000 years ago in Palestine, with Jesus of Nazareth.
- The sacred text for Christians is the Bible.
- While Jews, Christians and Muslims share many of same historical religious stories, their beliefs verge.
- While they recognize Christ as an important historical figure, their traditions don't believe he's the son of God, and their faiths see the prophecy of the messiah's arrival as not yet fulfilled.
- Although monotheistic, Christians often describe their god through three manifestations that they call the Holy Trinity: the father (God), the son (Jesus), and the Holy Spirit.

Islam

- Islam is monotheistic religion and it follows the teaching of the prophet Muhammad, born in Mecca, Saudi Arabia, in 570 C.E.
- The followers of Islam, whose U.S. population is projected to double in the next twenty years (Pew Research Forum 2011), are called Muslims.
- The sacred text for Muslims is the Qur'an (or Koran).
- As with Christianity's Old Testament, many of the Qur'an stories are shared with the Jewish faith.
- Divisions exist within Islam, but all Muslims are guided by five beliefs or practices, often called "pillars": 1) Allah is the only god, and Muhammad is his prophet, 2) daily prayer, 3) helping those in poverty, 4) fasting as a spiritual practice, and 5) pilgrimage to the holy center of Mecca.

Hinduism

- The oldest religion in the world, Hinduism originated in the Indus River Valley about 4,500 years ago in what is now modern-day India.
- It arose contemporaneously with ancient Egyptian and Mesopotamian cultures.
- With roughly one billion followers, Hinduism is the third-largest of the world's religions.
- Hindus believe in a divine power that can manifest as different entities. Three main incarnations—Brahma, Vishnu and Shiva—are sometimes compared to the manifestations of the divine in the Christian Trinity.
- Multiple sacred texts, collectively called the Vedas, contain hymns and rituals from ancient India and are mostly written in Sanskrit.

Buddhism

◄ Buddhism was founded by Siddhartha Gautama around 500 B.C.E.

◄ Siddhartha was said to have given up a comfortable, upper-class life to follow one of poverty and spiritual devotion.

◄ At the age of thirty-five, he famously meditated under a sacred fig tree and vowed not to rise before he achieved enlightenment (*bodhi*).

◄ After this experience, he became known as Buddha, or "enlightened one."

◄ Followers were drawn to Buddha's teachings and the practice of meditation, and he later established a monastic order.

Confucianism

◄ Confucianism was the official religion of China from 200 B.C.E. until it was officially abolished when communist leadership discouraged religious practice in 1949.

◄ The religion was developed by Kung Fu-Tzu (Confucius), who lived in the sixth and fifth centuries B.C.E.

◄ An extraordinary teacher, his lessons—which were about self-discipline, respect for authority and tradition, and *jen* (the kind treatment of every person)—were collected in a book called the *Analects*.

Taoism

◄ In Taoism, the purpose of life is inner peace and harmony.

◄ Tao is usually translated as "way" or "path." The founder of the religion is generally recognized to be a man named Laozi, who lived sometime in the sixth century B.C.E. in China.

◄ Taoist beliefs emphasize the virtues of compassion and moderation.

Judaism

◄ After their Exodus from Egypt in the thirteenth century B.C.E., Jews, a nomadic society, became monotheistic, worshipping only one God.

◄ The Jews' covenant, or promise of a special relationship with Yahweh (God), is an important element of Judaism, and their sacred text is the Torah, which Christians also follow as the first five books of the Bible.

◄ Talmud refers to a collection of sacred Jewish oral interpretation of the Torah.

◄ Jews emphasize moral behaviour and action in this world as opposed to beliefs or personal salvation in the next world.

Top Religions of the World (as of 2020)

Religion	Adherents	Percentage
Christianity	2.382 billion	31.11%
Islam	1.907 billion	24.9%
Secular/Nonreligious/Agnostic/Atheist	1.193 billion	15.58%
Hinduism	1.161 billion	15.16%
Buddhism	506 million	5.06%
Sikhism	26 million	0.30%
Judaism	14.7 million	0.18%
Bahá'í	5.0 million	0.07%
Jainism	4.2 million	0.05%

Major Languages of the World

Although there are currently more than 7,000 languages, only 23 cover more than half of the world's population. This is not just a matter of statistics: it is a fundamental fact when planning a global expansion strategy. Whether for work or personal use, knowledge of other languages opens up new horizons.

English — 1.5 Billion Speakers

- **Official language in:** Antigua and Barbuda, Australia, Bahamas, Barbados, Botswana, Brunei, Burundi, Cameroon, Canada, Dominica, Eswatini, Fiji, Gambia, Ghana, Grenada, Guyana, Hong Kong, India, Ireland, Jamaica, Kenya, Kiribati, Lesotho, Liberia, Malawi, Malta, Marshall Islands, Mauritius, Namibia, Nauru, New Zealand, Nigeria, Pakistan, Palau, Papua New Guinea, Philippines, Rwanda, Saint Kitts and Nevis, Saint Lucia, Saint Vincent and the Grenadines, Samoa, Seychelles, Sierra Leone, Singapore, Solomon Islands, Somaliland, South Africa, South Sudan, Sudan, Tanzania, Tonga, Trinidad and Tobago, Tuvalu, Uganda, UK, United States, Vanuatu, Zambia

- **Regional language in:** Honduras in the Bay Islands, Micronesia except for Kosrae, Netherlands in Saint Maarten, Saint Eustatius and Saba islands

- **Widely spoken in:** Cyprus, Ethiopia, Indonesia, Israel, Palestine, Switzerland.

- The English language dates back to the 5th century AD, when Germanic tribes invaded the isle of Britain. Today, nearly 1.5 billion people speak it, including 480 million native English speakers. That's 20 percent of the world.

Mandarin Chinese — 1.3 Billion Speakers

- **Official language in:** China, Singapore, Taiwan

- **Widely spoken in:** Malaysia

- Of all the 297 living languages spoken in China, Mandarin Chinese is by far the most common, with 1.3 billion speakers.

- There is much debate about Mandarin eventually surpassing English to become the language of international business, but as most people outside of Asia do not have a basic understanding of Mandarin, experts do not predict this will happen.

Spanish — 661 Million Speakers

- **Official language in:** Argentina, Bolivia, Chile, Colombia, Costa Rica, Cuba, Dominican Republic, Ecuador, El Salvador, Equatorial Guinea, Guatemala, Honduras, Mexico, Nicaragua, Panama, Paraguay, Peru, Sahrawi Arab Democratic Republic, Spain, Uruguay, Venezuela

- **Minority language in:** Andorra

- **Regional language in:** Belize

- ◄ **Widely spoken in:** Philippines, United States

- ◄ The Spanish language extended its reach quickly around the world as conquests were made to discover new lands. Commonly found in South America, Central America and the Caribbean, it is today spoken by millions of people in many different countries.

- ◄ The majority of Spanish speakers in the world are in Mexico. Across the border in the United States, where English is the official language, 41 million people speak Spanish as their first language. Nearly 12 million Americans are bilingual, as well, and studies predict that the U.S. will topple Mexico as the largest Spanish-speaking county by 2050.

Hindi — 544 Million Speakers

- ◄ **Official language in:** Fiji and India (Hindi);

- ◄ Hindustani refers to both the Hindi and Urdu languages, which are direct descendants of Sanskrit.

- ◄ Hindi is spoken by so many people in large part because it's an official language in India, the second-most-populous country on Earth.

Arabic — 422 Million Speakers

- ◄ **Official language in:** Algeria, Bahrain, Chad, Comoros, Djibouti, Egypt, Iraq, Jordan, Kuwait, Lebanon, Libya, Mauritania, Morocco, Oman, Palestine, Qatar, Sahrawi Arab Democratic Republic, Saudi Arabia, Somalia, Somaliland, Sudan, Syria, United Arab Emirates, Yemen

- ◄ **Regional language in:** Israel

- ◄ **National language in:** Cyprus (Cypriot Arabic), Niger, South Sudan, Tunisia

- ◄ **Widely spoken in:** Eritrea, Indonesia, Philippines

- ◄ A Semitic language from the Arabian Peninsula, Arabic began as a language used by nomadic tribes to converse with one another. Today, it is particularly dominant in the Middle East and nearby Asian and African countries.

- ◄ Although Hebrew, a similar language, began with tribes in the same area, it is not considered Arabic as it was influenced by Slavic, Roman and German dialects. It is spoken in Israel and by Jewish communities globally, whereas Arabic is mostly used in Muslim communities.

Malay — 281 Million Speakers

- ◄ **Official language in:** Brunei, Malaysia, Singapore, Indonesia

- ◄ Indonesian is the most widely used of the Malay dialects, spoken by some 170 million people. Standard Malay, by comparison, is spoken by about 18 million people.

- ◄ It's believed that Malay began on the Asian island of Borneo around 1000 BC.

Russian — 267 Million Speakers

- ◄ **Official language in:** Belarus, Georgia, Kazakhstan, Kyrgyzstan, Russia, Transnistria

- ◄ **Regional language in:** Moldova

- ◁ **Minority language in:** Poland
- ◁ **Widely spoken in:** Israel, Tajikistan, Turkmenistan, Ukraine, Latvia, Estonia
- ◁ Russia is a large country, and it was even larger when it was the Soviet Union — so it should come as no surprise that Russian is one of the most commonly spoken languages in the world. Its speakers can be found not only in modern-day Russia, but in nations that received independence when the Soviet Union collapsed, such as Poland and the Czech Republic.

Bengali — 261 Million Speakers

- ◁ **Official language in:** Bangladesh
- ◁ **Regional language in:** India
- ◁ In Bangladesh, nearly 100 million people speak Bengali, the Indo-Ayran language of the country. Another 85 million speak it in India, primarily in the states of West Bengal, Assam and Tripura.
- ◁ Like many languages on this list, Bengali has been spread around the world thanks to sizable Bangladeshi and Indian immigrant communities in the United Kingdom, the United States and the Middle East.

Portuguese — 229 Million Speakers

- ◁ **Official language in:** Angola, Brazil, Cape Verde, East Timor, Equatorial Guinea, Guinea-Bissau, Macau, Mozambique, Portugal, Sao Tome and Principe
- ◁ **Minority language in:** Andorra, Spain
- ◁ Though Portugal is a relatively small country, the reach of its language is vast, thanks in large part to the abundance of Portuguese colonizers, traders and missionaries who brought it to other corners of the world. A Romance language with similarities to Spanish and Italian, Portuguese is today found in parts of South America, Africa, Asia and Europe.
- ◁ Though it's not widespread enough to earn a spot on the map, Portuguese is also used more than you may think in North America. More than half a million speak it in the U.S., making it the 12th most-spoken language in the country.

French — 229 Million Speakers

- ◁ **Official language in:** Benin, Burkina Faso, Burundi, Cameroon, Canada, Central African Republic, Chad, Comoros, Democratic Republic of the Congo, Republic of the Congo, Djibouti, Equatorial Guinea, France, Gabon, Guinea, Haiti, Ivory Coast, Luxembourg, Madagascar, Mali, Monaco, Niger, Rwanda, Senegal, Seychelles, Switzerland, Togo, Vanuatu
- ◁ **Regional language in:** Belgium, Italy (in Aosta Valley), Spain, UK (Guernsey and Jersey)
- ◁ **Minority language in:** Andorra, Spain
- ◁ **National language in:** Mauritius
- ◁ **Widely spoken in:** Algeria, Mauritania
- ◁ Another Romance language, French is heavily used around the world due to France's many conquests and settlements. Started by the Germanic tribe of Franks,

it incorporates German and Latin and is spoken in territories that were home to the tribe, as well as later colonies of France.

- In Canada, French is one of two official languages. In Quebec, 78.4 percent of locals speak the language as their mother tongue.

Hausa — 150 Million Speakers

- **National language in:** Niger, Nigeria
- The native people of Nigeria and Niger known as the Hausa are the largest ethnic group in western Africa, and this is their native tongue.

Punjabi — 148 Million Speakers

- **Widely spoken in:** Pakistan
- **Regional language in:** India
- This Indo-Aryan language is the official tongue of the Punjab state of India, where the population nears 30 million. It also has 70 million speakers in Pakistan.

German — 129 Million Speakers

- **Official language in:** Austria, Germany, Liechtenstein, Luxembourg, Slovakia, Switzerland
- **Regional language in:** Belgium, Brazil, Italy, Namibia, Romania
- **Minority language in:** Denmark, Hungary, Poland
- **National language in:** Czech Republic
- German has been enormously influential; English, for one, has its roots in Germanic languages. As seen on the map, it's also a language with extensive reach.
- Surprised to see Brazil highlighted? That's due to German being spoken, along with Portuguese, by a vast majority of residents in the Brazilian municipality of Pomerode. Known as the "most German city in Brazil," its inhabitants are largely of German descent.
- Not shown here are the many countries where German is not widely spoken, but still has a decent presence. This list includes Argentina, Australia, Canada, Chile, Denmark, Ecuador, Greece, Hungary, Kazakhstan, Kyrgyzstan, Liechtenstein, Luxembourg, Paraguay, Poland, Romania, Russia, Ukraine, the United States and Uruguay.

Japanese — 129 Million Speakers

- **Official language in:** Japan
- **Regional language in:** Palau
- In addition to (obviously!) being the official language of Japan, Japanese is spoken in the state of Angaur in Palau. It's also spoken quite a lot — though not enough to earn it a spot on the map — in the U.S., specifically in the state of Hawaii, and in Brazil, where there are sizable Japanese immigrant communities.

Persian — 121 Million Speakers

- **Official language in:** Iran, Afghanistan, Tajikstan
- **National language in:** Kuwait
- Also known as Farsi, Persian heavily influenced the Arabic language.
- In Afghanistan, the official language is a variety of Persian called Dari; in Tajikstan, it's a variety called Tajik.

Swahili — 107 Million Speakers

- **Official language in:** Rwanda, Uganda
- **National language in:** Democratic Republic of the Congo, Kenya, Tanzania
- **Widely spoken in:** Burundi, Mozambique
- The first language of the Swahili people, this Bantu dialect is found primarily in eastern and southeastern Africa. In Burundi, it's specifically spoken widely in the African Great Lakes Region.

Vietnamese — 95 Million Speakers

- **National language in:** Czech Republic, Vietnam
- **Minority language in:** Cambodia
- While the 75 million people of Vietnam make up the majority of Vietnamese speakers, the language is found in communities across the world.
- The influx of Vietnamese immigrants has made it a minority language in Cambodia and a national language in the Czech Republic.

Telugu — 92 Million Speakers

- **Regional language in:** India
- Another Indian language making the list is Telugu, spoken in the central southeastern states. Considered the largest of the Dravidian languages, Telugu dates back to the 6th century.

Italian — 87 Million Speakers

- **Official language in:** Italy, Malta, San Marino, Switzerland, Vatican City
- **Minority language in:** Slovenia
- **National language in:** Croatia
- **Widely spoken in:** Albania, Eritrea
- A Romance language, Italian was used as a collective means of communication to bridge the gap between many regional dialects. Its speakers include 800,000 inhabitants of Albania, making it the most spoken foreign language in that country.

Javanese — 84 Million Speakers

- **Widely spoken in:** Indonesia
- On the Indonesian island of Java, which has more than 100 million inhabitants, the native language of the indigenous people is Javanese. About two-thirds of the people of Java speak this Austronesia language.

Wu Chinese — 80 Million Speakers

◁   **Widely spoken in:** China

◁   Known as the language of the Shanghainese, Wu is spoken in Shanghai and its communities of people in Jiangsu and Zhejiang. The population of these communities equates to nearly 8 percent of the Chinese population speaking Wu.

◁   Wu is also spoken in the Chinese cities of Hangzhou, Suzhou, Ningpo and Wenzhou.

Korean — 77 Million Speakers

◁   **Official language in:** North Korea, South Korea

◁   No surprise here: South Korea, with 48 million people, and North Korea, with 24 million people, are home to the vast majority of Korean speakers.

◁   Immigrants have also taken the language, which dates back to the 15th century, to nearby China and Japan, as well as across the United States, although it's not considered a major language in any of those countries.

Tamil — 75 Million Speakers

◁   **Official language in:** Singapore, Sri Lanka

◁   **Widely spoken in:** India

◁   In India, Tamil is mostly spoken in the state of Tamil Nadu and the union territory of Puducherry (Pondicherry). To a lesser extent (not enough to earn it a spot on the map), it's additionally spoken in Malaysia, Mauritius, Fiji and South Africa.

◁   24. Marathi — 74 Million Speakers

◁   **Regional language in:** India

◁   Derived from Sanskrit, Marathi is an Indo-Aryan language of western India. Spoken in the Indian states of Maharashtra and Goa, the language is native to the Marathi people.

◁   It's also spoken in Israel and Mauritius, though not pervasively.

Yue Chinese — 72 Million Speakers

◁   **Regional language in:** China

◁   Yue is the de facto official language of Hong Kong and Macau, both Special Administrative Regions of the People's Republic of China, and is additionally spoken in the Guangdong and Guangxi provinces of China.

◁   Chinese immigrants have made it a language of growing influence in Southeast Asia, Canada, Australia, the UK and the United States as well.

Awards & Honours

NOBEL PRIZE

NOBEL PRIZE

- The Nobel Prize is an international award administered by the Nobel Foundation in Stockholm, Sweden, and based on the fortune of Alfred Nobel, Swedish inventor and entrepreneur. He left most of his estate, more than 31 million Swedish kronor (SEK) to be converted into a fund and invested in "safe securities." The income from the investments was to be "distributed annually in the form of prizes to those who during the preceding year have conferred the greatest benefit to mankind."

- It is awarded in Physics, Chemistry, Medicine or Physiology, Literature and Peace. In 1968, Sveriges Riksbank established, the Sveriges Riksbank Prize in Economic Sciences in Memory of Alfred Nobel, founder of the Nobel Prize. Each prize consists of a medal, a personal diploma, and a cash award. The Nobel Prize amount for 2021 is set at 10.0 million Swedish kronor per full Nobel Prize.

- Till 2021, the Nobel Prizes and the Sveriges Riksbank Prize in Economic Sciences in Memory of Alfred Nobel were awarded 609 times to 975 people and organisations.

- The winners include 25 organisations and 58 women. The youngest one to receive the Nobel Prize is Malala Yousafzai who was awarded for Peace in 2014 at the age of 17 years. The Oldest Nobel Laureate is John B. Goodenough, the winner of 2019-Nobel Prize in Chemistry.

INTERNATIONAL GANDHI PEACE PRIZE

- The International Gandhi Peace Prize is an annual award instituted by the Government of India since 1995, the 125th Birth Anniversary commemoration year of Mahatma Gandhi. The award is open to all persons regardless of nationality, race, language, caste, creed or sex. The award is given to individuals and institutions for their outstanding contributions towards social, economic and political transformation through non-violence, and other Gandhian methods, for amelioration of human sufferings particularly of the less privileged sections of the society, contributing social justice and harmony.

- Normally recent works achieved during ten years immediately preceding the nomination are considered. Older work may also be considered if its significance has become apparent only recently. A written work, in order to be eligible for consideration should have been published during the last ten years. The nominations are invited from various eminent persons and institutions every year mentioned in code of procedure.

◅ The Jury for Gandhi Peace Prize is chaired by Prime Minister of India and comprises of two ex-officio members, namely the Chief Justice of India and Leader of the single largest Opposition Party in Lok Sabha. Two eminent members are also part of the Jury.

◅ The award carries an amount of Rs. 1 crore, a citation, a plaque and an exquisite traditional handicraft/ handloom item.

◅ The past awardees include luminaries like Dr. Julius Nyerere, Former President of Tanzania; Dr. Gerhard Fischer, Federal Republic of Germany; Ramakrishna Mission; Baba Amte (Murlidhar Devidas Amte); Late Dr. Nelson Mandela, former President of South Africa; Grameen Bank of Bangladesh; Archbishop Desmond Tutu of South Africa; Chandi Prasad Bhatt & Indian Space Research Organisation. Vivekananda Kendra, India; Akshaya Patra Foundation, India and Sulabh International (Jointly); Ekal Abhiyan Trust, India, Yohei Sasakawa, Japan, Sheikh Mujibur Rahman (Posthumously), Bangladesh.

THE RAMON MAGSAYSAY AWARD

The Ramon Magsaysay Award is Asia's premier prize and highest honour. It is named after former Philippine President Ramon Magsaysay. The Award is presented in formal ceremony in Manila, Philippines on August 31st, the birth anniversary of the former Philippine President whose ideals inspired the Award's creation in 1957.

The Ramon Magsaysay Award was conceived to honour greatness of spirit shown in service to the peoples of Asia—regardless of race, gender, or religion.

The Ramon Magsaysay Awardees, annually selected by the RMAF board of trustees, are presented with a certificate and a medallion with an embossed image of Ramon Magsaysay facing right in profile.

Since 1958, the Ramon Magsaysay Award has been bestowed upon over three hundred outstanding individuals and organizations whose selfless service has offered their societies, Asia, and the world successful solutions to some of the most challenging problems of human development.

From 1958 to 2008, the Award was given in six categories annually:

◅ Government Service, to recognize outstanding service in the public interest in any branch of government, including the executive, judicial, legislative, or military;

◅ Public Service, to recognize outstanding service for the public good by a private citizen;

◅ Community Leadership, to recognize leadership of a community toward helping the disadvantaged have fuller opportunities and a better life;

◅ Journalism, Literature, and Creative Communication Arts, to recognize effective writing, publishing, or photography or the use of radio, television, cinema, or the performing arts as a power for the public good;

◅ Peace and International Understanding, to recognize contributions to the advancement of friendship, tolerance, peace, and solidarity as the foundations for sustainable development within and across countries; and

◁   Emergent Leadership, to recognize an individual, forty years of age or younger, for outstanding work on issues of social change in his or her community, but whose leadership may not yet be broadly recognized outside of this community.

The category of Emergent Leadership was inaugurated in 2000 and is supported by a grant from the Ford Foundation.

Starting in 2009, the Ramon Magsaysay Award is no longer being given in fixed Award categories, except for Emergent Leadership.

SEOUL PEACE PRIZE

The Seoul Peace Prize has been awarded biennially to those individuals who have made their mark through contributions to the harmony of mankind, reconciliation between nations and to world peace.

The Seoul Peace Prize was established in 1990 to commemorate the success of the 24th Olympic Games held in Seoul. The award was established to crystalise Korean people's yearning for peace on the Korean peninsula and in the rest of the world.

Past laureates include former UN Secretary Generals Kofi Annan and Ban Ki-Moon, IOC President Thomas Bach, Indian Prime Minister Narendra Modi, German Chancellor Angela Merkel and renowned international relief organizations like Doctors Without Borders and Oxfam.

RIGHT LIVELIHOOD AWARD

Each year since 1980, The Right Livelihood Award is bestowed to courageous change-makers across the world. It was started in 1980 and are typically given to four change makers in the form of three cash awards of 1 million Swedish kronor each and one honorary award.

The Award recognises individuals and organisations that have greatly contributed to a more just, peaceful and sustainable world through a variety of practical and innovative solutions in different fields across the world. In recognising the diversity and interconnectivity of challenges in the world and likewise the solutions to them, the Award has no set categories for which Laureates are considered or honoured.

The cash awards are intended to directly support the Laureates' cause and expand the impact of their work. The honorary prize is intended to recognise equally outstanding achievements – although, where the benefit is seen through the recognition and support provided as a result of the Award.

The Award immediately connects Laureates with the dozens of leading change-makers who are already part of the Right Livelihood community. It can also serve as a protective tool for Laureates whose lives and liberties are at risk, through greater international attention on themselves and their causes as well as the lifelong support offered to Laureates.

PULITZER PRIZE

The Pulitzer Prize is given for achievements in the field of Media and Journalism in the category of newspaper, magazine, online journalism, literature and musical composition mainly within the United States. The award was established in 1917 by provisions in the will of Joseph Pulitzer, who had made his fortune as a newspaper publisher.

The award is administered by Columbia University and Prizes are given annually in twenty-one categories. Except one category each winner receives a certificate and a US$15,000 cash award while the winner in the public service category is honoured with a Gold Medal.

BOOKER PRIZE

Man Booker Prize formerly known as Booker McConnell Prize is a prestigious British award given annually to a full-length novel in English.

The Award was established in 1968 by Booker McConnell, a multinational company, to provide a counterpart to the Prix Goncourt in France. Initially, only English-language writers from the United Kingdom, the Republic of Ireland, and the Commonwealth countries were eligible, but now open to English-language writers worldwide from 2014. The award was administered by the Book Trust until 2002, when oversight passed to the Man Group PLC, an investment management firm.

OSCARS/ ACADEMY AWARDS

Oscars or Academy Award is a prestigious award that recognises personalities with artistic and technical merit in the movie industry. It is presented annually by the Academy of Motion Picture Arts and Sciences.

The award was founded in 1927, but the presentation was first started in 1929, and winners since then receive a gold-plated statuette commonly called Oscar.

The members of the Academy of Motion Picture Arts and Sciences can only nominate and vote for the winners. As a film production is divided into various branches for its making, the nominees are chosen by the members of the branch. To determine the best picture, the entire academy panel nominates and votes.

The winners are chosen from 24 categories, these are Best Picture, Best Actor, Best Actress, Best Supporting Actor, Best Supporting Actress, Best Director, Best Original Screenplay, Best Adapted Screenplay, Best Cinematography, Best Production Design, Best Editing, Best Original Score, Best Original Song, Best Costume Design, Best Makeup and Hairstyling, Best Sound Mixing, Best Sound Editing, Best Visual Effects, Best Foreign Language Film, Best Animated Feature Film, Best Animated Short, Best Live Action Short, Best Documentary Feature and Best Documentary Short

GRAMMY AWARD

The Grammy Award is presented by the Recording Academy to recognize achievement in the field of music industry. It is considered as one of the four major annual American entertainment awards, along with the Academy Awards, the Emmy Awards, and the Tony

Awards. The first Grammy Awards ceremony was held in 1959 as Gramophone award as the trophy depicts a gilded gramophone.

The Golden Globe Awards are presented by the Hollywood Foreign Press Association and bestowed on the persons excelling in both American and international film and television. It was established in 1944. The annual ceremony is normally held every year in January. The eligibility period for the Golden Globes corresponds to the calendar year. The awards ceremony ranks as the third most-watched awards show each year, behind only the Oscars and the Grammy Awards.

The British Academy Film Awards or BAFTA Film Awards are presented in an annual award show hosted by the British Academy of Film and Television Arts (BAFTA). The award honours the best British and international contributions to the film industry. The British Academy of Film and Television Arts (BAFTA) was founded in 1947 and the first award was presented in 1949. The award ceremony currently took place in February most commonly at the Royal Albert Hall in London.

The UN Environment Programme's Champions of the Earth award is the UN's highest environmental honour. The awards are given in categories like Policy leadership, Inspiration and action Entrepreneurial vision, Science and innovation and Lifetime Achievement Award. The Award recognizes the heroes who inspire, encourage others to join them, and defend a cleaner future.

For the past 15 years, the Champions of the Earth award has shone a spotlight on the work of people and organizations that have dedicated their lives to working for a healthier, more just and more sustainable planet. Laureates have ranged from heads of state and community activists to captains of industry and pioneering scientists. Some of these are The National Geographic Society, NASA's Goddard Space Flight Center, Indian Prime Minister Narendra Modi, Bangladesh Prime Minister Sheikh Hasina, Former New Zealand Prime Minister Helen Clark, Former Indonesian President Susilo Bambang Yudhoyono.

The Award was established in 1972 by Sir John Templeton. It honours individuals whose exemplary achievements advance Sir John Templeton's philanthropic vision: harnessing the power of the sciences to explore the deepest questions of the universe and humankind's place and purpose within it. The Templeton Prize winners have come from all major faiths and dozens of countries and have included Nobel Prize winners, philosophers, theoretical physicists, and one canonized saint.

ABEL PRIZE

The Abel Prize recognizes the research involved in the field of mathematics. The award is granted in commemoration of the 19th-century Norwegian mathematician Niels Henrik Abel. The King of Norway awards annually one or more outstanding mathematicians. It is directly modelled after the Nobel Prizes and comes with a monetary award of 7.5 million Norwegian kroner.

KYOTO PRIZE

The Kyoto Prize is an international award of Japanese origin, presented to individuals who have made significant contributions in the fields of science and technology, as well as the arts and philosophy. The award is presented in the three categories of Advanced Technology, Basic Sciences, and Arts and Philosophy, each of which comprises four fields, making a total of 12 fields.

This internationally renowned award is given by the Inamori foundation and was born out of the sincere wish of Kazuo Inamori to "contribute to the progress of the future of humanity while maintaining a balance between the development of science and civilization and the enrichment of the human spirit."

Each laureate is presented with a diploma, a Kyoto Prize medal, and prize money of 100 million yen per category.

Sports

OLYMPICS

The Olympic Games are the world's only truly global, multi-sport, celebratory athletics competition. With more than 200 countries participating in over 400 events across the Summer and Winter Games, the Olympics are where the world comes to compete, feel inspired, and be together.

Modern Olympics is inspired by the ancient Olympic Games held in Olympia, Greece from the 8th century BC to the 4th century AD. Baron Pierre de Coubertin founded the International Olympic Committee (IOC) in 1894, leading to the first modern Games in Athens in 1896.

The evolution of the Olympic Movement during the 20th and 21st centuries has resulted in several changes to the Olympic Games. Some of these adjustments include the creation of the Winter Olympic Games for snow and ice sports.

The Mega sporting events are normally held every four years, alternating between the Summer and Winter Olympics every two years in the four-year period. Only due to World wars it was cancelled in 1916, 1940, and 1944 and postponement for one year in 2020 due to COVID-19 pandemic. XXXIIth Summer Olympics have been held till now with Tokyo being the last host city.

In each Olympic event, gold medals are awarded for first place, silver medals are awarded for second place, and bronze medals are awarded for third place.

The International Olympic Committee is the guardian of the Olympic Games and the leader of the Olympic Movement. IOC acts as a catalyst for collaboration between all Olympic stakeholders, including the athletes, the National Olympic Committees, the International Federations, Organising Committees for the Olympic Games, the Worldwide Olympic Partners and Olympic broadcast partners. It also collaborates with public and private authorities including the United Nations and other international organisations.

PARALYMPICS

The Paralympic Games provide a platform for Para athletes with a diverse range of impairments to showcase their outstanding abilities. The Paralympics/ Summer Paralympics is an international multi-sport event where athletes with physical disabilities compete. This includes athletes with mobility disabilities, amputations, blindness, and cerebral palsy. The Paralympic Games are held every four years, organized by the International Paralympic Committee. Medals are awarded in each event, with gold medals for first place, silver for second and bronze for third like that of Olympic Games.

The Asian Games are described as the second largest multi-sport event after the Olympic Games. It is a continental multi-sport event held every four years among athletes from all over Asia. The Games are governed by Olympic Council of Asia (OCA). The Games are recognized by the International Olympic Committee (IOC). Since 2010, host cities manage both the Asian Games and the Asian Para Games, the latter an event for athletes with physical conditions to compete with each other. The Asian Para Games are held immediately following the Asian Games, but the exclusion of Asian Para Games from any Asian Games host city contract means that both events will run independently of each other.

COMMONWEALTH GAMES

The Commonwealth Games is an international multi-sport event involving athletes from the Commonwealth of Nations. These games were earlier known as the British Empire Games from 1930 to 1950, the British Empire and Commonwealth Games from 1954 to 1966, and British Commonwealth Games from 1970 to 1974. The event was first held in 1930 and has taken place every four years since with exception during world war. The Commonwealth Games are overseen by the Commonwealth Games Federation (CGF), which also controls the sporting programme and selects the host cities. The games movement consists of international sports federations (IFs), Commonwealth Games Associations (CGAs), and organising committees for each specific Commonwealth Games.

There are several rituals and symbols, such as the Commonwealth Games flag and Queen's Baton Relay, as well as the opening and closing ceremonies. Over 5,000 athletes compete at the Commonwealth Games in more than 15 different sports and more than 250 events. The first, second, and third-place finishers in each event receive Commonwealth Games medals: Gold, Silver, and Bronze, respectively. Apart from many Olympic sports, the games also include some sports which are played predominantly in Commonwealth countries but which are not part of the Olympic programme, such as lawn bowls, netball, cricket and squash.

Presently 72 teams participate in the Commonwealth Games, as it is a feature of the Commonwealth Games that a number of dependent territories who do not compete separately at the Olympic Games, compete in the Commonwealth Games under their own flags. The four Home Nations of the United Kingdom (England, Scotland, Wales and Northern Ireland) also send separate teams.

FOOTBALL/ SOCCER

Football also known as Association football/ soccer is a team sport played with a spherical ball between two teams of 11 players each side. It is the world›s most popular sport and played by approximately 250 million players in over 200 countries and dependencies. The game is played on a rectangular field called a pitch with a goal at each end. The object of the game is to score more goals than the opposition by moving the ball beyond the goal line into the opposing goal, usually within a time frame of 90 or more minutes.

International Federation of Association Football (FIFA) is the international governing body of Football. FIFA is responsible for organising World Cups for men and women every four years. The men's FIFA World Cup has taken place every four years since 1930, with the exception of cancellation due to World War II in 1942 and 1946. It is the most prestigious men's football tournament in the world, and the most widely viewed and followed sporting event in the world, exceeding the Olympic Games.

Some of the Important international football competitions are Confederations Cup, Copa del Rey, or «King›s Cup,", FA Cup, UEFA Europa League, Copa America, UEFA European Championship, UEFA Champions League, Africa Cup of Nations and Copa Libertadores.

Some of the famous players are Pele, Diego Maradona, Ronaldo, Ronaldinho, Lionel Messi, Cristiano Ronaldo, Xavi, Sunil Chhetri, Carlos Ruiz, Zinedine Zidane, David Beckham, Bhaichung Bhutia, Zinedine Zidane and Garrincha.

TENNIS

Tennis or Lawn Tennis is a racket sport that can be played individually against a single opponent (singles) or between two teams of two players each (doubles).

Each player uses a tennis racket that is strung with cord to strike a hollow rubber ball covered with felt over or around a net and into the opponent's court. The object of the game is to manoeuvre the ball in such a way that the opponent is not able to play a valid return. The player who is unable to return the ball will not gain a point, while the opposite player will.

Tennis is played by millions of recreational players and is also a popular worldwide spectator sport. The Australian Open, the French Open, Wimbledon, and the US Open are known as the four Grand Slam tournaments.

The International Tennis Federation (ITF) is the governing body of world tennis. It also governs wheelchair tennis, and beach tennis. The ITF partners with the Women's Tennis Association (WTA) and the Association of Tennis Professionals (ATP) to govern professional tennis. The International Tennis Federation (ITF) is the governing body of world tennis, wheelchair tennis, and beach tennis. It was founded in 1913 as the International Lawn Tennis Federation by twelve national associations, and as of 2016, was affiliated with 211 national tennis associations and six regional associations.

Arthur Ashe, Boris Becker, Andre Agassi, Martina Navratilova, Björn Borg, Jimmy Connors, Steffi Graf, Venus Williams, Novak Djokovic, Leander Paes, Mahesh Bhupathi, Stefan Edberg, Serana Williams Roger Federer, Goran Ivanišević, Rod Laver, Ivan Lendl, Ashleigh Barty, Helen Wills Moody, Maria Sharapova, Arantxa Sánchez Vicario, Sania MIrza and Naomi Osaka are some of the important tennis players.

BADMINTON

Badminton is a racquet sport played using racquets to hit a shuttlecock across a net. It is also a technical sport, requiring good motor coordination and the development of sophisticated racquet movements.

Badminton is played on a rectangular indoor court. Points are scored by striking the shuttlecock with the racquet and landing it within the opposing side's half of the court.

Each side may only strike the shuttlecock once before it passes over the net. Play ends once the shuttlecock has struck the floor or if a fault has been called by the umpire, service judge, or (in their absence) the opposing side.

The game developed in British India from the earlier game of battledore and shuttlecock. Since 1992, badminton has been a Summer Olympic sport with four events: men's singles, women's singles, men's doubles, and women's doubles.

The Badminton World Federation (BWF) is the internationally recognized governing body of sports. Five regional confederations associated with the BWF are Badminton Asia Confederation (BAC), Badminton Confederation of Africa (BCA), Badminton Pan Am (BPA), Badminton Europe (BE) and Badminton Oceania (BO).

TABLE TENNIS

Table tennis/ ping-pong is a table-ball sport in which two or four players hit a lightweight ball, back and forth across a table using small rackets. The game takes place on a hard table divided by a net. International Table Tennis Federation (ITTF) is the international governing body regulating the Table tennis. The federation have more than 200 member associations.

The most important international competitions of the Table Tennis in addition to Olympics are the World Table Tennis Championships, the Table Tennis World Cup, and the ITTF World Tour.

European Championships, Europe Top-16, the Asian Championships, and the Asian Games are continental competitions include the following:

CRICKET

Cricket is one of the most popular vat and ball game with over millions of viewers. It is played between two teams of eleven players on a field at the centre of a 22-yard pitch. There are different formats of cricket like T-20, with each team batting for a single innings of 20 overs, ODI of 50 overs of single innings for both teams and the Test match which lasts for five days and two innings for each team.

International Cricket Council (ICC) is the governing body of the Cricket worldwide with over 100 members. Twelve full members are eligible to play Test matches. The game's rules, the Laws of Cricket, are maintained by Marylebone Cricket Club (MCC) in London. The sport is followed in South Asia where India, Pakistan, Bangladesh and Sri Lanka are test playing nations. Other test playing nations are England, Australia, New Zealand, South Africa and the West Indies. Women's cricket, which is organised and played separately, has also achieved international standard.

Important tournaments are ICC ODI world Cup, T-20 World Cup, Test Championship, Champions Trophy, Ashes Series, Border-Gavaskar Trophy, Asia Cup. Now days regional T-20 leagues like IPL, CPL, Super-Smash, Big-Bash league, SLPL are also becoming popular.

HOCKEY

Hockey or Field Hockey is one of the popular games which is played at global level. It is an important part of Olympics game. The sport is played between two teams which play against each other by trying to manoeuvre a ball into the opponent's goal using a hockey stick.

The game is played on various surfaces including natural grass or on artificial turf. The game is popular in Europe, Asia, Australia, New Zealand, South Africa, and Argentina.

The International Hockey Federation (FIH) is the governing body of the Field Hockey world wide. The hockey is a part of Summer Olympic Games since 1908 with the exception of 1912 and 1924.

Important tournaments are Hockey World Cup which held every four years, in between the Olympics, Hockey Champions Challenge, FIH Pro League, Commonwealth Games, Sultan Azlan Shah Hockey Tournament.

The field hockey is dominated initially by India which dominated in the Olympics in the sixties and later by Argentina and Germany. In the Hockey world cup Pakistan Netherlands and Australia are the most successful teams.

VOLLEYBALL

It is a team sport in which two teams of six players are separated by a raised net. Each team on one side this net, tries to "volley" a ball onto the ground of the opposing team's side for points. Each team tries to score points by grounding a ball on the other team's court under organized rules. The game has a following of 900 million people, mostly in North America and Western Europe. There are variants of Volleyball including the most popular, beach volleyball that is played on sand with two people on each team, as opposed to regular volleyball, where there are normally six players on each team.

The Fédération Internationale de Volleyball (FIVB) is the global governing body responsible for all forms of volleyball. The federation plays a key role to provide leadership to over 500 million players and 33 million licensed athletes.

Misty May-Treanor, Kerri Walsh Jennings, Regla Torres, Sheila Castro, Lorenzo Bernardi, Kim Yeon-koung, Karch Kiraly, Giba, Saeid Marouf, Ricardo Lucarelli Souza are some of the famous players.

BASKETBALL

Basketball is played worldwide and has an estimated following of 825 million. In this game two teams attempt to dribble a ball up a court and shoot it into a raised, hoop-shaped net to score points.

The International Basketball Federation (FIBA) is the international association of national organizations which governs the sport of basketball worldwide. FIBA defines the rules of basketball, specifies the equipment and facilities required, organises international competitions, regulates the transfer of athletes across countries, and controls the appointment of international referees.

Some of the important tournaments in addition to Olympics are World Cup, Naismith Trophy, EuroBasket, FIBA Americas Championship, Asia Championship, African Championship, Oceania Championship, World Olympic Qualifying Tournament and NBA league.

Some important basketball players are Michael Jordan, Kobe Bryant, Magic Johnson, Shaquille O'Neal, Bill Russell, LeBron James and Sim Bhullar.

TOKYO OLYMPICS

Tokyo Olympics or the XXXII Summer Olympics held from 23 July to 8 August 2021 in Tokyo, Japan. The Olympics was scheduled to be in 2020 but postponed to 2021 due to Covid-19 pandemic, though the name Tokyo-2020 was retained. The 2020 Games were the fourth Olympic Games to be held in Japan, following the Tokyo 1964 (summer), Sapporo 1972 (winter) and Nagano 1998 (winter) games. Tokyo became the first city in Asia to hold the Summer Games twice.

The Tokyo 2020 Games were an unprecedented demonstration of unity and solidarity as the world came together for the first time following the onset of the COVID-19 pandemic.

The Tokyo 2020 Games showcased the evolution of the Olympic programme, introducing new sports and events that strengthened the timeless appeal of the Olympic Games for a new generation. Tokyo 2020's 339 events in 33 sports—the most in Olympic history—included the Olympic debut of sports such as skateboarding, sport climbing, surfing and karate, as well as events such as BMX freestyle and 3x3 basketball. Tokyo 2020 became the first Olympics which was largely held behind closed doors with no public spectators permitted due to the pandemic. It also became the most expensive Olympics ever, with total spending of over $20 billion.

Opening and Closing Ceremony

The opening ceremony of the Olympics took place at Olympic Stadium, Tokyo, and was formally opened by Emperor Naruhito. As mandated by the Olympic Charter, the proceedings combined the formal and ceremonial opening of this international sporting event, including welcoming speeches, hoisting of the flags and the parade of athletes, with an artistic spectacle to showcase the host nation's culture and history. The vast majority of the artistic spectacle was pre-recorded, with live segments performed with a small VIP audience and performers adhering to social distancing. The ceremony marked the 125th anniversary of the 1896 Summer Olympics in Athens—the inaugural edition of the modern Olympic Games. The motto of the Tokyo 2020 was 'United by Emotion' and it was intended to "reaffirm the role of sport and the value of the Olympic Games. The ceremony focused on responses to the pandemic by the athlete community, including themes of lament, restoration and hope. For the first time in an Olympic opening ceremony, a moment of silence was observed in honour of Israeli athletes and officials murdered in the Munich Massacre at the 1972 Summer Olympics.

"*Moving Forward*" was the consistent theme for both 2020 Opening and Closing Ceremonies, as announced by Tokyo 2020. The Opening and Closing Ceremonies was produced by Takayuki Hioki. As the originator of the Olympics, the Greek team entered first. The Refugee Olympic Team, composed of refugees from several countries, was the second nation to enter. Other teams entered in order of the Gojūon system based on the names of countries in the Japanese language. Following tradition, the delegation from the host nation Japan entered last.

Officially hailed as the ambassador of the Games, Miraitowa was the official mascot of the Tokyo Olympics, and it comes with surprising powers the athletes can only envy.

The Tokyo Games became the "first gender-balanced Games in history as almost 49% of the women athletes competed. For the first time, each team had the option to allow two flag bearers, one male and one female, in an effort to promote gender equality.

Japanese tennis player Naomi Osaka lit the Olympic cauldron while Japanese badminton player Ayaka Takahashi lit another cauldron, outside the stadium which was off–limits to guests.

The closing ceremony of the 2020 Summer Olympics took place in the Olympic Stadium in Tokyo on August 8, 2021. The closing ceremony was held without spectators. The scale was also reduced compared to past ceremonies as athletes were required to leave the Olympic Village 48 hours after their competitions finished.

The proceedings combined the formal ceremonial closing of this international sporting event with an artistic spectacle to showcase the culture and history of the current and next host nation (France) for the 2024 Summer Olympics in Paris. The theme of the Olympic Ceremonies was *"Moving Forward"*, referencing the Covid-19 pandemic, with the closing ceremony theme being *"Worlds we share"*.

Medals

The first gold medal of the Tokyo Olympics goes to Qian Yang from China, after the 21-year-old came out on top in the women's 10 meter air rifle competition. Yang narrowly beat out Russia's Anastasiia Galashina and set an Olympic record. The bronze medal went to Swiss shooter Nina Christen.

Momiji Nishiya of Japan won the first-ever gold medal in women's street skateboarding. USA's Carissa Moore won gold in the first-ever women's surfing competition while Ítalo Ferreira claimed the top spot on the men's side. In karate, Gold went to Japan's Ryo Kiyuna. In sport climbing, Slovenia's Janja Garnbret and Spain's Alberto Ginés López won the first Golds.

Naohisa Takato won host Japan's first gold medal, beating Taiwan's Yang Yung-wei in the men's 60-kilogram judo final.

Due to the COVID-19 pandemic, athletes were presented with their medals on trays, and were asked to put them on themselves (or each other, in case of team winners), rather than having them placed around their necks by a dignitary.

The United States won the most gold medals, as well as the most overall medals. China finished second while host Japan finished third.

Country	Position	Gold	Silver	Bronze	Total
United States	1	39	41	33	113
China	2	38	32	18	88
Japan	3	27	14	17	58
Great Britain	4	22	21	22	65

ROC	5	20	28	23	71
Australia	6	17	7	22	46
Netherlands	7	10	12	14	36
France	8	10	12	11	33
Germany	9	10	11	16	37
Italy	10	10	10	20	40
Canada	11	7	6	11	24
Brazil	12	7	6	8	21
New Zealand	13	7	6	7	20
Cuba	14	7	3	5	15
Hungary	15	6	7	7	20
South Korea	16	6	4	10	20
Poland	17	4	5	5	14
Czech Republic	18	4	4	3	11
Kenya	19	4	4	2	10
Norway	20	4	2	2	8

Top International Companies

Since the COVID-19 crash, global equity markets have seen a strong recovery. The 100 biggest companies in the world were worth a record-breaking **$31.7 trillion** as of March 31 2021, up 48% year-over-year. As a point of comparison, the combined GDP of the U.S. and China was $35.7 trillion in 2020.

In today's graphic, we use PwC data to show the world's biggest businesses by market capitalization, as well as the countries and sectors they are from.

THE TOP 100, RANKED

PWC ranked the largest publicly-traded companies by their market capitalization in U.S. dollars. It's also worth noting that sector classification is based on the FTSE Russell Industry Classification Benchmark, and a company's location is based on where its headquarters are located.

Here is the top 100 ranking of the biggest companies in the world, organized from the biggest to the smallest.

(Data as of March 31, 2021)

Rank	Company Name	Location	Sector	Market Capitalization
1	APPLE INC	United States	Technology	$2.1T
2	SAUDI ARAMCO	Saudi Arabia	Energy	$1.9T
3	MICROSOFT CORP	United States	Technology	$1.8T
4	AMAZON.COM INC	United States	Consumer Discretionary	$1.6T
5	ALPHABET INC	United States	Technology	$1.4T
6	FACEBOOK INC	United States	Technology	$839B
7	TENCENT	China	Technology	$753B
8	TESLA INC	United States	Consumer Discretionary	$641B
9	ALIBABA GRP	China	Consumer Discretionary	$615B
10	BERKSHIRE HATHAWAY	United States	Financials	$588B
11	TSMC	Taiwan	Technology	$534B
12	VISA INC	United States	Industrials	$468B

Rank	Company Name	Location	Sector	Market Capitalization
13	JPMORGAN CHASE	United States	Financials	$465B
14	JOHNSON & JOHNSON	United States	Health Care	$433B
15	SAMSUNG ELECTRONICS	South Korea	Technology	$431B
16	KWEICHOW MOUTA	China	Consumer Staples	$385B
17	WALMART INC	United States	Consumer Discretionary	$383B
18	MASTERCARD INC	United States	Industrials	$354B
19	UNITEDHEALTH GRP	United States	Health Care	$352B
20	LVMH MOET HENNESSY	France	Consumer Discretionary	$337B
21	WALT DISNEY CO	United States	Consumer Discretionary	$335B
22	BANK OF AMERICA	United States	Financials	$334B
23	PROCTER & GAMBLE	United States	Consumer Staples	$333B
24	NVIDIA CORP	United States	Technology	$331B
25	HOME DEPOT INC	United States	Consumer Discretionary	$329B
26	NESTLE SA	Switzerland	Consumer Staples	$322B
27	IND & COMM BK	China	Financials	$290B
28	PAYPAL HOLDINGS	United States	Industrials	$284B
29	ROCHE HOLDING	Switzerland	Health Care	$283B
30	INTEL CORP	United States	Technology	$261B
31	ASML HOLDING NV	Netherlands	Technology	$255B
32	TOYOTA MOTOR	Japan	Consumer Discretionary	$254B
33	COMCAST CORP	United States	Telecommunications	$248B
34	VERIZON COMMUNICATIONS	United States	Telecommunications	$241B

Rank	Company Name	Location	Sector	Market Capitalization
35	EXXON MOBIL CORP	United States	Energy	$236B
36	NETFLIX INC	United States	Consumer Discretionary	$231B
37	ADOBE INC	United States	Technology	$228B
38	COCA-COLA CO	United States	Consumer Staples	$227B
39	MEITUAN	China	Technology	$226B
40	PING AN	China	Financials	$219B
41	CISCO SYSTEMS	United States	Telecommunications	$218B
42	AT&T INC	United States	Financials	$216B
43	L'OREAL	France	Consumer Discretionary	$215B
44	CHINA CONSTRUCTION BANK	China	Financials	$213B
45	ABBOTT LABS	United States	Health Care	$212B
46	NOVARTIS AG	Switzerland	Health Care	$212B
47	NIKE INC	United States	Consumer Discretionary	$209B
48	ORACLE CORP	United States	Technology	$202B
49	PFIZER INC	United States	Health Care	$202B
50	CHEVRON CORP	United States	Oil & Gas	$202B
51	CHINA MERCH	China	Financials	$196B
52	PEPSICO INC	United States	Consumer Staples	$195B
53	SALESFORCE.COM	United States	Technology	$195B
54	MERCK & CO	United States	Health Care	$195B
55	ABBVIE INC	United States	Health Care	$191B
56	BROADCOM INC	United States	Technology	$189B
57	PROSUS NV	Netherlands	Technology	$181B
58	RELIANCE INDS	India	Energy	$180B
59	THERMO FISHER	United States	Health Care	$180B
60	ELI LILLY & CO	United States	Health Care	$179B

Rank	Company Name	Location	Sector	Market Capitalization
61	AGRICULTURAL BANK OF CHINA	China	Financials	$178B
62	SOFTBANK GROUP	Japan	Telecommunications	$176B
63	ACCENTURE PLC	Ireland	Industrials	$176B
64	TEXAS INSTRUMENT	United States	Technology	$174B
65	MCDONALDS CORP	United States	Consumer Discretionary	$167B
66	VOLKSWAGEN AG	Germany	Consumer Discretionary	$165B
67	BHP GROUP LTD	Australia	Basic Materials	$163B
68	WELLS FARGO & CO	United States	Financials	$162B
69	TATA CONSULTANCY	India	Technology	$161B
70	DANAHER CORP	United States	Health Care	$160B
71	NOVO NORDISK	Denmark	Health Care	$160B
72	MEDTRONIC PLC	Ireland	Health Care	$159B
73	WULIANGYE YIBI	China	Consumer Staples	$159B
74	COSTCO WHOLESALE	United States	Consumer Discretionary	$156B
75	T-MOBILE US INC	United States	Telecommunications	$156B
76	CITIGROUP INC	United States	Financials	$152B
77	HONEYWELL INTL	United States	Industrials	$151B
78	QUALCOMM INC	United States	Technology	$151B
79	SAP SE	Germany	Technology	$151B
80	BOEING CO	United States	Industrials	$149B
81	ROYAL DUTCH SHELL	Netherlands	Oil & Gas	$148B
82	NEXTERA ENERGY	United States	Utilities	$148B
83	UNITED PARCEL	United States	Industrials	$148B
84	UNION PAC CORP	United States	Industrials	$148B
85	UNILEVER PLC	United Kingdom	Consumer Staples	$147B

Rank	Company Name	Location	Sector	Market Capitalization
86	AIA	Hong Kong SAR	Financials	$147B
87	LINDE PLC	United Kingdom	Basic Materials	$146B
88	AMGEN INC	United States	Health Care	$144B
89	BRISTOL-MYER SQB	United States	Health Care	$141B
90	SIEMENS AG	Germany	Industrials	$140B
91	BANK OF CHINA	China	Financials	$139B
92	PHILIP MORRIS INC	United States	Consumer Staples	$138B
93	LOWE'S COS INC	United States	Consumer Discretionary	$136B
94	CHARTER COMMUNICATIONS	United States	Telecommunications	$135B
95	CHINA MOBILE	Hong Kong SAR	Telecommunications	$134B
96	SONY GROUP CORP	Japan	Consumer Discretionary	$132B
97	ASTRAZENECA PLC	United Kingdom	Health Care	$131B
98	ROYAL BANK OF CANADA	Canada	Financials	$131B
99	STARBUCKS CORP	United States	Consumer Discretionary	$129B
100	ANHEUSER-BUSCH	Belgium	Consumer Staples	$128B

- In total, 59 companies were headquartered in the United States, making up 65% of the top 100's total market capitalization.
- China and its regions was the second most common location for company headquarters, with 14 companies on the list.

Risers and Fallers

- **Tesla's** market capitalization surged by 565% temporarily making Elon Musk the richest person in the world.
- Food delivery platform **Meituan** and **PayPal** benefited from growing e-commerce popularity with their market capitalizations growing by 221% and 151% respectively.

- ◄ Tech companies **TSMC** and **ASML Holdings** were also among the top 10 risers, thanks to a shortage of semiconductor chips and growing demand.

- ◄ Swiss companies **Nestlé, Novartis,** and **Roche Holding** were all among the bottom 10 companies by market capitalization growth.

- ◄ **China Mobile** was the only company to decline with a -12% change.

A Sector View

Across the 100 biggest companies in the world, some sectors had higher weightings.

Sector	Total Market Cap in Top 100	% of Top 100 Market Cap	Number of Companies in Top 100
Technology	$10.5T	33.0%	20
Consumer Discretionary	$6.0T	18.9%	17
Financials	$3.4T	10.8%	14
Health Care	$3.3T	10.5%	16
Energy	$2.7T	8.5%	5
Consumer Staples	$2.0T	6.4%	9
Industrials	$2.0T	6.4%	9
Telecommunications	$1.3T	4.1%	7
Basic Materials	$0.3T	1.0%	2
Utilities	$0.1T	0.5%	1

- ◄ Technology had the highest market capitalization and was also the most common sector, with Big Tech dominating the top 10.

- ◄ Companies in the consumer discretionary, financials and health care sectors also had a strong representation in the ranking.

- ◄ Despite having only five companies on the list, the energy sector amounted to almost 10% of the top 100's market capitalization, mostly due to Aramco's whopping valuation.

- ◄ Basic materials and industrials, both cyclical sectors, were high performers in the top 100 and outperformed their respective industry indexes.

- ◄ Technology companies also outperformed, and accounted for **$255 billion** or 31% of all shareholder distributions by the top 100, far more than any other sector.

- ◄ Apple alone spent $73 billion on share buybacks and $14 billion in dividends in the 2020 calendar year.

- ◄ On the other hand, the worst-performing sectors in the top 100 were health care, utilities and energy.

- ◄ While the index performance for health care and utilities was also relatively poor, the wider energy sector performed fairly well.

- ◄ It's perhaps not surprising that all sectors saw positive returns since their low levels in March 2020, buoyed by fiscal stimulus and central bank policies.

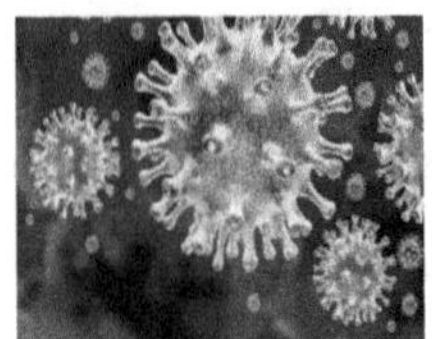

The Novel Coronavirus (COVID-19)

- COVID-19 is the disease caused by SARS-CoV-2, the coronavirus that emerged in December 2019.
- COVID-19 can be severe, and has caused millions of deaths around the world as well as lasting health problems in some who have survived the illness.
- The coronavirus can be spread from person to person. It is diagnosed with a laboratory test.
- COVID-19 vaccines have been authorized for emergency use by the U.S. Food and Drug Administration, and vaccination programs are in progress across the U.S. and in many parts of the world.
- Prevention involves physical distancing, mask-wearing, hand hygiene and staying away from others if you feel sick.
- Some health care systems are becoming overwhelmed and there may be limited access to adequate medical care in affected areas; as of 6 October 2021, 235,673,032 confirmed cases of COVID-19 and 4,814,651 deaths have been reported to the World Health Organization
- As of 6 October 2021, 46.1% of the World population has received at least one dose of COVID-19 vaccine.

How Does Coronavirus Spread?

As of now, researchers know that the coronavirus is spread through droplets and virus particles released into the air when an infected person breathes, talks, laughs, sings, coughs or sneezes. Larger droplets may fall to the ground in a few seconds, but tiny infectious particles can linger in the air and accumulate in indoor places, especially where many people are gathered.

How Coronavirus Started?

The first case of COVID-19 was reported Dec. 1, 2019, and the cause was a then-new coronavirus later named SARS-CoV-2. SARS-CoV-2 may have originated in an animal and changed (mutated) so it could cause illness in humans.

Incubation Period

Symptoms show up in people within two to 14 days of exposure to the virus. A person infected with the coronavirus is contagious to others for up to two days before symptoms appear, and they remain contagious to others for 10 to 20 days, depending upon their immune system and the severity of their illness.

Symptoms

COVID-19 symptoms include: Cough, fever or chills, shortness of breath or difficulty breathing, muscle or body aches, sore throat, new loss of taste or smell, diarrhea, headache, new fatigue, nausea or vomiting, congestion or runny nose, etc.

Some people infected with the coronavirus have mild COVID-19 illness, and others have no symptoms at all. In some cases, however, COVID-19 can lead to respiratory failure, lasting lung and heart muscle damage, nervous system problems, kidney failure or death.

How COVID-19 diagnosed?

COVID-19 is diagnosed through a laboratory test. Diagnosis by examination alone is difficult since many COVID-19 signs and symptoms can be caused by other illnesses. Some people with the coronavirus do not have symptoms at all.

COVID-19 Treatment

Treatment for COVID-19 addresses the signs and symptoms of the infection and supports people with more severe disease. For mild cases of coronavirus disease, some measures such as fever reducers or over-the-counter medications are recommended.

More severe cases may require hospital care, where a patient may receive a combination of treatments that could include steroids, oxygen, mechanical breathing support and other COVID-19 treatments in development. Infusions of monoclonal antibodies given to certain patients early in the infection may reduce the symptoms, severity and duration of the illness.

Protection from Coronavirus

Vaccines are now authorized to prevent infection with SARS-CoV-2, the coronavirus that causes COVID-19. But until more is understood about how the vaccines affect a person's ability to transmit the virus, precautions such as mask-wearing, physical distancing and hand hygiene should continue regardless of a person's vaccination status to help prevent the spread of COVID-19.

All about Masks

Masks should be used as part of a comprehensive strategy of measures to suppress transmission and save lives; the use of a mask alone is not sufficient to provide an adequate level of protection against COVID-19.

Wearing a mask is a normal part of being around other people. The appropriate use, storage and cleaning or disposal of masks are essential to make them as effective as possible. Clean your hands before you put your mask on, as well as before and after you take it off, and after you touch it at any time. Make sure it covers both your nose, mouth and chin.

When you take off a mask, store it in a clean plastic bag, and every day either wash it if it's a fabric mask, or dispose of a medical mask in a trash bin. Don't use masks with valves.

Vaccine

A COVID-19 vaccine is a vaccine intended to provide acquired immunity against severe acute respiratory syndrome coronavirus 2 (SARS-CoV-2), the virus that causes coronavirus disease 2019 (COVID-19). The initial focus of SARS-CoV-2 vaccines was on preventing symptomatic, often severe illness.

Many countries have implemented phased distribution plans that prioritize those at highest risk of complications, such as the elderly, and those at high risk of exposure and transmission, such as healthcare workers. Single dose interim use is under consideration to extend vaccination to as many people as possible until vaccine availability improves.

- As of 31 October 2021, 7.04 billion doses of COVID-19 vaccines have been administered worldwide based on official reports from national public health agencies.
- AstraZeneca anticipates producing 3 billion doses in 2021, Pfizer–BioNTech 1.3 billion doses, and Sputnik V, Sinopharm, Sinovac, and Janssen 1 billion doses each.
- Moderna targets producing 600 million doses and Convidecia 500 million doses in 2021.
- By December 2020, more than 10 billion vaccine doses had been preordered by countries, with about half of the doses purchased by high-income countries comprising 14% of the world's population.

How the Pandemic Changed the Economy?

The impact of COVID-19 on the global economy has been immense, and it could be many more months before it returns to pre-pandemic levels. Prior to the coronavirus, forecasts showed that growth rates in real gross domestic product (GDP) would increase by 2.9 percent in 2020. However, due to COVID-19, real output fell by 3.4 percent.

As a result of job losses and rising unemployment, there have been significant changes in the income tiers of people due to the coronavirus – more than 130 million people worldwide have been added to the 'poor' tier.

Many industries have felt the full force of the economic downturn, but COVID-19's impact on the travel and tourism industry has been particularly hard. Airlines have witnessed an unprecedented drop in passengers, while countries and cities that rely on business from tourism have experienced substantial job and revenue losses.

Total Coronavirus Cases (by 31st October 2021) : 247,463,597

Deaths: 5,014,976; Recovered: 224,135,386

Top 20 Countries Affected by Covid-19

S.No.	Country	Total Cases	Total Deaths	Total Recovered
	World	**247,463,597**	**5,014,976**	**224,135,386**
1	USA	46,823,938	766,299	36,715,313
2	India	34,285,814	458,470	33,668,560
3	Brazil	21,810,855	607,860	20,996,772
4	UK	9,057,629	140,632	7,356,576

S.No.	Country	Total Cases	Total Deaths	Total Recovered
5	Russia	8,513,790	238,538	7,358,539
6	Turkey	8,032,988	70,611	7,490,125
7	France	7,166,877	117,683	6,939,948
8	Iran	5,924,638	126,303	5,508,815
9	Argentina	5,288,807	115,950	5,155,184
10	Spain	5,011,148	87,368	4,864,318
11	Colombia	5,002,387	127,281	4,845,554
12	Italy	4,771,964	132,100	4,557,417
13	Germany	4,607,958	96,259	4,275,500
14	Indonesia	4,244,358	143,405	4,088,635
15	Mexico	3,807,211	288,365	3,168,911
16	Poland	3,025,247	76,999	2,706,968
17	Ukraine	2,922,302	67,729	2,436,213
18	South Africa	2,922,116	89,177	2,814,264
19	Philippines	2,787,276	43,172	2,698,871
20	Malaysia	2,471,642	28,912	2,374,761

OMICRON VARIANT

The World Health Organization found out about B.1.1.529 on Nov. 24 and within two days labelled it "Omicron" and designated it a "variant of concern".

The variant was little known to the public until November 24, when South African officials reported it to the WHO. "This variant has a large number of mutations, some of which are concerning. Preliminary evidence suggests an increased risk of reinfection with this variant, as compared to other" variants of concern, the organization said in a statement.

As of Nov. 29, the variant has been detected in at least 15 countries on five continents, including Canada. (Dutch state broadcaster NOS reported that among 600 passengers from two quarantined flights out of South Africa, 10% tested positive for some version of the coronavirus.)

Media reports indicated that multiple of the confirmed cases were in vaccinated people, though South African doctors noted that the vast majority of the infected were unvaccinated.

- The World Coal Association estimates that there are more than one trillion tonnes of coal reserves worldwide, enough to last 150 years at current rates of production.

- China has consistently led the world in production – the country was responsible for 3.3 billion tonnes in 2016 – this was down 16% from the 3.9 billion tonnes produced in 2012.

- Chinese coal output slumped below the 3.4 billion tonne-threshold predicted in 2016 and the trend may continue, as renewable energy sources become more widespread.

- India is second on the list of the world's largest coal-producing countries, producing around 783 million tonnes in 2019 – just under 10% of the global share.

- State-owned Coal India, the world's largest coal-mining company, accounts for around 80% of the country's output, and has more than 360 mines in operation.

- Coal production has increased in Australia and Russia in the last five years, both South Africa and the US have seen sharp declines in production of anthracite and bituminous coal.

- American coal production in particular has fallen from over 900 million tonnes in 2012 to 782 million in 2016, the lowest figure since 1979.

Top 10 Countries by Coal Production (million tonnes)

Country	2020	2019
China	3,902.0	3,846.3
India	756.5	753.9
Indonesia	562.5	616.2
United States	484.7	640.8
Australia	476.7	504.1
Russia	399.8	440.9
South Africa	248.3	258.4
Kazakhstan	113.2	115.0
Germany	107.4	131.3
Poland	100.7	112.4

◄   According to recent data collected by the Energy Information Administration (EIA), total oil production averaged more than 94.185 million barrels per day (b/d) in 2020.

◄   According to the most recent data, the top five oil-producing nations are the United States, Saudi Arabia, Russia, Canada, and China.

◄   The top five oil-producing nations are responsible for nearly half of the world's production of crude oil as well as all other petroleum liquids, biofuels and products resulting from the refinery process.

◄   The United States overtook Russia in 2017 for the second-place spot and surpassed former leader Saudi Arabia a year later to become the world's top oil producer.

◄   Global oil production is expected to rise from 80 million b/d in 2018 to 100 million b/d in 2050.

◄   Thanks to oil sands, Canada is expected to have some of the highest growth in oil production, percentage-wise, over the next three decades.

◄   The United States is the top oil-producing country in the world, with an average of 18.6 million b/d, which accounts for 20% of the world's production.

◄   The Kingdom of Saudi Arabia contributes 10.82 million b/d, representing 11% of the world's total production.

◄   While Russia has fallen in the ranks, it remains one of the world's top oil producers, with an average of 10.5 million b/d in 2020, accounting for 11% of total world production.

◄   Canada holds the fourth spot among the world's leading oil producers, with an average production of 5.26 million b/d in 2020, accounting for 6% of global production.

◄   China produced an average of 4.93 million b/d of oil in 2020, which accounts for 5% of the world's production.

Top 10 Countries by Oil Production

Country	Oil production 2020 (bbl/day)	Oil production per capita 2017 (bbl/day/million people)
United States	11,307,560	35,922
Russia	9,865,495	73,292
Saudi Arabia (OPEC)	9,264,921	324,866
Canada	4,201,101	100,931
Iraq (OPEC)	4,102,311	119,664
China	3,888,989	2,836
United Arab Emirates (OPEC)	3,138,249	335,103
Brazil	2,939,950	12,113

Country	Oil production 2020 (bbl/day)	Oil production per capita 2017 (bbl/day/million people)
Iran (OPEC)	2,665,809	49,714
Kuwait (OPEC)	2,625,145	721,575

Top 10 largest oil consumers & share of total world oil consumption in 2018

Country	Million barrels per day	Share of world total
United States	20.51	21%
China	13.89	14%
India	4.77	5%
Japan	3.79	4%
Russia	3.56	4%
Saudi Arabia	3.08	3%
Brazil	3.06	3%
South Korea	2.57	3%
Canada	2.53	3%
Germany	2.33	2%
Total top 10	60.08	60%
World total	100.05	

NATURAL GAS

- As of 2020, the United States was the biggest producer of natural gas in the world. With a production of approximately 915 billion cubic meters that year.

- U.S. natural gas production was roughly 240 billion cubic meters more than the second biggest producer - Russia.

- These two nations are by far the biggest contributors to natural gas production on the planet.

- In 2019, global natural gas production reached a peak of four trillion cubic meters.

- Global proved natural gas reserves totalled more than seven quadrillion cubic feet in 2019.

- The Middle East and the Commonwealth of Independent States are home to the largest regional natural gas reserves.

- The country with the largest proved natural gas reserves is Russia, which holds 38 trillion cubic meters.

- Russia's state-owned energy group Gazprom held a 16.3 percent share of global natural gas in 2019.

- In addition to having the largest natural gas reserves, Russia is also the world's leading gas exporting country.

≺ The majority of Russia's gas exports are via pipelines, and in 2019 it exported approximately 217 billion cubic meters through this method.

≺ In comparison, Qatar is the second largest natural gas exporter, but is the leading LNG exporting country.

Top 10 Countries by Natural Gas Production

(Source: The World Factbook 2015 est.)

Rank	Country	Continent	Annual NG Production (million m^3)
1	USA	North America	766,200
2	Russia	Europe	598,600
3	Iran	Asia	184,800
4	Qatar	Asia	164,000
5	Canada	North America	149,900
6	China	Asia	138,400
—	European Union	Europe	118,200
7	Norway	Europe	117,200
8	Saudi Arabia	Asia	102,300
9	Indonesia	Asia	86,940
10	Turkmenistan	Asia	83,700

Important Books & their Authors

A Bend in the River : V. S. Naipaul

A Billion is Enough : Ashok Gupta

A Brief History of Time : Stephen Hawking

A Bunch of Old Letters : Jawaharlal Nehru

A China Passage : John Kenneth Galbraith

A Contribution to the Critique of Political Economy : Karl Marx

A Critique of Pure Reason : Immanuel Kant

A Doll's House : Henrik Ibsen

A Fine Balance : Rohinton Mistry

A House Divided : Pearl S. Buck

A Midsummer Night's Dream : William Shakespeare

A Pair of Blue Eyes : Thomas Hardy

A Passage to England : Nirad C. Chaudhuri

A Passage to India : E. M. Forster

A Personal Adventure : Theodore H. White

A Sense of Time : S. H. Vatsyayan

A Spaniard in the Works : John Lennon

A. Study of History : Arnold Toynbee

A Suitable Boy : Vikram Seth

A Tale of Two Cities : Charles Dickens

A View from Delhi : Chester Bowles

A Week with Gandhi : Louis Fischer

A Bend in the Ganges : Manohar Malgonkar

Against the Grain : Boris Yeltsin

Ain-i-Akbari : Abul Fazal

Airport : Arthur Hailey

Ajatshatru : Jai Shankar Prasad

Akbarnama : Abul Fazal

Alexander the Great : John Gunther

Algebra of Infinite Justice : Arundhati Roy

All Is Well That Ends Well : William Shakespeare

All Things Bright and Beautiful : James HerrQit

All Under Heaven : Pearl S. Buck

American Capitalism : J. K. Galbraith

An Admiral's Fall : Wilson John

An American Dilemma : Gunnar Myrdal

An Area of Darkness : V. S. Naipaul

An Unfinished Dream : Dr. Verghese Kurien

Anandmath : Bankim Chandra Chatterjee

Anna Karenina : Leo Tolstoy

Another Life : Derek Walcott

Antic Hay : Aldous Huxley

Antony and Cleopatra : William Shakespeare

Ape and Essence : Aldous Huxley

Arabian Nights : Sir Richard Burton

Arms and the Man : George Bernard Shaw

Around the World in Eighty Days : Jules Verne

Arthashastra : Kautilya

As You Like It : William Shakespeare

Ascent of the Everest : Sir John Hunt

Ashtadhyayi : Panini

Asia and Western Dominance : K. M. Panikkar

Asian Drama : Gunnar Myrdal

Aspects of the Novel : E. M. Forster

Back to Methuselah : George Bernard Shaw

Bang-i-Dara : Mohammad Iqbal

Beast and Man : Murry Midgley

Beginning of the Beginning : Acharya Rajneesh

Bermuda Triangle : Charles Berlitz

Betrayal of Pearl Harbour : James Rusbridger and Eric Nave

Beyond Belief : V. S. Naipaul

Beyond Peace : Richard Nixon

Bharat Bharati : Maithili Sharan Gupta

Birth and Evolution of the Soul : Annie Besant

Black Holes and Baby Universes : Stephen Hawking

Black Sheep : Honore de Balzac

Bleak House : Charles Dickens

Blind Ambitions : John Dean

Blind Beauty : Boris Pasternak

Broken Wings : Sarojini Naidu

Buddha Charitam : Ashvaghosha

Burial At Sea : Khushwant Singh

Business at the Speed of Thought : Bill Gates

Caesar and Cleopatra : George Bernard Shaw

Candida : George Bernard Shaw

Child Who Never Grew : Pearl S. Buck

Childe Harold's Pilgrimage : George Byron

Childhood : Maxim Gorky

Children of the Sun : Maxim Gorky

Chithrangada : R. N. Tagore

Chitra : Rabindranath Tagore

Christabel : Samuel Taylor Coleridge

Christmas Tales : Charles Dickens

City of Joy : Dominique Lapierre

City of Saints : Sir Richard Burton

City of the Yellow Devil : Maxim Gorky

Comedy of Errors : William Shakespeare

Common Sense : Thomas Paine

Communist Manifesto : Karl Marx

Comus : John Milton

Conquest of Self : M. K. Gandhi

Court Dancer : Rabindranath Tagore

Crescent Moon : Rabindranath Tagore

Crossing the River : Caryl Phillips

Crossing the Threshold of Hope : Pope John Paul II

Daniel Deronda : George Eliot

Das Kapital : Karl Marx

David Copperfield : Charles Dickens

Days of His Grace : Eyvind Johnson

Death and after : Annie Besant

Death Be Not Proud : John Gunther

Death in the Castle : Pearl S. Buck

Decline of the West : O' Spengler

Descent of Man : Charks Darwin

Deserted Village : Oliver Goldsmith

Detective : Arthur Hailey

Devdas : Sharat Chandra Chatterjee

Development As Freedom : Amartya Sen

Diana - Her Time Story in Her Own Words : Andrew Martin

Diplomacy in Peace and War : J. N. Kaul

Discovery of India : Jawaharlal Nehru

Distant Neighbours : Kuldip Nayar

Divine Comedy : A. Dante

Divine Life : Swami Sivananda

Doctor's Dilemma : George Bernard Shaw

Durgesh Nandini : Bankim Chandra Chatterjee

Earth in the Balance - Forging a New Common Purpose : Al Gore

East West : Salman Rushdie

East Wind : Pearl S. Buck

Echoes from Old Calcutta : H. E. Busteed

Eminent Victorians : Lytton Strachey

Emma : Jane Austen

Empire of the Soul - Some Journeys in India : Paul William Roberts

Ends and Means : Aldous Huxley

Enemies : Maxim Gorky

Erewhon : Samuel Butler

Escape : John Forsyte

Essay on Life : Samuel Butler

Essays on Gita : Aurobindo Ghosh

Ethics : Aristotle

Far From the Madding Crowd : Thomas Hardy

Farewell the Trumpets : James Morris

Forty-nine Days : Amrita Pritam

Freedom in Exile : Dalai Lama

Gandhi and Stalin : Louis Fisher

Gandhi - A Sublime Failure : S. S. Gill

Geet Govinda : Jaya Dev

Gita Rahasya : Bal Gangadhar Tilak

Gitanjali : Rabindranath Tagore

Godaan : Prem Chand

Golden Threshold : Sarojini Naidu

Gone with the Wind : Margaret Mitchell

Good Earth : Pearl S. Buck

Great Expectations : Charles Dickens

Gul-e-N aghma : Raghupati Sahai 'Firaq' Gorakhpuri

Gulistan Bostan : Sheikh Saadi

Hamlet : William Shakespeare

Hamsters : C. P. Snow

Hannibal : Thomas Harris

Happy Death : Albert Camus

Hard Times : Charles Dickens

Henry Esmond : William M. Thackeray

Hind Swaraj : M. K. Gandhi

Hindu-Muslim Unity : Ian Bryant Wells

Idols : Sunil Gavaskar

Imperial Woman : Pearl S. Buck

In the Company of Women : Khushwant Singh

Inconceivable : Ben Elton

India Divided : Rajendra Prasad

Indian Home Rule : M. K. Gandhi

Indomitable Spirit : Dr. A.P.J. Abdul Kalam

Inferno : Alighieri Dante

Ink : John Preston

Ivanhoe : Sir Walter Scott

Ivanov : Anton Chekhov

Jurassic Park : Michael Crichton

Kamayani : Jai Shankar Prasad

Kulliyat : Ghalib

Kumar Sambhava : Kalidas

L'Allegro : John Milton

La Divine Comedia : A. Dante

La Peste : Albert Camus

Lady Chatterley's Lover : D. H. Lawrence

Lady of the Lake : Sir Walter Scott

Lady with the Lapdog : Anton Chekhov

Lajja : Taslima Nasreen

Leaders : Richard Nixon

Life Divine : Aurobindo Ghosh

Long Walk to Freedom : Nelson Mandela

Lycidas : John Milton

Macbeth : William Shakespeare

Mahabhashya : Patanjali

Major Barbara : George Bernard Shaw

Man for Moscow : G Wynne

Man of Destiny : George Bernard

Maneaters of Kumaon : Jim Corbett

Mansfield Park : Jane Austen

Maurice : E. M. Forster

Mein Kampf : Adolf Hitler

Mill on the Floss : George Eliot

Modern Painters : John Ruskin

Moonwalk : Michael Jackson

Mother : Maxim Gorky

Murder in the Cathedral : T. S. Eliot

My Experiments with Truth : M. K. Gandhi

Odyssey : Homer

Oliver Twist : Charles Dickens

Paradise Lost : John Milton

Paradise Regained : John Milton

Pavilion of Women : Pearl S. Buck

Politics : Aristotle

Ramayana : Maharishi Valmiki

Republic : Plato

Resurrection : Leo Tolstoy

Satyartha Prakash : Swami Dayanand

Silas Marner : George Eliot

The Animal Farm : George Orwell

The Cocktail Party : T. S. Eliot

The Confidential Clerk : T. S. Eliot

The Dark Room : R. K. Narayan

Truth, Love and A Little Malice : Khushwant Singh

Unhappy India : Lala Lajpat Rai

Untouchable : Mulk Raj Anand

Wake up India : Annie Besant

War and Peace : Tolstoy

Waste Land : T.S. Eliot

Wealth of Nations : Adam Smith

Wonder That Was India : A.L. Basham

International Agreements, Treaties & Pacts

The Vienna Convention for the Protection of the Ozone Layer

"The Vienna Convention for the Protection of the Ozone Layer" (note1) is a treaty on the framework for international cooperation concerning the protection of the ozone layer, which was adopted in 1985 and entered into force in 1988. It provides observations, research and information exchange on the ozone layer.

Montreal Protocol

The Montreal Protocol on Substances that Deplete the Ozone Layer is the landmark multilateral environmental agreement that regulates the production and consumption of nearly 100 man-made chemicals referred to as ozone depleting substances (ODS). Adopted on 15 September 1987, the Protocol is to date the only UN treaty ever that has been ratified every country on Earth - all 198 UN Member States.

UN Framework Convention on Climate Change

The UNFCCC entered into force on 21 March 1994. Today, it has near-universal membership. The 197 countries that have ratified the Convention are called Parties to the Convention. Preventing "dangerous" human interference with the climate system is the ultimate aim of the UNFCCC.

UN Convention to Combat Desertification

The United Nations Convention to Combat Desertification (UNCCD), adopted in 1994, is the sole legally binding international agreement linking environment and development to sustainable land management. The Convention addresses specifically the arid, semi-arid, and dry sub-humid areas, known as the drylands, where some of the most vulnerable ecosystems and peoples can be found.

Geneva Conventions: First, Second, Third, Fourth

The Geneva Conventions are a series of treaties on the treatment of civilians, prisoners of war (POWs) and soldiers who are otherwise rendered hors de combat (French, literally "outside the fight"), or incapable of fighting. In 1949, after World War II, two new Conventions were added, and the Geneva Conventions entered into force on 21 October 1950.

United Nations Charter

The Charter of the United Nations was signed on 26 June 1945, in San Francisco, at the conclusion of the United Nations Conference on International Organization, and came into force on 24 October 1945. The United Nations can take action on a wide variety of issues due to its unique international character and the powers vested in its Charter, which is considered an international treaty. The UN Charter codifies the major principles of international relations, from sovereign equality of States to the prohibition of the use of force in international relations.

The Convention concerning the Protection of the World Cultural and Natural Heritage

The Convention concerning the Protection of the World Cultural and Natural Heritage entered into force on 17 December 1975. In 1966, UNESCO's General Conference adopted resolution 3.342, by which it instructed the Director-General to coordinate and secure the international adoption of appropriate principles and scientific, technical and legal criteria for the protection of cultural property, monuments and sites.

The Chemical Weapons Convention

The Chemical Weapons Convention (CWC) is a multilateral treaty that bans chemical weapons and requires their destruction within a specified period of time. The treaty is of unlimited duration and is far more comprehensive than the 1925 Geneva Protocol, which outlaws the use but not the possession of chemical weapons. CWC negotiations started in 1980 in the UN Conference on Disarmament. The convention opened for signature on January 13, 1993, and entered into force on April 29, 1997.

The Vienna Convention on Diplomatic Relations

The Vienna Convention on Diplomatic Relations of 1961 is an international treaty that defines a framework for diplomatic relations between independent countries. It specifies the privileges of a diplomatic mission that enable diplomats to perform their function without fear of coercion or harassment by the host country. This forms the legal basis for diplomatic immunity. As of June 2020, it has been ratified by 193 states.

Kyoto Protocol

The Kyoto Protocol operationalizes the United Nations Framework Convention on Climate Change by committing industrialized countries and economies in transition to limit and reduce greenhouse gases (GHG) emissions in accordance with agreed individual targets.

The Kyoto Protocol was adopted on 11 December 1997. Owing to a complex ratification process, it entered into force on 16 February 2005. Currently, there are 192 Parties to the Kyoto Protocol.

Paris Agreement

The Paris Agreement entered into force on 4 November 2016, thirty days after the date on which at least 55 Parties to the Convention accounting in total for at least an estimated 55% of the total global greenhouse gas emissions have deposited their instruments of ratification, acceptance, approval or accession with the Depositary.

192 Parties out of 197 Parties to the Convention are Parties to the Paris Agreement. On 5 October 2016, the threshold for the entry into force of the Paris Agreement was achieved.

Treaty on the Non-Proliferation of Nuclear Weapons

The Treaty on the Non-Proliferation of Nuclear Weapons (NPT), which entered into force in March 1970, seeks to inhibit the spread of nuclear weapons. Its 190 states-parties are classified in two categories: nuclear-weapon states (NWS), consisting of the United States, Russia, China, France, and the United Kingdom, and non-nuclear-weapon states (NNWS). Under the treaty, all states-parties commit to pursue general and complete disarmament and the NNWS agree to forgo developing or acquiring nuclear weapons.

UN Convention against Illicit Traffic in Narcotic Drugs and Psychotropic Substances

This Convention provides comprehensive measures against drug trafficking, including provisions against money laundering and the diversion of precursor chemicals. It provides for international cooperation through, for example, extradition of drug traffickers, controlled deliveries and transfer of proceedings. The Convention entered into force on November 11, 1990. As of June 2020, there are 191 Parties to the Convention. These include 186 out of 193 United Nations member states.

International Convention for the Suppression of the Financing of Terrorism

The Terrorist Financing Convention (formally, the International Convention for the Suppression of the Financing of Terrorism) is a 1999 United Nations treaty designed to criminalize acts of financing acts of terrorism. The convention also seeks to promote police and judicial co-operation to prevent, investigate and punish the financing of such acts. As of October 2018, the treaty has been ratified by 188 states.

International Convention against Doping in Sport

The International Convention against Doping in Sport is a multilateral UNESCO treaty by which states agree to adopt national measures to prevent and eliminate drug doping in sport. The convention was adopted at the General Conference of UNESCO in Paris on 19 October 2005. It entered into force on 1 February 2007 after it had been ratified by 30 state parties. As of February 2018, the convention has been ratified by 187 states, which includes 185 UN member states plus the Cook Islands and State of Palestine.

International Convention on the Elimination of All Forms of Racial Discrimination

The International Convention on the Elimination of All Forms of Racial Discrimination is the centerpiece of the international regime for the protection and enforcement of the right against racial discrimination. The convention was adopted and opened for signature by the United Nations General Assembly on 21 December 1965, and entered into force on 4 January 1969. As of July 2020, it has 88 signatories and 182 parties.

Comprehensive Nuclear-Test-Ban Treaty

The Comprehensive Nuclear-Test-Ban Treaty (CTBT) is a multilateral treaty that bans nuclear weapons test explosions and any other nuclear explosions, for both civilian and military purposes, in all environments. It was adopted by the United Nations General

Assembly on 10 September 1996, but has not entered into force, as eight specific nations have not ratified the treaty.

LIST OF OTHER TREATIES BY NUMBER OF PARTIES

Treaty	Year concluded	Topic	Total Members
Convention on the Rights of the Child	1989	Human rights	**196**
Convention on Biological Diversity	1992	Environment (species preservation; sustainable development)	**196**
Constitution of the United Nations Educational, Scientific and Cultural Organisation	1945	Organizational (UNESCO); education; science; culture	**195**
Constitution of the Food and Agriculture Organization	1945	Organizational (FAO); agriculture; food	**195**
Constitution of the World Health Organization	1946	Organizational (WHO); health	**193**
Chicago Convention on International Civil Aviation	1944	Organizational (ICAO); air transport	**193**
Convention on the Elimination of All Forms of Discrimination against Women	1979	Human rights	**189**
United Nations Convention against Transnational Organized Crime	2000	Organized crime; international criminal law	**190**
Constitution of the International Labour Organization	1919/1945[p]	Organizational (ILO); labour	**187**
Basel Convention	1992	Environmental (hazardous waste disposal)	**187**
Tokyo Convention	1969	Terrorism, air transport	**186**
United Nations Convention against Corruption	2003	International criminal law	**186**

Treaty	Year concluded	Topic	Total Members
Biological Weapons Convention	1972	International humanitarian law; arms control	183
Worst Forms of Child Labour Convention	1999	Human rights; labour	186
Stockholm Convention on Persistent Organic Pollutants	2001	Environmental (persistent organic pollutants)	184
WHO Framework Convention on Tobacco Control	2003	Health	181
Vienna Convention on Consular Relations	1963	Privileges and immunities; diplomatic relations	181
Paris Convention for the Protection of Industrial Property	1883	Intellectual property	177
Convention on the Rights of Persons with Disabilities	2006	Human rights	181
Agreement establishing the International Fund for Agricultural Development	1976	Organizational (IFAD); development	176
International Convention against the Taking of Hostages	1979	Terrorism	176
Berne Convention for the Protection of Literary and Artistic Works	1886	Intellectual property (copyright)	176
Convention establishing a Customs Co-operation Council	1950	Organizational (WCO); customs	175[s]
Protocol for the Suppression of Unlawful Acts of Violence at Airports serving International Civil Aviation	1988	aviation; terrorism	175

Treaty	Year concluded	Topic	Total Members
Abolition of Forced Labour Convention	1957	Human rights; labour	**173**
International Covenant on Civil and Political Rights	1966	Human rights	**172**
Statute of the International Atomic Energy Agency	1956	Peaceful use of nuclear energy	**172**
Cartagena Protocol on Biosafety	2000	Environment (species preservation; biological technology)	**172**
Convention on Wetlands of International Importance especially as Waterfowl Habitat[84]	1971	Environment (species preservation; waterfowl; wetlands)	**170**
International Convention for the Suppression of Terrorist Bombings	1997	Terrorism	**170**

LIST OF ENVIRONMENTAL CONVENTIONS

Name	Year of Establishment
Ramsar Convention	1971
Stockholm Convention	2001
CITES	1973
Convention on Biological Diversity	1992
Bonn Convention	1979
Vienna Convention	1985
Montreal Protocol	1987
Kyoto Protocol	1997
United Nations Framework Convention on Climate Change (UNFCCC)	1992
Rio Summit	1992
UNCCD	1994
Basel Convention	1989

Cartagena Protocol on Biosafety	2000
UN-REDD	2008
Nagoya Protocol	2010
COP24	2018
COP21	2016
Kigali Amendment	2016
Minamata Convention	2013
Rotterdam Convention	1998
COP25	2019
COP26	2021